First World War
and Army of Occupation
War Diary
France, Belgium and Germany

31 DIVISION
Divisional Troops
B Squadron 1/1 Lancashire Hussars,
Divisional Cyclist Company,
165, 169 and 171 Brigade Royal Field Artillery
28 February 1916 - 26 March 1916

WO95/2349/1-5

The Naval & Military Press Ltd
www.nmarchive.com
Published in association with The National Archives

Published by

The Naval & Military Press Ltd

Unit 10 Ridgewood Industrial Park,

Uckfield, East Sussex,

TN22 5QE England

Tel: +44 (0) 1825 749494

www.naval-military-press.com

www.nmarchive.com

This diary has been reprinted in facsimile from the original. Any imperfections are inevitably reproduced and the quality may fall short of modern type and cartographic standards.

© Crown Copyright
Images reproduced by permission of The National Archives, London, England, 2015.

Contents

Document type	Place/Title	Date From	Date To
Heading	WO95/2349/1		
Heading	31st Division Divl Troops 'B' Son Lanc Hussars 1916 Feb-1916 Apr To 8 Corps Box 828		
Heading	B Squad Lane Hussars Vol I 31st Div		
Heading	H/Qrs 31st Division		
War Diary		28/02/1916	30/03/1916
War Diary		06/03/1916	26/03/1916
Heading	WO95/2349/2		
Heading	31st Division Divl Troops 31st Divl Cyclist Coy, 1916 Feb-May 1916		
War Diary	El Kab	19/02/1916	10/03/1916
War Diary	Etalminil	11/03/1916	30/03/1916
War Diary	Bertrancourt	01/04/1916	30/04/1916
War Diary	Kantara	25/01/1916	19/02/1916
War Diary	El Kab	19/02/1916	10/03/1916
War Diary	Etalminil	11/03/1916	30/03/1916
War Diary	Bertrancourt	03/04/1916	06/05/1916
Heading	WO95/2349/3		
Heading	31st Division Divl Artillery 165th Brigade R.F.A. Mar 1916-May 1919		
War Diary	Kantara	02/03/1916	05/03/1916
War Diary	Port Said	06/03/1916	14/03/1916
War Diary	France	14/03/1916	20/03/1916
War Diary	Fontaine	21/03/1916	29/03/1916
War Diary	Englebelmer	02/04/1916	07/04/1916
War Diary	Orville	07/04/1916	16/04/1916
War Diary	Courselles	16/04/1916	30/04/1916
War Diary	165 Brigade R.F.A. D.A.G. 3rd October	02/06/1915	02/06/1915
War Diary	Kantara Egypt	01/05/1916	02/05/1916
War Diary	Courcelles	01/05/1916	31/05/1916
War Diary	165 Brigade R.F.A. O.G 3rd Echelon Base	03/07/1916	03/07/1916
War Diary		01/06/1916	30/06/1916
Heading	31st Division. War Diary 165th Brigade R.F.A. July 1916		
Heading	War Diary 165th Bde R.F.A. July 1st To 31st 1916 Vol.5		
War Diary		01/07/1916	31/07/1916
Heading	Confidential War Diary. Of 165th Brigade R.F.A. From August 1st, 1916 To August 31st, 1916 Volume VIII		
War Diary	In The Field	01/08/1916	29/08/1916
War Diary	Field	30/08/1916	31/08/1916
War Diary	Field	01/08/1916	31/08/1916
Heading	Confidential. War Diary Of 165th Bde. R.F.A. From 1st September 1916 To 30th September 1916. Volume IX		
War Diary	Lacouture	01/09/1916	14/09/1916
War Diary	Le Touret	18/09/1916	30/09/1916
Heading	Confidential War Diary Of 165th Brigade R.F.A. From 1st October To 31st October, 1916 Volume X Vol 8 31 Div		
War Diary	Le Touret	01/10/1916	31/10/1916

Heading	Confidential. War Diary Of 165 Brigade. R.F.A. From November 1st 1916 To November 30th 1916 (Volume XI) Vol 9		
Miscellaneous	165th Bde. R.F.A. H.Q. 31st D.A.	02/11/1916	02/11/1916
War Diary		01/11/1916	30/11/1916
Heading	Confidential War Diary Of 165th Brigade R.F.A. From 1st December 1916 To 31st December 1916. Volume XII Vol 10		
War Diary		01/12/1916	31/12/1916
Heading	Confidential War Diary Of 165th Brigade R.F.A. From 1st January 1917 To 31st January 1917. Volume XIII. Vol XI		
War Diary	In The Field	01/01/1917	01/02/1917
Heading	Confidential War Diary Of 165th Brigade R.F.A. From 1st February 1917 To 28th February 1917. Volume XIV Vol 12		
War Diary	St. Queen	01/02/1917	24/02/1917
War Diary	Bayencourt	26/02/1917	28/02/1917
Heading	Confidential War Diary Of 165th Brigade R.F.A. From 1st March 1917 To 31st March 1917. Volume XV. Vol 13		
Miscellaneous	165 Bde. R.F.A. W 23/4 H.Q 31st D.A	02/04/1917	02/04/1917
War Diary	Bayencourt	01/03/1917	06/03/1917
War Diary	Hebuterne	10/03/1917	31/03/1917
Heading	Confidential War Diary Of 165th Brigade R.F.A. From 1st April 1917 To 30th April 1917. Volume XVI Vol 14 31 Div		
War Diary	Ecoivres	01/04/1917	01/04/1917
War Diary	La Targette	02/04/1917	08/04/1917
War Diary		03/04/1917	15/04/1917
War Diary	Roclincourt	16/04/1917	30/04/1917
Heading	Confidential War Diary Of 165th Brigade R.F.A. From 1st May 1917 To 31st May 1917. Volume XVII Vol 15 31st		
War Diary	Gavrelle	01/05/1917	03/05/1917
War Diary	Bailleul	04/05/1917	28/05/1917
Heading	Confidential. War Diary Of 165th Brigade R.F.A. From 1st June 1917 To 30th June 1917. Volume XVIII. Vol 16		
Miscellaneous	165 Bde R.F.A. N 23/4 H.Q 31st D.A	04/07/1917	04/07/1917
War Diary	Bailleul	01/06/1917	30/06/1917
Heading	Confidential. War Diary Of 165th Brigade R.F.A. From 1st July To 31st July, 1917 Volume XIX Vol 17		
War Diary	Bailleul	01/07/1917	23/07/1917
War Diary	Vimy	24/07/1917	31/07/1917
Heading	Confidential War Diary Of 165th Brigade R.F.A. From 1st August To 31st August, 1917. Volume XX. Vol 18 31Div		
War Diary	S. Se of Vimy	01/08/1917	31/08/1917
War Diary		30/08/1917	30/08/1917
Heading	Confidential War Diary Of 165 Brigade R.F.A. From 1st Sept. To 30th Sept. 1917. Volume XXI. Vol 19		
Miscellaneous	165th Bde R.F.A. W 23/4 H.Q. 31st D.A	08/10/1917	08/10/1917
War Diary	S. Se of Vimy	01/09/1917	07/09/1917
War Diary	Farbus & Willerval	08/09/1917	30/09/1917

Heading	Confidential War Diary Of 165th Brigade R.F.A. From 1st October To 31st October, 1917. Volume XXII Vol 20		
Miscellaneous	165th Bde R.F.A. N 23/4 H.Q 31 D.A	05/11/1917	05/11/1917
War Diary	Willerval & Farbus	01/10/1917	31/10/1917
Heading	Confidential War Diary Of 165th Brigade R.F.A. From 1st November To 30th November, 1917 Volume XXIII Vol 21		
Miscellaneous	165th Bde R.F.A. N23/4 H.Q 31st D.A.	04/12/1917	04/12/1917
War Diary	Farbus & Willerval	01/11/1917	30/11/1917
Heading	Confidential War Diary Of 165th Brigade R.F.A. From 1st December To 31st December 1917. Volume XXIV. Vol 22		
Miscellaneous	165th Bde R.F.A. N23/4 H.Q. 31 D.A.	03/01/1918	03/01/1918
War Diary	Willerval And Farbus	01/12/1917	31/12/1917
Heading	Confidential War Diary Of 165 Brigade R.F.A. From 1st January To 31st January, 1918. Volume XXV Vol 23		
Miscellaneous	165th Bde R.F.A. N23/4 H.Q 31st D.A.	03/02/1918	03/02/1918
War Diary	Farbus & Willerval	01/01/1918	31/01/1918
Heading	Confidential War Diary Of 165th Brigade R.F.A. From 1st February To 28th February, 1918 Volume XXVI Vol 24		
War Diary	Farbus & Willerval	01/02/1918	28/02/1918
Heading	31st Divisional Artillery War Diary 165th Brigade R.F.A. March 1918		
Heading	Confidential War Diary Of 165th Brigade R.F.A. From 1st March 1918 To 31st March 1918. Volume XXVII. Vol 25		
War Diary	Douchy	25/03/1918	31/03/1918
Heading	31st Divisional Artillery. 165th Brigade R.F.A. :: April 1918		
Heading	Confidential War Diary Of 165th Brigade R.F.A. From 1st April To 30th April, 1918. Volume XXVIII Vol 26		
War Diary	Douchy Valley	01/04/1918	30/04/1918
Heading	Confidential War Diary Of 165 Brigade R.F.A. From 1st May To 31st May, 1918. Volume XXIX. Vol 27		
Miscellaneous	165th Bde R.F.A. W.23/4 H.Q. 31st D. A	05/06/1918	05/06/1918
War Diary	Douchy Valley	01/05/1918	30/05/1918
War Diary	Humbercourt	31/05/1918	31/05/1918
Heading	Confidential War Diary Of 165th Brigade R.F.A. From 1st June To 30th June, 1918. Volume XXX. Vol 28		
Miscellaneous	165th Bde R.F.A. W 23/4 H.Q. 31st Div	02/04/1918	02/04/1918
War Diary	Humbercourt	01/06/1918	15/06/1918
War Diary	Vicinity of Rabbit Wood Sheet 51c X 19	16/06/1918	30/06/1918
Miscellaneous	165th Bde R.F.A. No W23/4 H.Q. 31st D.A.	03/08/1918	03/08/1918
Heading	Confidential War Diary Of 165th Brigade R.F.A. From 1st July To 31st July, 1918. Volume XXXI Vol 29		
War Diary	C22A Sheet 36A	01/07/1918	02/07/1918
War Diary	E 19 a E 20 Sheet 36 A	03/07/1918	31/07/1918
Heading	Confidential War Diary Of 165th Brigade R.F.A. From 1st August To 31st August, 1918 Volume XXXII. Vol 30		
War Diary	Nieppe Forest	01/08/1918	31/08/1918

Heading	Confidential. War Diary Of 165th Brigade R.F.A. From 1st September To 30th September, 1918 Volume XXXIII. Vol 31		
Miscellaneous	165th Brigade R.F.A. H.Q. 31st D.A	07/10/1918	07/10/1918
Heading	War Diary Of Headquarters 31st Divisional Artillery. From 1st. October To 31st. October, 1918. Volume XXXIV Vol 32		
Heading	Confidential War Diary Of 165th Brigade R.F.A. From 1st. October To 31st. October, 1918 Volume XXXIV Vol 32		
Miscellaneous	165th Bde. R.F.A. H.Q., 31st Div Art.	09/11/1918	09/11/1918
War Diary	Ploegsteert	01/10/1918	18/10/1918
War Diary	Caestre	18/10/1918	25/10/1918
War Diary	Vichte	27/10/1918	31/10/1918
Miscellaneous	165th Brigade R.F.A. H.Q., 31st Div. Arty.	15/12/1918	15/12/1918
Heading	Confidential. War Diary Of 165th Brigade R.F.A. From 1st November To 30th November, 1918 Volume XXXV. Vol 33		
War Diary	Avelghem Cotinghem Area	01/11/1918	02/11/1918
War Diary	Bousbecque	03/11/1918	07/11/1918
War Diary	Avelghem	08/11/1918	10/11/1918
War Diary	Russeignies	11/11/1918	29/11/1918
War Diary	Wizernes Near St. Omer	30/11/1918	30/11/1918
Heading	Confidential. War Diary Of 165th Brigade R.F.A. From 1st December To 31st December, 1918. Volume XXXVI Vol 34		
Miscellaneous	165th Bde R.F.A. N.23/4 H.Q 31 D.A.	06/01/1919	06/01/1919
War Diary	Wizernes Near St. Omer	01/12/1918	31/12/1918
Heading	Confidential. War Diary Of 165 Brigade R.F.A. From 1st January To 31st January, 1919. Volume XXXVII. Vol 35		
Miscellaneous	165th Bde R.F.A. W 23/4 H.Q. 31 D.A	04/01/1919	04/01/1919
War Diary	Wizernes Near St. Omer	01/01/1919	31/01/1919
Heading	Confidential. War Diary Of 165th Brigade R.F.A. From 1st February To 28th February, 1919 Volume XXXVIII. Vol 36		
Miscellaneous	165th Bde. R.F.A. W. 23/4 H.Q. 31st D.A.	05/03/1919	05/03/1919
War Diary	Wizernes France	01/02/1919	28/02/1919
Heading	Confidential. War Diary Of 165th Brigade R.F.A. From 1st March To 31st March, 1919. Volume XXXIX. Vol 37		
Miscellaneous	165th. Bde. R.F.A. H.Q. 31st Div Art.	06/04/1919	06/04/1919
War Diary	Wizernes France	01/03/1919	31/03/1919
Heading	Confidential. War Diary Of 165th Brigade R.F.A. From 1st April To 30th April, 1919 Volume. XI Vol 38		
Miscellaneous	165th Bde. R.F.A. W. 23/4. H.Q. 31st D.A.	03/05/1919	03/05/1919
War Diary	Wizernes France	01/04/1919	30/04/1919
War Diary	Wizernes	01/05/1919	17/05/1919
Heading	WO95/2349/4		
Heading	31st Division Divl Artillery 169th Brigade R.F.A. Mar 1916- Jan 1917 Broken Up		
War Diary	Alexandria	01/03/1916	01/03/1916
War Diary	Marseilles	06/03/1916	09/03/1916
War Diary	Pont Remy	10/03/1916	10/03/1916
War Diary	Frucourt	11/03/1916	27/03/1916
War Diary	Belloy	28/03/1916	28/03/1916

War Diary	Naours.	29/03/1916	29/03/1916
War Diary	Amplier	31/03/1916	31/03/1916
Heading	Confidential War Diary Of 169th Bde R.F.A. From 1st April 1916 To 30th April 1916		
War Diary	Amplier	01/04/1916	02/04/1916
War Diary	Colincamps	06/04/1916	28/04/1916
Heading	War Diary Of 169th Bde R.F.A. From May 1st 1916 To May 31st 1916 (Sheet 7)		
War Diary	Colincamps	03/05/1916	27/05/1916
Heading	Confidential War Diary Of 169th Brigade R.F.A. From 6 June 1916 To 30 June 1916 Volume 1. Sheets 8 & 9		
War Diary	Colincamps	03/04/1916	30/04/1916
Heading	War Diary 169th Brigade R.F.A. 1st to 31st July 1916. 31st Division.		
Heading	War Diary Of 169th Bde R.F.A. July 1st To 31st 1916 Vol 5		
War Diary	Colincamps	01/07/1916	07/07/1916
War Diary	Autheux	09/07/1916	09/07/1916
War Diary	Haverskerke	10/07/1916	15/07/1916
War Diary	Laventie	15/07/1916	19/07/1916
War Diary	Laventie (Pont Du Hem)	21/07/1916	30/07/1916
War Diary	Quentin	31/07/1916	31/07/1916
Heading	Confidential. War Diary. Of 169th Brigade R.F.A. From August 1st, 1916 to August 31st, 1916. Volume VIII Vol 6		
War Diary	Quentin	03/08/1916	24/08/1916
War Diary	Mazingarbe	24/08/1916	30/08/1916
War Diary	Mazingarbe And Fosse	30/08/1916	30/08/1916
War Diary	Mazingarbe	30/08/1916	30/08/1916
Heading	War Diary 169 Bde R.F.A.		
Miscellaneous	Defence Scheme Neuve Chapelle & Ferme du Bois Sections Appendix A		
Miscellaneous	Defence Scheme Neuve Chapelle & Ferme du Bois Sections Village. St. Vaast-Croix Barbee System.		
Miscellaneous	14 Bis Group Appendix B.	28/08/1916	28/08/1916
Miscellaneous	Appendix C.	29/08/1916	29/08/1916
Miscellaneous	Appendix E	30/08/1916	30/08/1916
Heading	Confidential. War Diary Of 169th Bde. R.F.A. From 1st September 1916 to 30th September 1916. (Volume IX)		
War Diary	Le Touret	01/09/1916	18/09/1916
War Diary	Loisnes	20/09/1916	30/09/1916
Miscellaneous	Re-Organization, 31st Divisional Artillery.	27/08/1916	27/08/1916
Miscellaneous	Centre Group Appendix 2	27/09/1916	27/09/1916
Miscellaneous	Objective. Appendix 3		
Heading	War Diary Of 169th Brigade R.F.A. From 1st October To 31st October, 1916. Volume X		
Heading	War Diary Of 169 Brigade R.F.A. Pages. 27-35 Vol 10 From 1-31 October 1916		
War Diary	Loisnes	03/10/1916	08/10/1916
War Diary	Merville	09/10/1916	09/10/1916
War Diary	Courcelles	10/10/1916	13/10/1916
War Diary	Colincamps K 19c 6 1/2. 1/2	14/10/1916	31/10/1916
War Diary	Colincamps	31/10/1916	31/10/1916
Heading	War Diary Of 169 Brigade. R.F.A. From November 1st 1916 To November 30th 1916. (Volume XI)		
War Diary	Colincamps K 19c 6 1/2. 1/2	01/11/1916	18/11/1916

War Diary	Colincamps	19/11/1916	23/11/1916
War Diary	Colincamps K 19c 6 1/2.1/2	24/11/1916	30/11/1916
Heading	War Diary Of 169th Brigade R.F.A. From 1st December 1916 To 31st December 1916. Volume XII		
War Diary	Colincamps K 19c 6 1/2.1/2	01/12/1916	01/12/1916
War Diary	Sailly J 18 C 6.2	02/12/1916	03/12/1916
War Diary	Sailly J 18c 6 1/2.2	03/12/1916	31/12/1916
Heading	War Diary Of The 169th Brigade R.F.A. From January 1st To January 31st 1917. Volume XIII		
War Diary	Sailly J18c 6 1/2.2	01/01/1917	16/01/1917
War Diary	Frohen-Le-Petit	17/01/1917	31/01/1917
Miscellaneous	O/C Battery.	01/01/1917	01/01/1917
Miscellaneous	Appendix II	02/01/1917	02/01/1917
Miscellaneous	Appendix III	01/01/1917	01/01/1917
Miscellaneous	Appendix 4	04/01/1917	04/01/1917
Miscellaneous	Appendix 5	07/01/1917	07/01/1917
Miscellaneous	Appendix 6	08/01/1917	08/01/1917
Miscellaneous	Communication Sheet Night 8/9th		
Operation(al) Order(s)	31st Divisional Artillery Order No. 54	07/01/1917	07/01/1917
Miscellaneous	Programme "X" Day		
Miscellaneous	Table Of Objectives Table "B"		
Miscellaneous	Appendix 8	12/01/1917	12/01/1917
Miscellaneous	Programme Of Night Showing 12/13 January 1917	12/01/1917	12/01/1917
Heading	WO95/2349/5		
Heading	31st Division Divl Artillery 171st (How) Bde R.F.A. 1916 Mar-1916 Aug		
War Diary	Alexandria	01/03/1916	07/03/1916
War Diary	Marseilles	08/03/1916	10/03/1916
War Diary	Allery (Abbeville Distract)	11/03/1916	11/03/1916
War Diary	Allery (Somme) France	12/03/1916	20/03/1916
War Diary	Allery	20/03/1916	26/03/1916
War Diary	Yseux	27/03/1916	27/03/1916
War Diary	Wargenies	28/03/1916	28/03/1916
War Diary	Sarton & Orville	29/03/1916	29/03/1916
War Diary	Sarton	30/03/1916	31/03/1916
Miscellaneous	Appendix A	26/03/1916	26/03/1916
Miscellaneous	D.A.G. 3rd Echelon	13/05/1916	13/05/1916
War Diary	Headquarters Sarton (France)	01/04/1916	23/04/1916
War Diary	Beaussart	29/04/1916	30/04/1916
Heading	171 How Brigade R.F.A. 31st Div. VIII Corps Fourth Army Vol IV Month Of April 16		
War Diary	Mailly	01/05/1916	12/05/1916
War Diary	Hdqrs Mailly-Maillet	15/05/1916	22/05/1916
War Diary	Mailly-Maillet		
War Diary	Hdqrs Mailly-Maillet	01/06/1916	24/06/1916
War Diary	Battle HQ. Near Mailly	25/06/1916	30/06/1916
Heading	War Diary 171 Brigade R.F.A. Vol VI June/16		
Heading	War Diary 171st Brigade R.F.A. (How) 1st To 31st July 1916		
Heading	War Diary Of 171st Bde R.F.A. 31st Division July 1st To 31st 1916. Vol 5		
War Diary	Battle Hdqrs	01/07/1916	01/07/1916
War Diary	Battle H.Q. Near Mailly	01/07/1916	07/07/1916
War Diary	Amplier	08/07/1916	15/07/1916
War Diary	Hd Qrs St Venant	15/07/1916	20/07/1916
War Diary	Merville	22/07/1916	24/07/1916

War Diary	Lestrom HQ	25/07/1916	27/07/1916
War Diary	France Near La Touret	29/07/1916	31/07/1916
Heading	War Diary 171 Brigade R.F.A. Vol VII July/16		
Heading	War Diary. Of 171st Brigade R.F.A. From August 1st. 1916 To August 31st, 1916. Volume VIII		
War Diary	Headquarters Farm Near Le Touret (Ferme Du Bois Sector)	01/08/1916	30/08/1916
Heading	War Diary 171 Brigade R.F.A. Original Vol 8 August /16		
Heading	171 R.F.A. Vol 1		

WO 95/23490

WO 95/23490

31ST DIVISION
DIVL TROOPS

'B' SQN LANC HUSSARS

1916 FEB - 1916 APR

TO 8 CORPS

Box 828

B Sera
Jane Hussas
Vol I

H/qrs.   4/
31st Division

[stamp: HEADQUARTERS, 31st D. No. 485.A. Date 5.5.16]

Herewith copy of War Diary
asked for

T. Algrade

France 5/5/1916   Lt Colonel
                         1/1st Lancashire
                         Hussars Yeomy.

Headquarters 1/1st Lancashire
M/Gun Section Hussars Yeomy
"H" Sqdn.

13 Jan Hume Vol 1
War Diary for March 1916

WAR DIARY
or
INTELLIGENCE SUMMARY
(Erase heading not required.)

Army Form C. 2118

XXXI

Place	Date	Hour	Summary of Events and Information	Remarks and references to Appendices
Egypt	28/2/16		H/qrs M/Gun Section and "H" Squadron left EGYPT on H.M.T. NORTHLAND on 28th February leaving 2nd Lt. Dixon in charge of 21 Officers chargers to proceed later.	
	6/3/16		Arrived MARSEILLES and entrained for ROUEN same day, there received horses and re-equipped, receiving re-inforcement to complete establishment.	
	13th to 15th		Proceeded to 31st Divisional concentration area. Headquarters to HALLENCOURT, M/Gun section and "H" Squadron to LIMEUX, the 31st Division being in VIII Corps and 4th Army.	
	17		Officers chargers arrived at MARSEILLES on H.M.T. Knight Templar and rejoined Headquarters at HALLENCOURT.	
	18		First line Transport received at ABBEVILLE.	
	20		Lt. Col. Eale received appointment as O/C Divisional Mounted Troops	
	21st		Leave opened to 31st Division.	
	25		31st Division commenced move to front line.	

26th	Squadron ordered to march to ACHEUX-en-VIMEU for attachment to Secunderabad Brigade 2nd Indian Cavalry Division for 14 days training
27th	Squadron went to ACHEUX-en-VIMEU
28th	M/G and H/Qrs left HALLENCOURT and marched to CANAPLES, midday
29th	" " " " arrived BEAUVAL "
30th	" " " " " BUS-LE-ARTOIS.

T. O. Jones
Lt Colonel
1/1st Lancashire Hussars Y/o

HEADQUARTERS
M/G SECTION   "LANCASHIRE
"B" SQUADRON   HUSSARS,

Army Form C. 2118

WAR DIARY For Month of
or
INTELLIGENCE SUMMARY MARCH - 1916 -

Instructions regarding War Diaries and Intelligence attached to
Summaries are contained in F.S. Regs., Part II. 31 Division
and the Staff Manual respectively. Title Pages B.E.F. FRANCE
will be prepared in manuscript.
(Erase heading not required.)

31st
2B 3/16

Place	Date	Hour	Summary of Events and Information	Remarks and references to Appendices
	MARCH 6th		Headquarters, M/G Section, and "B" Squadron left EGYPT on H.M.T. NORTHLAND on 28th February, leaving 2nd Lt DIXON in charge of 21 officers chargers to proceed later.	
	4th 13-15		Arrived at MARSEILLES and entrained for ROUEN. Same day. There they received horses and re-equipped, receiving reinforcement to complete establishment. Proceeded to 31st Divisional Concentration Area - H.Q. to HALLENCOURT. M/G Section and "B" Squadron to LIMEUX; The 31st Division being in VIII CORPS and Fourth Army.	
	10		Officers chargers arrived at MARSEILLES on H.M.T. KNIGHT TEMPLAR and rejoined HdQrs at HALLENCOURT.	
	12th		First Line Transport received at ABBEVILLE,	
	13th		Lt Col. Earle resumed appointment as O/C Divisional Mounted Troops.	
	20th		Leave opened to 31st Division.	
	21st		Division commenced move to Front Line.	
	25th		Squadron ordered to to ACHEUX-en-VIMEU for attachment to Secunderabad Brigade, 2nd INDIAN Cavalry Division for 14 days leaving HdQRS	

1/1st LANCASHIRE HUSSARS) attached to
Head Quarters   31st Division
M/G Section   B.E.F. France
B Squadron

B Leares Hendon

WAR DIARY for the month of April 1916. Army Form C. 2118.
or
INTELLIGENCE SUMMARY
(Erase heading not required.)

Instructions regarding War Diaries and Intelligence
Summaries are contained in F. S. Regs., Part II.
and the Staff Manual respectively. Title pages
will be prepared in manuscript.

Vol 2.

Hour, Date, Place	Summary of Events and Information	Remarks and references to Appendices
April 1st BUS.	Head Quarters and M/G Section arrived at BUS-LES-ARTOIS on 30th March. B Squadron at ACHEUX-EN-VIMEU attached to 2nd Indian Cavalry Division from 27th March	
3rd to 10th	Major & Quartermaster Mountford appointed Town Major of BUS. 5a Squadron carried out daily tactical schemes with dismounted Brigade practising	
10th ACHEUX.	advanced & rear guards, attack and protection of convoys, observation & reconnaissance duties.	
11th BUS.	Captain A. R. Wood reported in Squadron as Supplying officer on arrival from the Base.	
12th St OUEN.	Squadron marched to St OUEN and billets for the night.	
14th AMPLIER.	Squadron arrived at AMPLIER rejoining 31st Division.	
16th SARTON.	Captain Aspinall appointed Town Major of SARTON. Squadron moved to SARTON.	
18th	2nd Lt Hornby and 2 N.C.O. proceeded to HOTCHKISS Gun Class at CAMIERS.	
19th	2nd Lt Ahart and 30 other Ranks proceeded to BUS for police duties under A.P.M.	
21st COLINCAMPS.	16 N.C.O.'s and men went to ENGLAND on months furlough (re-engaged men) 1 N.C.O & 6 men proceeded to COLINCAMPS to be attached to 93rd Inf Bde for observation duties.	
24th BUS.	2 N.C.O's and 10 men to BUS for course at Bombing School. 2 Vickers guns received by M/9 Section in place of one Lewis (returned to ordnance).	
25th MARIEUX	Lt J. W. Earle appointed Temporary A.D.C. to G.O.C. VIIIth Corps.	
26th BUS-SARTON	All horses of M/9, M/9 & Squadron mallein tested. 2 each Hornby and NCO returned from CAMIERS.	

T. Aspinall
O.C. 1/1st Lanc. Hussars.
Lieut Colonel

W309/2349(2)

W309/2349(2)

31ST DIVISION
DIVL TROOPS

31ST DIVL CYCLIST COY.
1916 FEB ~~OCT 1915~~ – MAY 1916

WAR DIARY or INTELLIGENCE SUMMARY

Army Form C. 2118

Vol I BEF

Place	Date	Hour	Summary of Events and Information	Remarks and references to Appendices
EL KAB	Feby 19th to Feby 28th		Company remained at EL KAB, on outpost - no alarm indicated -	
	July 18th	14.30	Moved back to KANTARA by barge, preparatory to embarking for France.	
	July 29th		Lt Hall + 114 Men embarked from ALEXANDRIA, per H.T. "KNIGHT TEMPLAR" for MARSEILLE - + 12 Bicycles -	
	Jul 29		Capt COATSWORTH - Lt HUDSON - 2/Lt WHINPRIZE, 2/Lt WK PEACE + 2/Lt WILSON embarked from PORT SAID per H.T. "TUNISIAN" for MARSEILLE - 13 Men - (5 Rations + 8 from duty in PORT SAID). + 90 Bicycles	
	March 7th	Noon	TUNISIAN party landed in MARSEILLE - stayed thru the night +	
	"	6"	left by train for Northern France.	
	"	14.00		
	"	10th	arrived at PONT REMY - + stayed the night in Billets at HOCQUINCOURT	
		15.00		

WAR DIARY
or
INTELLIGENCE SUMMARY

Army Form C. 2118

Place	Date	Hour	Summary of Events and Information	Remarks and references to Appendices
ETAPLES	Mar 8th	11th	Moved up to ETAPLES & entrained in Cattle trucks.	
	9th	10th	"KNIGHT TEMPLAR" Party arrived in MARSEILLE - stayed there till Mar 10th.	
			When the entrained for the NORTH.	
	12th	12.30	Arrived SONT REMY & proceeded to billets in ETALMINIL.	
			Continuing tiny readjusting Gear - & general re-equipment.	
			To Mentioning detached for duty with Divisional Signal Co. & 6 M Cos	
			136 Men for duty under A.P.M. on Road Control work. Movements	
			All	
	Mar 18th to 26		At ETALMINIL, continuing general Colist Training - Rifle Marches, discipline - Musketry - A. & Gas Drill - Road reconnaissance & Map Reading.	

WAR DIARY or INTELLIGENCE SUMMARY

Army Form C. 2118

Place	Date	Hour	Summary of Events and Information	Remarks and references to Appendices
May	27	8.0 a	Company left by Road for LONGPRÉ-les-Corps-Saints — Billeted there for the night	
"	28	8.0 a	Left LONGPRÉ — Arrived CANAPLES 9.45 a.m. Billeted there for the night	
"	29	8.30 a.m	Left CANAPLES, arrived at BEAUVAL 10.30 a.m. Billeted there for the night —	
"	30	8.15 a.m	Left BEAUVAL and arrived at our destination, BERTRANCOURT, at 11.0 a.m. every man completing the march — In fairly comfortable Billets — Company's work in BERTRANCOURT — 50 O.R. detailed to act as Traffic Control Posts at various Road Junctions in the Divisional Area, under the direction of the A.P.M. A number of men also attached to act as G.cyclist orderlies to Div. Sigwe Coy — DADOS. D.M.T. Town Major — Divisional H.Q. Party of 2 Officers + 20 O.R. attended Divisional Bombing School for a 4 days course —	OK

WAR DIARY
or
INTELLIGENCE SUMMARY
(Erase heading not required.)

Army Form C. 2118

Vol 2

Place	Date	Hour	Summary of Events and Information	Remarks and references to Appendices
BEAUQUESNE	Apr 1st		Company paraded through Chlorine Gas. With Pte Helwell. No Helwell.	
	Apr 3		Company moved into 67 Anti. into Battels in Rue de l'Eglise -	
	19		A Serjeant H19 O.R. on duty as Guard at H.Q. Chateau - returned 10.4.16.	
	20		A Serjeant & 19 O.R. detailed for duty opening / attending Observation Posts, Augers	
	22		2/Lt Millson assumed charge of this party.	
	22		2/Lt REED with a Serjeant & 6 Men on Observation Duty - under Capt. Woods Intelligence Officer D.M.T.	
	24		1 Serjeant & 19 Men attached to Corps Bombing Course at Divisional Bombing School.	
	25		2/Lt HUDSON & 130 R/attached for duty at H.Q. VIII Corps. MARIEUX	
	25		2/Lt MAINPRIZE returned from Divisional Bombing School for duty with the Company.	
			& assumed Officer's charge.	
	30		2/Lt REED handed over charge of Observation Post to Lieut Dixon of L.H.Y.	

30/4/16.

T. Argyle
Lieut Colonel.
O.Comdg 31st D.M.T.

Commdg. 31st Divnl. Cyclist Coy.
Captain,

WAR DIARY
INTELLIGENCE SUMMARY

Army Form C. 2118

Place	Date	Hour	Summary of Events and Information	Remarks and references to Appendices
KANTARA	Jan 25th		Company placed under O.C. Divisional Squadron for Discipline & Administration. Reported to him personally at KANTARA 10.30 a.m. — He instructed me to carry on as previously — for the present. — Very cold weather prevailing — Strong N.W. Wind. & squalls of Rain. — (Only 12 Cycles brought to KANTARA — the Remainder 169 being left in PORT SAID at Ordnance Depot.)	
"	Feby 19th		Company left KANTARA 6 mile up position at EL KAB relieving A. Coy. 10th R.Y.R. Left KANTARA by Barge at 8.45 a.m. & arrived — Immediately took over. —	
EL KAB	"		The same May at 10.00 a.m. recieved position of pickets etc. — Encamped under canvass. Weather fine. — Cloudy. — Stiff West Breeze. —	

Army Form C. 2118

● **WAR DIARY**
or
● **INTELLIGENCE SUMMARY**
(Erase heading not required.)

Instructions regarding War Diaries and Intelligence Summaries are contained in F. S. Regs., Part II. and the Staff Manual respectively. Title Pages will be prepared in manuscript.

Place	Date	Hour	Summary of Events and Information	Remarks and references to Appendices
EL KAB	Feb. 19th		Position taken up is shown in the rough sketch:—	

Sketch:

← TINA 10 Kilom.   PUMP GUARDS N. ↓   No. 2 Piquet ↙ picket line   No. R. Piquet ↓   Mounting Patrol N. ↘   No. 1 Piquet   Mounting Patrol S. →   TO KANTARA 10 Kilom. →

KILO. 30.000   KILO. 32.200   E. Bank of SUEZ CANAL   Landing Stage   KILO. 35.420

N / W–E / S

W. Bank of CANAL.

Sweet Water Canal.

Landing Stage   Gare du CAP   Lookout Post in MAST   Bridge   Bridge

RAILWAY

WAR DIARY
or
INTELLIGENCE SUMMARY
(Erase heading not required.)

Army Form C. 2118

Place	Date	Hour	Summary of Events and Information	Remarks and references to Appendices
EL KAB	May 14th to Feb 25th		Company remained at EL KAB, on outpost - as also indicated -	
	Feb 28th	1430	Moved back to KANTARA, by lorry. Preparations for embarking for France.	
	Feb 29th		2/Lt Molt + 174 Men entrained from ALEXANDRIA, per H.T. "KNIGHT TEMPLAR" for MARSEILLE - + 12 Bicycles -	
	Feb 29		Capt COATSWORTH - Lt HUDSON - 2/Lt MANNPRIZE; 2/Lt Wk PEACE + 2/Lt MILLSON embarked from PORT SAID per H.T. "TUNISIAN" for MARSEILLE + 13 Men - (5 Batmen + 8 from duty in PORT SAID) + 190 Bicycles	
	March 7	Noon	Tunisian party landed in MARSEILLE - stayed there the night +	
	" 6th	1400	left Train for Northern FRANCE.	
	" 10th	15.00	Arrived at PONT REMY - + stayed the night Bellah at HOCQUINCOURT	

Army Form C. 2118

WAR DIARY
or
INTELLIGENCE SUMMARY
(Erase heading not required.)

Place	Date	Hour	Summary of Events and Information	Remarks and references to Appendices
ETAMINIL	Mar 8th	11th	moved up to ETALMINIL & established in billet there —	
	Mar 8th	10th	"KNIGHT TEMPLAR" Party arrived in MARSEILLE — stays there till Mar 10th	
	" 10th		Went the entraines for the NORTH.	
	" 12th	18.30	Arrive SONT REMY & proceeded to billet in ETALMINIL. Continuing try readjusting Gear — & general re-equipment — 12 Machinery attached for duty with Divisional Signal Co. — & 6 NCOs & 36 Men for duty under A.P.M. on Road Control work. under Z	
	Mar 15th to 26.		AT ETALMINIL, continuing general Colist Training — Rifle Macho discipline — Musketry — Arms Drill — Road Reconnaissance & Map Reading —	

WAR DIARY or INTELLIGENCE SUMMARY

Army Form C. 2118

Place	Date	Hour	Summary of Events and Information	Remarks and references to Appendices
May	27	8.0a	Company left by Road for LONGPRÉ - to toplants - Billets thin for the night.	
"	28	8.0a	Left LONGPRÉ - Y arrived CANAPLES 9.45am. Billets thin for the night.	
"	29	6.30am	Left CANAPLES, arrived at BEAUVAL 10.30am. Billets thin for the night.	
"	30	8.15am	Left BEAUVAL and arrived at our destination, BERTRANCOURT, at 11.0am very near completing the march. In fairly comfortable Billets - Company's work in BERTRANCOURT - 50 O.R. detailed to act as Traffic Control Posts at various Road junctions in the Divisional Area, under the direction of the A.P.M. A number of men also attached to act as Cyclist Orderlies to Dr Signal Co - D.A.D.O.S. D.M.T. Town Major - Divisional H.Q. Party of 2 Officers + 20 O.R. attended Divisional Bombing School, for a 4 days course.	

WAR DIARY or INTELLIGENCE SUMMARY

Army Form C. 2118

Place	Date	Hour	Summary of Events and Information	Remarks and references to Appendices
BERTRANCOURT	April 3rd		The Company moved out of the Huts E. of the Village in which they were billeted - & occupied Billets, [including] quite dry barns in Rue de l'Eglise. A.D.M.S. repeated urgent representations to H.Q. I obtained a Motor Cart & Horses from the 93rd Field Ambulance. It would appear to me that a Motor (bus: should be included in the W.E. of every Gclut [Gas] Company. It is absolutely indispensable. The Company - is all available, have put through a recent Chlorine Gas - P.H. Helmets were worn - for all effect than tested by any one	MG

WAR DIARY
or
INTELLIGENCE SUMMARY

Army Form C. 2118

Place	Date	Hour	Summary of Events and Information	Remarks and references to Appendices
BERAN COURT	April 9th		A/Sergeant & 19 O.R. now detailed to be attached to H.Q. (returned on Apl 19th) as Guard & Orderlies at the General's Chateau. The remainder of the Company continued to be employed as indicated in last month's diary.	1197
	20th		A/Sergeant & 19 Men detailed for duty repairing & altering Observation Posts.	
	22		2/Lt PINKSON took charge of this party — which goes out nightly.	
	☐		2/Lt REED — with A/Sergeant & 16 Men on duty at	

Army Form C. 2118

WAR DIARY
or
INTELLIGENCE SUMMARY
(Erase heading not required.)

Instructions regarding War Diaries and Intelligence Summaries are contained in F.S. Regs., Part II. and the Staff Manual respectively. Title Pages will be prepared in manuscript.

Place	Date	Hour	Summary of Events and Information	Remarks and references to Appendices
BEAUMONT	April 22		Observation Post. (Map 57.D. K.33.b.8.8.) dawn to dusk - men	
"	24		Capt WOOD - Intelligence Officer L.H.Y. 1 Sergeant & 19 Men attended Army Bombing Course at Divisional Bombing School at BUS.	
"	25		Lieut HUDSON & 13 O.R. detailed for duty at H.Q. VIII Corps at MARIEUX.	
"	25		2 Lieut MAJOPRIZE returned from Divisional Bombing School. In div - with the Company - and	
"	27		day working in the park, working on Observation Posts	

WAR DIARY or INTELLIGENCE SUMMARY

Army Form C. 2118

Place	Date	Hour	Summary of Events and Information	Remarks and references to Appendices
BERANCOURT	April 30th		Construction of dug outs. 2/Lt REED handed over charge of Observation Post, as above, to Lieut DIXON of L.H.Y. Lieut HALL - 2nd reinforcement - has been posted under the A.P.M. of the Division. The whole of this month — The general health of the Company this month has been very good — Weather, until the 23rd, very cold, with snow every day — since that day - warm & sunny. Again diary conducted by instructions of O.C. D.M.T. MW7. — See next page —	

Army Form C. 2118

WAR DIARY
or
INTELLIGENCE SUMMARY
(Erase heading not required.)

Instructions regarding War Diaries and Intelligence Summaries are contained in F.S. Regs., Part II. and the Staff Manual respectively. Title Pages will be prepared in manuscript.

Date	Hour	Summary of Events and Information	Remarks and references to Appendices
BERNANCOURT Apr 1		Company passed through Chlorine Gas - With P.H. Helmets. No ill effects -	
Apr 3.		Company moved out of Huts into Billets in Rue de l'Eglise -	
19		A Sergeant + 19 O.R. on duty as Guard at H.Q. Chateau - returned 19.4.16 -	
20		A Sergeant + 19 O.R. detailed for duty, repairing / altering Observation Posts, I August -	
22		2/Lt Willson assumed charge of this Party.	
22		2/Lt REED with a Sergeant + 6 Men on Observation duty - under Capt Wood Intelligence Officer D.M.T.	
24		1 Sergeant + 19 Men attended a day Bombing Course at Divisional Bombing School.	
25		Lt HUDSON + 130.R. detailed for duty at H.Q. VIII Corps. MARIEUX.	
25		2/Lt MANPRIZE returned from Divisional Bombing School - for duty with the Company.	
		& assumed Altimate charge, with 2/Lt Willson, of men working on Aug. Posts.	
30		2/Lt REED handed over charge of Observation Post to Lieut DIXON of L.H.Y.	

[signature]

Places	Date	Hour	Summary of Events and Information	Remarks and references to Appendices
BERTRANCOURT.	May 6th	11.0 a.m.	The Company moved into BUS-LES-ARTOIS — In Billets [and good accommodation] —	

Army Form C. 2118

WAR DIARY
or
INTELLIGENCE SUMMARY
(Erase heading not required.)

May 1916.

Instructions regarding War Diaries and Intelligence Summaries are contained in F. S. Regs., Part II. and the Staff Manual respectively. Title Pages will be prepared in manuscript.

Place	Date	Hour	Summary of Events and Information	Remarks and references to Appendices
Berneville	May 6	11 v.	The Company moved into BUS-LES-ARTOIS — In Billets. Had good accommodation —	

WO95/23498

WO95/23498

31ST DIVISION
DIVL ARTILLERY

165TH BRIGADE R.F.A.
MAR 1916-MAY 1919

WAR DIARY or INTELLIGENCE SUMMARY

Army Form C. 2118

165 Bde R.F.A.
Mar -16
May '19

Place	Date	Hour	Summary of Events and Information	Remarks and references to Appendices
KANTARA	2-3-16		Received of "D" D Batteries ord. by 7.10 am from PORT SAID. Men of A.B.C. & D Batteries under 2/Lt Roberts. KANTARA station to collect. Rearg horses Capt. Roberts Echelon in Camp & proceeded to ALEXANDRIA. Horses embarked on H.T. "NESMAN", the party returning to PORT SAID. and onward reaching to the H-unit. Encamped Port SAID until the evening of the 5th inst.	
N3 LH	5-3-16		Embarked on H.T. "IVERNIA" 12 noon	

Army Form C. 2118

WAR DIARY
or
INTELLIGENCE SUMMARY
(Erase heading not required.)

Instructions regarding War Diaries and Intelligence Summaries are contained in F. S. Regs., Part II. and the Staff Manual respectively. Title Pages will be prepared in manuscript.

Place	Date	Hour	Summary of Events and Information	Remarks and references to Appendices
PORT SAID	6-3-16		Left Port Said 5:30am and arrived MALTA onshore alongside.	
	9-3-16		Left MALTA about 7.30am	
	11-3-16		Arrived MARSEILLES 11.0am and proceeded to disembark. Entrained at No 2 point and left at 9.35pm for Pont-Remy.	
	13-3-16		Arrived PONT REMY midnight.	
	14-3-16		Arrived COCQUERELLE 4.0am. FONTAINE { COCQUERELLE Coys & Battns & BHQ billeted at FONTAINE. A. B. Coys Battns billeted at COCQUEREL	

Army Form C. 2118

WAR DIARY
or
INTELLIGENCE SUMMARY
(Erase heading not required.)

Instructions regarding War Diaries and Intelligence Summaries are contained in F. S. Regs., Part II. and the Staff Manual respectively. Title Pages will be prepared in manuscript.

Place	Date	Hour	Summary of Events and Information	Remarks and references to Appendices
France	18-3-16		Fireworks field.	
		16	Reconnaissance to FONTAINE.	
16	19-3-16	79	horses cart.	
17	20-3-16	179	horses received to make up to strength	
18			8 Officers 25 Other ranks (NCO) proceed to Proven	
			In 3 days.	
			1052 Shrapnel returned to Dump for exchange	
			for High Explosive.	

1875 Wt. W593/826 1,000,000 4/15 I.B.C. & A. A.D.S.S./Forms/C. 2118.

WAR DIARY
or
INTELLIGENCE SUMMARY
(Erase heading not required.)

Instructions regarding War Diaries and Intelligence Summaries are contained in F. S. Regs., Part II. and the Staff Manual respectively. Title Pages will be prepared in manuscript.

Place	Date	Hour	Summary of Events and Information	Remarks and references to Appendices
FONTAINE 21 22 23 24	25/3/16		Brigade moved by road to BELLOY & billeted for the night.	
	26/3/16		Left BELLOY at 9.0am and proceeded by road to NAOURS, billeted for the night.	
	27/3/16		Left NAOURS at 9.0am and proceeded by road to ORVILLE	
	28/3/16		Batteries commenced to move to gun position at INGLEBEAMER	

D. Burns
Capt. 165 Bde RFA

165 RFA
Army Form C. 2118
VOL 2

WAR DIARY
or
INTELLIGENCE SUMMARY
(Erase heading not required.)

Place	Date	Hour	Summary of Events and Information	Remarks and references to Appendices
ENGLEBELMER	2/4/16	—	Brigade H.Q. to take over 10.p.m. the exchange of wagon lines commenced at 9.0 am and finished 10.0 am. S.A.A. section of B.A.C. commenced at 9 am and finished 10 am. Guns taken over from 26th Div Arty north gun testing sheets leo DIAL SIGHTS. Guns handed over to 36th Div Arty with gun testing sheets leo DIAL SIGHTS.	
	3/4/16		Early morning Quiet. Lieut Hartai reported active asphyxiating with 6" Stokes trench mortar at 11.45 pm received report from one of F.O.Os that mortar was again located — called on 11th Siege Bde, who fired and the mortar shut up for the night. At 5.0 pm "B" Battery fires on the Saline trenches and it is believed	

1875 Wt. W593/826 1,000,000 4/15 J.B.C. & A. A.D.S.S./Forms/C.2118.

WAR DIARY or INTELLIGENCE SUMMARY

Army Form C. 2118

(Erase heading not required.)

Place	Date	Hour	Summary of Events and Information	Remarks and references to Appendices
ENGLEBELMER	3/4/16		decoyed some equipment by a direct hit - casualty reported. Rounds of mining of Redoubt - 22 shells expended. - 495 received from D.A.C.	
	4/4/16		One heavy Trench Mortar Shell - MARY. REDAN. - 16th Essex Company ordered to fire on it. Slipped firing for a time. At 7 pm fire of Trench Mortar Reported. Signal by the fire of W D. Battery 16's "Bee" KOs at request of Infantry.	
	5/4/16		Enemy's Mortars fired from 12 cm mortar 1-30 pm destributing bombs along line of trenches. 7 Sounds from Trench Mortar fire in our sector at 2-30 pm - 49 Shells expended - 43 Shells received	

WAR DIARY or INTELLIGENCE SUMMARY

Army Form C. 2118

Place	Date	Hour	Summary of Events and Information	Remarks and references to Appendices
ENGLEBELMER	6/7/16		Slight artillery duel - commenced at about 9·0pm. German Artillery bombarded heavily MARY REDAN - also had severe (direct hit on "A" Battery 165th Bde R.F.A. shot reserve done - also shelled heavily "A" 171st but no damage done, but range too long - no damage. Howr Battery, but range too long - no damage done - front effects fell on the eyes, the Germans used a quantity of "tear" shells. Firing ceased about 10·30pm - no casualties - reported 521 shells. Brigade handed over to 29th Divisional Artillery & also moved to ORVILLE, into billets.	
ORVILLE	7/7/16		Guns moved to GORN CAMPS to meet new gun positions.	
	8			
	9	11		
	10			

WAR DIARY
or
INTELLIGENCE SUMMARY

(Erase heading not required.)

Army Form C. 2118

Place	Date	Hour	Summary of Events and Information	Remarks and references to Appendices
ORVILLE	16/4/16		Brigade Headquarters moved to COURCELLES and went into billets.	
COURCELLES	17/4/16 to 30/4/16		Battery guns not working on new gun positions and O.P.s. Certify R.F. Stores from DUMP. Nothing on new gun positions and O.P.s	

C. Wilkinson
Lt. R.F.A. Adjutant,
165th (County Palatine) Brigade R.F.A.

165 Brigade R.F.A.

D.A.G.
3rd
Echelon

Herewith A.F. B.213 for
the month of May, 1916.

[Stamp: 165th BRIGADE, R.F.A. No. 76 Date 13]

_____ Lt. Col. R.F.A.
Commanding 165th (County Palatine) Brigade R.F.A.

WAR DIARY
or
INTELLIGENCE SUMMARY
(Erase heading not required.)

Army Form C. 2118

Place	Date	Hour	Summary of Events and Information	Remarks and references to Appendices
Kantara Egypt	1-5-16		One officer 50 other ranks 157 horses & 56 pair Jackets left by 7 am train for ALEXANDRIA. Mules on H.T. "TINTORETTO".	
			One Officer 50 other ranks 157 horses & 55 pair Jackets left by 9-15 for ALEXANDRIA. Mules on H.T. "TINTORETTO".	
			1 Officer 50 other ranks 144 horses 40 pair Jackets left by 11-40 am for ALEXANDRIA. Mules on H.T. "TINTORETTO". Also 6 other ranks and 6 horses of Divisional Headquarters.	
	2-5-16		Brigade Bell Tent Cart of A.I.B Batteries and Bell Tent Cart left by 2-15 am for PORT SAID	

165 Army Form C.2118
XX / VOL. 3

WAR DIARY
or
INTELLIGENCE SUMMARY
(Erase heading not required.)

Place	Date	Hour	Summary of Events and Information	Remarks and references to Appendices
COURCELLES	1/5/16		Working on new gun positions and O.Ps.	
	4/5/16		Two guns of L.D. Battery 169th replaced by 2 guns L.D. Bty 163rd Brigade R.F.A. — H.Q.: O.P. Ammunition Wagons of B.C.C. 169th Brigade R.F.A. at THIEVRES (relieved by wagons B.A.C. 165th Bde R.F.A. Relay Posts place at AUTHIE at noon on 4 May. Wagon lines of L.D. Bty 165th Bde R.F.A. moved to St. LEGER. Batteries in new gun positions 4.O.Ps.	
	6/5/16		Night of 4th and 5th. 2 guns L.D. Bty 165th Bde R.F.A. replaced remaining 2 guns of 169th Brigade R.F.A. B.C. D. Bty 165th Bde R.F.A. resumes the post of	

WAR DIARY
or
INTELLIGENCE SUMMARY

(Erase heading not required.)

Army Form C. 2118

Instructions regarding War Diaries and Intelligence Summaries are contained in F. S. Regs, Part II. and the Staff Manual respectively. Title Pages will be prepared in manuscript.

Place	Date	Hour	Summary of Events and Information	Remarks and references to Appendices
COURCELLES	5/5/16		Front from 9 am on the 5 inst. All ammunition for 4 wagons at THIEVRES supplied by 48th Division D.A.C. All ammunition by 48th Division. Batteries in new gun positions and O.P.s. Batteries in new gun positions and O.P.s.	
	14/5/16	6 to 14		
	15/5/16		D.A.C. transferred to D.A.C. C. Battery Attached to 169th Brigade R.F.A. and took over gun positions - wagon line moved to BUS-LES-ARTOIS - Batteries on new gun position 7098 dealing gun position & O.P.s A.T.B. Batteries	
	16		" " " "	
	17 to 21	21	" " " "	

WAR DIARY
or
INTELLIGENCE SUMMARY

(Erase heading not required.)

Army Form C. 2118

Place	Date	Hour	Summary of Events and Information	Remarks and references to Appendices
CORCELLES	22/5/16		The whole of "D" Battery personnel, horses, vehicles and ammunition transferred to 171st Brigade R.F.A.	
	23/5/16		The whole of A171st Howitzer Battery transferred to 165th Brigade R.F.A. Change took place at 12 noon. 22-4-16. Working on dugouts & O.Ps.	
	24/5/16		" " " " and new communication	
	25/5		" " " "	
			Trench.	
	26/5		Working on Gun pits, New communication	
	27/5		Working on Gun pits, New communication Trench, Cable 2nd Lieut. C.F. LYON killed in action 3.30pm	

WAR DIARY
or
INTELLIGENCE SUMMARY

Army Form C. 2118

Places	Date	Hour	Summary of Events and Information	Remarks and references to Appendices
COURCELLES	28 31/5 29 30 31 /16		Working on Gun pits and new Cable Trench.	

C. Wilkinson Lt RFA
Adjutant,
165th (County Palatine) Brigade R.F.A.

165th BRIGADE, R.F.A.
No. 1
Date 1-6-16.

165" Brigade R.F.A.

a.q.
3rd Echelon
Base

Army Form C2118 (War Diary) for the month of June 1916, forwarded to you, please.

3/7/16

A Henderson
....Lt. Col. R.F.A.
Commanding 165th (County Palatine) Brigade R.F.A.

June

CLXXI 165. R.F.A. Vol 4

Army Form C. 2118

WAR DIARY or INTELLIGENCE SUMMARY

(Erase heading not required.)

Instructions regarding War Diaries and Intelligence Summaries are contained in F. S. Regs., Part II. and the Staff Manual respectively. Title Pages will be prepared in manuscript.

Place	Date	Hour	Summary of Events and Information	Remarks and references to Appendices
	1/6		Working on Gun Pits, OPs & Cover trenches	
	2/6		" " " " " "	
	3/6		" " " " " "	
	4/6		" " " " " "	
	5/6		" " " " " "	
	6/6		" " " " " "	
	7/6		" Received to complete Establishment- collected from Base Force, A.Bty 4 - B.Bty 7 C.Bty 2 - D.Bty 1	

1875 Wt. W593/826 1,000,000 4/15 J.B.C. & A. A.D.S.S./Forms/C.2118.

Army Form C. 2118

WAR DIARY
or
INTELLIGENCE SUMMARY
(Erase heading not required.)

Instructions regarding War Diaries and Intelligence Summaries are contained in F. S. Regs., Part II. and the Staff Manual respectively. Title Pages will be prepared in manuscript.

Place	Date	Hour	Summary of Events and Information	Remarks and references to Appendices
	8/6/16		Working in Gun Pits, OPs, Cable Trench.	
	9/6/16		" " " " " " "	
	10/6/16		"D" Battery moved to BOS from SARTON. Guns taken to the position. Working on Cable Trench.	
	11/6/16		Working on Cable Trench and dug outs.	
	12/6/16		A 4.5 Battery guns moved up from ORVILLE to new positions. 100 Infantry working on trenches.	
	13/6/16		Working on trenches to Cable	
	14/6/16		Working on trenches for Cable. Ammunition drawn from D.A.C. E'65, 264A, 88 A.X.	

1875 Wt. W593/826 1,000,000 4/15 J.B.C. & A. A.D.S.S./Forms/C. 2118.

Place	Date	Hour	Summary of Events and Information	Remarks and references to Appendices
	16/6/18		Ammunition drawn from D.A.C. - "A" Battery A.24 AX.24 - expended on Registering A.37. "B" Battery A.156 - AX.62 rounds - expended "NIL" "A" 171 St. Bde R.F.A. A.988 AX.204 - expended A.23	
	17/6/18		Ammunition drawn from D.A.C. - "A" Bty A.582 AX.176. "B" Bty A.532 AX.176. "C" Bty. A.384 AX.128 and A.171 St. Bde. A.384 AX.128. For Special DUMP. "C" Battery received A.76 rounds for wagon line and the following expended on registering "A" Bty. A.18 "B" Bty. A.67 and A.171 St Bde R.F.A. A.40 AX.4.	

WAR DIARY or INTELLIGENCE SUMMARY

Army Form C. 2118

Place	Date	Hour	Summary of Events and Information	Remarks and references to Appendices
	14/6/16		A-171 — 264 A.— 88 A X. D165 * 500 B X.	
	15/6/16		Sending on Sunken Cable. Ammunition from D.A.C. "A" Brown. B 165 - 912 A - 304 A X. "A 171- 912 A 304 AX. D. 165 * 6000 B X. Ammunition drawn from R.A. Dump. "A" Bty 504 A — 152 AX — "B" Bty 342 A — 114 AX. A. 171 *× 525 A.— 176 AX.	
	16/6/16		Headquarters moved from Courcelles to Dug-out. "D" Battery Ammunition handed over to O.C. 171st Bde at 12 noon. B 197 — BX 648 rounds. "C" Battery 165th Bde Ammunition taken on Charge at 12 noon from O.C. 169 4/Bde R.F.A. A 3092 A.X. 1107.	

Place	Date	Hour	Summary of Events and Information	Remarks and references to Appendices
	18/6/16		"A" Bty. Ammunition received from D.A.C. "A" A.912 AX 608. "B" Bty. A.912 AX 608. ffor Special DUMP. The following ammunition received from D.A.C. for 13dg on line. A.171st Bde R.F.A. A.13½. AX 20. Ammunition expended "A" Battery A.20. "C" Battery A.33. "A" 171st Bde. A.97 AX 43, registering.	
	19/6/16		Ammunition received from D.A.C. "A" Battery A."48 AX 40. "B" Battery A."28 AX 40 for Special DUMP. The following ammunition received from D.A.C. for wagon line. "A" Battery A.100. Ammunition expended "A" Battery A.42 AX 4 "B" Battery A.24 AX 46. "C" Battery A.23 AXNK A.171. Bee Bde A 67 AX "CC"	

Army Form C. 2118

WAR DIARY
or
INTELLIGENCE SUMMARY
(Erase heading not required.)

Instructions regarding War Diaries and Intelligence Summaries are contained in F.S. Regs., Part II. and the Staff Manual respectively. Title Pages will be prepared in manuscript.

Place	Date	Hour	Summary of Events and Information	Remarks and references to Appendices
	20/6/16		Ammunition received from D.A.C. A171st Bde A152. Expended on registering 'B' Bty A.5. 'C' Bty A.14. A171st Bde A.41.	
	21/6/16		Ammunition received from D.A.C. 'C' Bty A.76. Expended on registering 'B' Bty A.51. 'C' Bty A.51. A171st Bde A.53. AX3.	
	22/6/16		Ammunition received from D.A.C. 'C' Bty A.76. A171st Bde AX4. Expended A Bty A.57. AX5. 'A' 171st Bde A.26. 'B' Bty A.47. AX3. 'C' Bty A.45.	
	23/6/16		Ammunition received from D.A.C. 'A' Bty A.76. 'B' Bty A.152. 'C' Bty A.76. A171st Bde A.100. Expended 'A' Bty A.12. 'B' Bty A.60. 'C' Bty A.100. A171st Bde A.3.	

Army Form C. 2118

WAR DIARY
or
INTELLIGENCE SUMMARY

(Erase heading not required.)

Instructions regarding War Diaries and Intelligence Summaries are contained in F. S. Regs., Part II. and the Staff Manual respectively. Title Pages will be prepared in manuscript.

Places	Date	Hour	Summary of Events and Information	Remarks and references to Appendices
"U" DAY	21/6/16		Wire cutting commenced at 6-0 am in accordance with programme of operations for the advance. Ammunition expended:— "A"By. A137 A.x30. "B" By. A305 A.x29. "C" By. A276 A.x N16. A171 Bcc A222 Ax 65. A/65. 2nd, 3rd, 4th Wire Lanes "Y" Satisfactorily cut. B/165. 2nd, 3rd, 4th Wire Lanes 2nd-2nd Wire fairly well cut, 3rd Line needs few more rounds, 4th Line not visible. C/65. 2nd 3rd 4th Wire Lanes W 2nd Wire appears Satisfactory, 3rd 4th not yet finished. A/171 B/C. 2nd 4/3 Sheet cut, fourth damaged but not yet finished.	

1875 Wt. W593/826 1,000,000 4/15 J.B.C. & A. A.D.S.S./Forms/C. 2118.

WAR DIARY
or
INTELLIGENCE SUMMARY

(Erase heading not required.)

Army Form C. 2118

Place	Date	Hour	Summary of Events and Information	Remarks and references to Appendices
	23/6	"V" DAY.	Ammunition received from D.A.C. "A" Battery A. 225 AX 76. "B" Bty. A.228 AX76, - "C" Battery A.380 - AX 76 - A.1718 13 de. A.304 AX 76. Expended 'A' Bty. A.571 AX 83. 'B' Bty. A.790 AX161, "C" Bty A.644 A.X 142 - A.171 13 de A.65g A.X 60. A/165 - Objective engaged during day - Lane 'y'. Cut through 2nd, 3rd, y 4th wires. Resistance to be encountered in subsequent day. 3rd Lane cut through. B/165 - Objective Lane 'z'. Cut through 2nd, 3rd, y 4th wires - No 3 wire needs a bit of clearing up. Good deal wire being about. This can be done during subsequent days. A/191 - Objective Lane x 1st y 2nd Cut through 2nd, 3rd y 4th wires - will be endorsed on subsequent days.	

WAR DIARY
or
INTELLIGENCE SUMMARY

(Erase heading not required.)

Army Form C. 2118

Place	Date	Hour	Summary of Events and Information	Remarks and references to Appendices
	16/1/16		Objective 'W' Lane. 2nd Line cut. 3rd Line; result difficult to see owing to a communication trench fairs crossing 3rd. Line parapet judging from personal observation of C.O. the bursts of shells and range were right to be cut, but aerial results cannot be seen. It would be well to pay special attention to this during bombardment. 4th. Line reported partially cut, and will be attacked during subsequent days. Aerial results hard to see. Casualties. Killed 4 O.R. Wounded 3. O.R.	

WAR DIARY
or
INTELLIGENCE SUMMARY
(Erase heading not required.)

Army Form C. 2118

Place	Date	Hour	Summary of Events and Information	Remarks and references to Appendices
	26/6/16		"W" Day. Ammunition received from D.A.C. - "A" Bty A229 - AX 76. "B" Bty A228 AX 76 6 Bty, A380 AX 76 - A171st Bde A228 AX 76 AX 76 - A513 AX33 Repaired A Bty A 636 AX 155 - B Bty - A513 AX 33 "B" Bty A499 AX 154. "A" Battery engaged on K29. 6 60. 75 am - K29 6 90. 68 this was effective, result believed to be satisfactory. Also direct hits on M.G. emplacements. "B" Battery engaged on Lane "t". Lane Tent & Dugouts were 15.30 wide. - It was difficult to observe practically cut - subsequent difficult to observe. "C" Battery engaged on 2", 3rd and 4th live wires. Effect good.	

WAR DIARY
or
INTELLIGENCE SUMMARY

(Erase heading not required.)

Army Form C. 2118

Place	Date	Hour	Summary of Events and Information	Remarks and references to Appendices
A 19 + B &c	26/6/16		Ro venche resulex. M.G. emplacement K.29.c.52.25" supposed to be through loophole about 6" square and one round through loophole. Have in fact 6" Junction 2nd and 3rd lines corrected and parapet front destroyed. Hostile Artillery active K.15a.1.7.2.2 - 5"9's fired in salvos of 4 - Cable in PYLON BUFFER. NAIRNE to EXEMA and CAMPION shelled by 5"9's. Trench mortars in TOUVENT. K.29.c.52.25"	

WAR DIARY
or
INTELLIGENCE SUMMARY
(Erase heading not required.)

Place	Date	Hour	Summary of Events and Information	Remarks and references to Appendices
	2/7/16		**X Day** Ammunition received from Jac. A. Bty A 228 A X 46. B Bty A 227 A X 46. Jac. A. Bty A 370 A X 76. A 117th Bde A 228 A X 76. A 22F A X 76. B Bty A 353. A X 7 - B Bty A 447 A X 53". Bye⊙ A Bty A 353. A X 7 - B Bty A 447 A X 53". A X 178 - A - 171st Bde A 504. A X 138. 'C' Battery A 442 A - X 178 - A - 171st Bde A 504. A X 138. 'A' Battery engaged on 'Y' Lane. 2 rounds lane cut - Otd widening amounts lane cut - Otd more to do. Good work done, but Otd more to do. 'B' Battery engaged on 'Z' Lane Lane cut and 2nd & 3rd series. 'C' Battery engaged on 'W' Lane. Lane cut - 30+ wide wire damaged for 30+ Lane.	

WAR DIARY or INTELLIGENCE SUMMARY

Army Form C. 2118

Place	Date	Hour	Summary of Events and Information	Remarks and references to Appendices
	27/6/16		A.111 & B.111 engaged in 1st line, were in Battery fire. All guns but were at back of first line. Fired only cut on planes. Hostile Artillery. Between 7am & 9am enemy shelled X roads at there Battle Hoargeard, into Gear Guard. Our troops between MARNE and CATEAU and front of CAMPION heavily shelled from 6–7 6.30, 10.25 am to 2pm with 5.9 and H.E. 11.0am and 2pm to 2 regts ROB ROY front, trenches heavily from 5–5.30pm onwards shelled with 5.9 H.2". 50 enemy balloons up to-day. M.F.R. Reference REBOTERNE 1/50000	

WAR DIARY or INTELLIGENCE SUMMARY

Army Form C. 2118

Place	Date	Hour	Summary of Events and Information	Remarks and references to Appendices
	28/6/16		**Y DAY.** Ammunition received from D.A.C. A Bty 608 rounds, B Bty 608 rounds, C Bty 608 rounds, D Bty 608 rounds. A 171st Bde 608 rounds. B Bty 681 rounds. Expended – A Bty 1090 rounds, B Bty 681 rounds. A 171st Bde 1034 rounds. C Bty 1286 rounds. "A" Battery, engaged on Zone Y 1, 2, 3, 44 lines. Widener's Lane – Progress slow but some damage done on 1st June wire. "B" Battery; engaged on Bosche line west on Battery Lane. Wire 10 + visible cuts, and some damage for about 100+. A/171 Battery; engaged on first line wire. 6 Bd 171 Bde, engaged on Zone W. Visible cuts & damage, Zone wire. Hostile fire. Very little.	

WAR DIARY or INTELLIGENCE SUMMARY

Army Form C. 2118

Place	Date	Hour	Summary of Events and Information	Remarks and references to Appendices
	29/9/16		Ammunition received from D.A.C. "A" Battery 912 rounds "B" Bty 912 rounds. "C" Bty 956 rounds. A.171 H Bde 912 rounds. Expended "A" Bty 083 rounds "B" Bty 360 rounds. "C" Bty 799 rounds. A.171 st Bde 676 rounds. "A" Battery engaged in front line wire. Left of were badly damaged Jan 10th - Right of these wire is being damaged. "B" Battery engaged on front line wire. Large piece of wire were seen to rise rests in eight of T.27 mile at K 26 C 60.81. "C" Battery engaged on front line wire. With exception of three small patches, front line were opened to be completely cut from K 29 C 23.23 to K 29 C 05-10.	

WAR DIARY
or
INTELLIGENCE SUMMARY
(Erase heading not required.)

Army Form C. 2118

Place	Date	Hour	Summary of Events and Information	Remarks and references to Appendices
	29/6/16		A. riflle engaged enemy front line. Another line strafed enfiladed through wire at K.29.6.8340. Special bombardment of enemy's 1st line and communication trenches between 5pm & 7pm later. "ho to" Artillery. 3.5pm – 3.30pm shelled K.27.0 with 5.9" 3. " " – 4. " K.31 " " 5.9" 4.40pm " K.30.17.15 6.9" 4.30pm " " Enemy replied to our bombardment by shelling trenches R.O.B R.O.Y. MONT & MARNE. Kite Balloon brought down by Zeppere 2.30pm Kite Balloons were seen SOUTHWARD as enemy as 18 Kite. During afternoon Captain G.J. Herman-Hodge & 2 O.R. wounded.	

WAR DIARY
or
INTELLIGENCE SUMMARY
(Erase heading not required.)

Army Form C. 2118

Place	Date	Hour	Summary of Events and Information	Remarks and references to Appendices
	30/6/16		Ammunition received. A. Battery 1016, "B" Bty. 1216 rounds, "C" Bty. 13, 16 rounds, A171st Bde.	
			1216 rounds	
			Expended "A" Battery 846 rounds, "B" Battery 654 rounds, "C" Battery 1052 rounds, A. 171st Bde	
			846 rounds.	
			Special bombardment 8.40 am to 9.20 am - objective 70 to 100 yards NORTH of point 46 - 9.20 am ceasefire received 9.25 am	

....
Lt. R.F.A.
Adjutant,
165th (County Palatine) Brigade R.F.A.

31st Division.

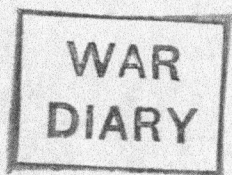

165th BRIGADE R. F. A.

JULY 1916

Confidential   Vol. IV

War Diary

165th Bde R.F.A.

July 1st to 31st
1916.

165 Bde. RFA   • 165 Bde RFA 31st January 4th note first army
Army Form C. 2118

WAR DIARY
or
INTELLIGENCE SUMMARY
(Erase heading not required.)

Volume VII. July 1916

Place	Date	Hour	Summary of Events and Information	Remarks and references to Appendices
	July 1st 1916.	6.25 a.m.	Opened fire with H.E. on German front line Trenches. BYF 15000.	
		7.13.	Germans reported in front line owing to white. Enemy replied heavily in front of 92½ Inf. Bde. too heavily on 93 2/3 4/5 Bde. Rifle fire a little but still impossible to observe fire.	
		7.20.	Infantry left our trenches & Germans steady. "B" reported all guns in action.	
		7.30	A/171 ob? two in action. Changed to shrapnel. Rifle commenced. Infantry & others showing activity.	
		7.39	Two waves at back of own Infantry reached front line. L.K. ment from no man's land. Double rounds occupation very difficult.	
		7.49	Signals appear to be away F.O.	
		7.50.	F.O.O. reported Infantry at work? across line.	
		7.56	Enemy fire became intense to our front line.	
		8.7	has from 2 PURPLE LINE. Some reported our front line on left of 92 & 93 Bde front.	
		8.15	Batteries firing on ORCHARD & TRENCHES NORTH OF SERRE.	
		8.16	A F.O.O. reported Infantry moving through SERRE.	
		8.24	No hostile fire on our Batteries so far -	
		8.30	Enemy barrage intense on own trenches.	
		8.36	Lt FENWICK & one Gunner reported wounded in no mans land while crossing to enemy front line.	
		8.41	242 ? Bde reported Germans still in front line enemy trenches.	
		9.0	Hostile barrage cut quite so intense. Situation very uncertain. Joint advance of Infantry did not appear to have been pushed ?.	

WAR DIARY or INTELLIGENCE SUMMARY

Army Form C. 2118

Place	Date	Hour	Summary of Events and Information	Remarks and references to Appendices
	1st July am	9.2	A cigarette of A/171 — DUNMOW reported 94 & 1.B. well into SERRE. Situation still very uncertain.	
		10.13	Still firing to our programme. Very little hostile fire W. of SERRE.	
		10.20	Visual message from TOUVENT FARM states 2 Lt DEIGHTON wounded in attack.	
		10.25	Hostile fire WEST of SERRE practically nil.	
		10.40	" " on our front line very heavy now.	
		10.46	Heavy shells falling in SERRE.	
		11.20	A few 4.2 shrapnel fell near batteries behind quarries.	
		11.30	Report from 94 & for S.F. BARRAGE — complied. BVF. 10 secs.	
		11.40	Message from F.O.O. B/165 reported hostile batteries & ammunition to 12 K y.k. very heavy.	
		12.35 pm	Shell fire on machine gun emplacements between points 60 & 96. Heavy machine gun fire & shelling of our infantry advance across no man's land. Great trouble with buffer springs, and fresh supplies unobtainable.	
		12.50	No hostile fire north and west of SERRE	
		4.10	94th I.B. reported to be holding from 29 to 68 and ORCHARD. A few Germans seen myself near French 1st & North of point 10.	
		5.0	A few Germans seen — the Battalion was chiefly engaged in bringing Germans over, they showed numbers and much had accrued for a great many.	
		6.15	Remainder in 2nd line between Points 64 & 40 from about point 10 east towards a lither-east line trenches opposite MARK COPSE.	

WAR DIARY
or
INTELLIGENCE SUMMARY.
(Erase heading not required.)

Army Form C. 2118.

Place	Date	Hour	Summary of Events and Information	Remarks and references to Appendices
Afns Plus als HEBUTERNE	July 1st 1916.	PM 6.30	Rec'd a message from the Hidden Gun Officer that 94" T.B. That horse and motor Transport could be seen moving on the ACHIET-BUCQUOY Road. Passed the information on to Heavy Artillery who opened fire with about 20 rounds and also own section. —	(Reg D/165)
		7.30	Germans been shooting our wounded in No Man's Land. Took a gun of A/171 Brigade forward to our front of German trenches and stopped them shooting any more. —	
			Just at dusk a movement of men noticed on flank of our front of 93rd.	
			T.B. our Batteries opened fire on hostile lines —	
			All Batteries barraging from 1 am. Till daylight	
	2nd	1 AM	Early in morning S.O.S. signal rec'd. All batteries fired — Nothing further reported.	
			With 94th I.B. ranged to say to how far we responded.	
			Enemy observed working on his trenches — sniped at all day whenever	
			Enemy seen — kept up a steady fire throughout the night —	
			Enemy's artillery quiet.	

Army Form C. 2118.

WAR DIARY
or
INTELLIGENCE SUMMARY.
(Erase heading not required.)

Instructions regarding War Diaries and Intelligence Summaries are contained in F.S. Regs., Part II and the Staff Manual respectively. Title pages will be prepared in manuscript.

Hour, Date, Place.	Summary of Events and Information	Remarks and references to Appendices
3/7/16.	Batteries firing on enemy's front-lines and outlying Machine Gun & Enemy observed working hard on trenches. Hostile Artillery very quiet.	
4/7/16.	Batteries firing on enemy's front lines and sniping Renches Gups. One direct hit observed. Enemy very busy on trenches – plenty of new earth being thrown up. Ammunition to be reduced to 300 rounds per gun – the remainder to be DUMPED with D.A.C.	

(73989) W4141—463. 400,000. 9/14. H.&J.Ltd. Forms/C. 2118/10.

Army Form C. 2118.

WAR DIARY
or
INTELLIGENCE SUMMARY.
(Erase heading not required.)

Instructions regarding War Diaries and Intelligence Summaries are contained in F.S. Regs., Part II. and the Staff Manual respectively. Title pages will be prepared in manuscript.

Hour, Date, Place	Summary of Events and Information	Remarks and references to Appendices
5/7/16	Men were observed in front of enemy's trench. Batteries firing on M.G. emplacements and damaging wire. Enemy very busy on trenches.	
6/7/16	Ammunition to be reduced to you down in battery wagons & 100 rounds to be fired for the 6th. Battery handed over to 48th DIVISIONAL ARTY.	
7 } 8 } 9/7/16	Brigade Left Bretons and proceeded by road to COUTRE BOIS and went into billets. Brigade moved by road and entrained at PREVENT at 15.22.	

WAR DIARY
or
INTELLIGENCE SUMMARY.
(Erase heading not required.)

Army Form C. 2118.

Hour, Date, Place	Summary of Events and Information	Remarks and references to Appendices
9/7/16	Arrived STEENBECQUE about 7.30pm, and marched to billets at HAVERSKERQUE.	
13/7/16	General's Inspection and Horse Inspection by D.D.V.S. & D.D.R. Classes formed for Engineers.	
14/7/16	"C" & "B" Batteries moved to PONT-DU-HEM and attached to 39th DIVISION	
15/7/16	"E" Battery move to PONT-DU-HEM and are attached to 169th Brigade. L.C. & G.S. Howitzers 165th Bde R.F.A. attached to 5th Australian Division	

Army Form C. 2118.

WAR DIARY
or
INTELLIGENCE SUMMARY.
(Erase heading not required.)

Instructions regarding War Diaries and Intelligence Summaries are contained in F.S. Regs., Part II and the Staff Manual respectively. Title pages will be prepared in manuscript.

Hour, Date, Place	Summary of Events and Information	Remarks and references to Appendices
16/7/16.	Headquarters & "D" Battery in Lawers. Cleaning - gun drill - semaphore.	
17th 2/6.	Headquarters & "D" Battery in Lawers. Cleaning - gun drill - semaphore - fuzing and sterliz.	
18/7/16	Headquarters cleaning Lewis - fuzing. Scores. "D" Battery working order.	
19/7/16	Headquarters cleaning Lewis - fuzing scores. "D" Battery - gun drill - semaphore - signalling.	

WAR DIARY
or
INTELLIGENCE SUMMARY.
(Erase heading not required.)

Army Form C. 2118.

Instructions regarding War Diaries and Intelligence Summaries are contained in F.S. Regs., Part II and the Staff Manual respectively. Title pages will be prepared in manuscript.

Hour, Date, Place	Summary of Events and Information	Remarks and references to Appendices
20/7/16	Headquarters. Cleaning horses - preparing and exercise. D. By. - Drill Order.	
21/7/16	Headquarters cleaning horses & stables. Telephone repairs. D. By. rough exercise.	
22/7/16	Headquarters - working order. D. By. rough exercise.	
23/7/16	Headquarters. Signals out with Telephone Cart on practice - paying exercise. D. By. rough exercise & stables.	

Army Form C. 2118.

WAR DIARY
or
INTELLIGENCE SUMMARY.
(Erase heading not required.)

Instructions regarding War Diaries and Intelligence Summaries are contained in F. S. Regs., Part II. and the Staff Manual respectively. Title pages will be prepared in manuscript.

Place	Date	Hour	Summary of Events and Information	Remarks and references to Appendices
	27/7/16		"D" Battery moved from HAVERSKERQUE and attached to 170th Brigade for tactical purposes.	
	27/7/16		"A" & "C" Batteries attached to 171st Brigade R.F.A. for tactical purposes. "B" Battery attached to 170th Brigade R.F.A. for tactical purposes. Headquarters moved from HAVERSKERQUE to ST ROBES	
	28/7/16		Headquarters Rough essence & Kobbes	
	29/7/16		Headquarters moved from ST ROBES to VIEILLE CHAPELLE.	
	28/7/16 to 31/7/16		Rough essence, Kobbes, and expects to Elsephele 30/7/16	

A.M. Wilson Lt. Col. R.F.A.
Commanding 165th (County Palatine) Brigade R.F.A.

T2134. Wt. W708—776. 500000. 4/15. Sir J. C. & S.

Vol 6

CONFIDENTIAL.

WAR DIARY.

of

165th BRIGADE R.F.A.

From AUGUST 1st, 1916 to AUGUST 31st, 1916.

VOLUME VIII

165 Bde R.F.A. Volume VIII.

Army Form C. 2118.

August 1916

WAR DIARY
or
INTELLIGENCE SUMMARY.

(Erase heading not required.)

Place	Date	Hour	Summary of Events and Information	Remarks and references to Appendices
In the Field	1/8/16 to 3/8/16		All available men from Headquarters on wire cutting fatigue. 2nd Lieut. R.H. Whittall joined "B" Battery 1-8-16. 2nd Lieut. H.T. Onward attached to "B" Battery returned to 31st D.A.C. 1-8-16	ibid
	4/8/16		All available men from Headquarters with available R.E. and 1 N.C.O & 6 men from 169th Brigade R.F.A. attached to "B" Battery, 1 N.C.O & 3 men from 170th Bde. also 1 N.C.O & 3 men from 171st Bde to be billeted at and attached for rations to 223rd R.E. Coy. All went to the carried out wire orders from Trench Mortar G.S. "Henderson" on wire on Hollow Battery & O.Ps.	ibid
	5/8/16 to 7/8/16		All available fuel on enemy's positions	ibid

T.2134. Wt. W703—776. 500000. 4/15. Sir J. C. & S.

WAR DIARY
or
INTELLIGENCE SUMMARY.
(Erase heading not required.)

Army Form C. 2118.

Instructions regarding War Diaries and Intelligence Summaries are contained in F.S. Regs., Part II. and the Staff Manual respectively. Title pages will be prepared in manuscript.

Place	Date	Hour	Summary of Events and Information	Remarks and references to Appendices
	8/6/16 to 10/6/16		Captain A.E. Barfords 14 days leave and then to report to War Office	oifkb
			Set on the night of the transportation Newcastle [crossed out]	
	11/6/16 to 16/6/16		Lieut H.E. McEnue attached to "B" Battery returned to 169" Bde	
	17/6/16		Major A.J. Claveley transferred to N°2 London C.C.S. All available men of Headquarters on New Cutting positions	oifkb
	18/6/16 to 19/8/16		Headquarters on New Cutting training. 2nd Lieut C.C. Deafe attached to "B" Battery 19-5-16. "C" Battery 165" Bde left for lieut D.M. Davies to report to War Office Leg cause on duty	oifkb
	20/6/16		R.S.M. Brotheau reported on duty 2nd Lieut C. B. Grey reported for duty Howitzer	oifkb

WAR DIARY
or
INTELLIGENCE SUMMARY.

(Erase heading not required.)

Army Form C. 2118.

Place	Date	Hour	Summary of Events and Information	Remarks and references to Appendices
	20/6/16		Cove - All available men of Headquarters men of Headquarters were cutting positions	initials
	21/6/16 to 24/6/16		All available men of Headquarters cutting positions	initials
	25/6/16		2nd Lieut. J.G.W. Sibold reported for duty - posted to "B" Battery. 2nd Lieut. C.B. Deeps attached to "B" Battery. 160th Brigade returned to 169th Brigade All available men of Headquarters on wire cutting positions. "B" Battery took part in bombardment of enemy infantry & gun emplacements at - @ 11, @ 9. - S.11.a.11. S.11.a.11½.1½	initials

Army Form C. 2118.

WAR DIARY
or
INTELLIGENCE SUMMARY.
(Erase heading not required.)

Place	Date	Hour	Summary of Events and Information	Remarks and references to Appendices
	26/6/16 to 29/6/16		All available men of Headquarters on wire cutting parties.	July

Army Form C. 2118.

WAR DIARY
or
INTELLIGENCE SUMMARY.
(Erase heading not required.)

Instructions regarding War Diaries and Intelligence Summaries are contained in F.S. Regs., Part II. and the Staff Manual respectively. Title pages will be prepared in manuscript.

Place	Date	Hour	Summary of Events and Information	Remarks and references to Appendices
Lille	30th		Brigade reorganized as from noon 30th with the following changes:— A/165 is enlarged by 1 section of B/171. B/165 is enlarged by 1 section of B/171, & Capt. Roper, S.G. as second in command. C/165 is enlarged by 1 section of B/171. D/165 is enlarged by addition of Major Sir Eric Hixon Bart, who assumes command from to-day's date, vice Capt. Belcher (late B.C.) as second in command. All three 15pr batteries thus become 6 gun batteries and the 4.5" How. battery remains as before in establishment. On reorganization taking place the following officers came over with their sections and are posted to the Brigade as follows:— 2/Lt. G.J. Elliott } To A/165 from B/171. 2/Lt. J.A. Robinson } 2/Lt. G.J. Tanner } To B/165 from B/171. 2/Lt. S.W. Lorthouse } To B/165 from B/171.	

Place	Date	Hour	Summary of Events and Information	Remarks and references to Appendices
Fields	30th		Continued. 2/Lt R.S. Knott-Thomas } To B/165 from B/171. 2/Lt R.C.C. Scott-Stirring } On this date Batteries (B & A) changed position on reorganisation as follows:- 'A'/165 occupied position at S.13.d.25.40. (late of 171.) B/165 " " S.7.d.80.70. (" B/171) C & D/165 remained in same positions	
"	31st		During the month the C.O. has been supervising & carrying out the rebuilding & additions to the O.P.s on the Divisional Front, as in addition to this, has been constructing Lines connecting observing positions as follows:- Personnel engaged on this work are detailed from Batteries & HQrs.	

O.C.

WAR DIARY
or
INTELLIGENCE SUMMARY.

Army Form C. 2118.

Place	Date	Hour	Summary of Events and Information	Remarks and references to Appendices
Field	1st to 31st August		All batteries of this Brigade have been detailed during this month as stated in War Diary for July. A & C batteries to Right Centre Group, 31st Div. Arty, and B & D batteries to Left Group 31st Div. Arty. All four batteries have been engaged in "holding the line" and have been in positions as follows:—	
			A/165 S 7 b 39.	
			B/165 M 31 b 95.60. (1 gun detached at S 14 b 69)	
			C/165 S 2 d 48.	
			D/165 M 32 b 43.	
			A/165 X 9 c 45, changed to R 34 c 8.3	
			B/165 R 31 D 27,	
			C/165 M 25 d 46, changed to R 34 c 9.3.	
			D/165 R 35 a 05.	

Adjutant,
165th (County Palatine) Brigade R.F.A.

Vol 7

CONFIDENTIAL.

WAR DIARY

OF

165th Bde. R.F.a.

From 1st September 1916 to 30th September 1916.

(VOLUME IX)

165th Bde RFA
1-30 Sept 1916
Vol. IX

Army Form C. 2118.

WAR DIARY
INTELLIGENCE SUMMARY.
(Erase heading not required.)

Place	Date	Hour	Summary of Events and Information	Remarks and references to Appendices
LACOUTURE	1.9.16		A/165 Battery became RFA gun batteries. 2/Lieut remains the Bn. Major Sir C.S.Nixon took over command of 3/165 from Capt. J.R. Fletcher	
		1.58	C/165 fired about 120 rounds in retaliation from a raid by 2nd & 3rd Inf. Bde. on 16 Suff.	1/9/16
			2 Lt C.B. Gray proceeded on T.M. Course prior to going to Egypt.	
			A/165 fired about 120 rounds on alarm	
	2.9.16		C/165 fired about 30 rounds in support of T.M's answering – Considerable aeroplane activity	2/9/16
	3.9.16		A/165 (operate) with T.M's good effect. Our heavy T.M fired three ronds from L. Berry retaliated on FACTORY & vicinity	3/9/16
	4.9.16		A/165 fired 95H a very wire which was considerably damaged 9/165 fired on T.M. 2nd Lieut R.C.C. Scot SCURVING proceeded to Offrs.	
	5.9.16		9/165 fired on enemy T.M. Much material flung into air	
			C/165 placed 4 3gr. in neutralising position on S87E0, keeping it up to ask to retire obtaining good target.	5/9/16
	6.9.16		C/165 cut wire at S9 6 63 55, making gap but not clearing same off.	
			A/165 also wire cutting.	

WAR DIARY or INTELLIGENCE SUMMARY

Army Form C. 2118.

(Erase heading not required.)

Place	Date	Hour	Summary of Events and Information	Remarks and references to Appendices
	7.9.16	12.5 am	B/165 intermittent B.C. fired bursts of fire on enemy front line, roads etc.	
		1.30 am	Catch working parties. Considerable hostile artillery activity. C/165 opened O.P.'s on very bad ground. "BX"	OPEN O.P. "BX"
			shells. B/165 fired on active trench mortars. "B" were very bad ground.	
			Les & 9nd ret 9.28, 9.600 6nd.	
	8.9.16	12.27	C/165 fired about 170 rounds in support of raid on enemy right. Difficulty	
		am	Difficulty in locating enemy trenches. Prisoner states who died after being captured.	
		1.30	B/165 out wire, with good effect, much timber torn in air, parapet breached.	
			B & B/165 fired on 7 P.M. entering enemy camp N39 c17 963 at S16a 9235, also observed him go in wire.	
			Working party opened by C/165 at S16a 9235, also observed him go in wire.	
			Lieut. H.A. LEE transferred to 1st Signal Artillery C/165	C/165
			2Lieut. V.C. MARTIN " " "	B/165
			Lieut. F.H. WOODHOUSE " " "	B/165
	9.9.16	10 PM	Batteries fired bursts during night to catch working parties	
			Centre Group became Right Group. C/Br's worken they few opened battery	
			B/165 fired during night 130 to assist 93rd Inf. Bde to carry out wire	
			cut enough as far as known at present.	

WAR DIARY
or
INTELLIGENCE SUMMARY
(Erase heading not required.)

Army Form C. 2118.

Place	Date	Hour	Summary of Events and Information	Remarks and references to Appendices
	9.9.16		B/165 fired on enemy wire with good effect.	
			Major Sir G.M. NIXON (killed) to command B/165 vice Major R.E. Staveley (wounded).	
			Capt FLETCHER assumed command of D/165.	
	10.9.16	12:30am	Heavy hostile 9th/165 Batteries bombarded — end of 93 & left 139c as above.	
		1:55am	Batteries opened bursts of fire to catch enemy working parties.	
	11.9.16	12noon	B/165 fired on working parties in open with excellent effects when firing on enemy wire, previous fire having been registered.	
			C/165 came to (?) area for BEAU PUITS to support for [?] at [?] area D.	
			C/165 went from S.O.H. obsg heavy S. return.	
	12.9.16		B/165 fired on usual target & wire.	
		R30 to 11:51am	Batteries fired bursts of fire during night to catch working parties.	
			Test 'R'.	
			Organized shoots did not take place by T.M. in FERME du BOIS.	
			B/165 dispersed high velocity party at 5224 area D.	
	13.9.16		Still & rainy. Very quiet day.	

Army Form C. 2118.

WAR DIARY
or
INTELLIGENCE SUMMARY.
(Erase heading not required.)

Instructions regarding War Diaries and Intelligence Summaries are contained in F. S. Regs., Part II. and the Staff Manual respectively. Title pages will be prepared in manuscript.

Place	Date	Hour	Summary of Events and Information	Remarks and references to Appendices
	14.9	2.50 a.m.	Bomb & rifle fire on right bank to catch working parties. 5/65 finds a active trench mortars. 5/65 in one fire in prepared position at 17.26.6.91. Enemy quiet day. All quiet except for shelling of R.H70 crater. 2/ R.C.C. Rest. Showing a tendency in bombs & rifles. 2/ C.B. Group above off strength neck effect from 30.6.16.	

T2134. Wt. W708—776. 500000. 4/15. Sir J. C. & S.

Army Form C. 2118.

WAR DIARY
or
INTELLIGENCE SUMMARY.
(Erase heading not required.)

Instructions regarding War Diaries and Intelligence Summaries are contained in F. S. Regs., Part II. and the Staff Manual respectively. Title pages will be prepared in manuscript.

Place	Date	Hour	Summary of Events and Information	Remarks and references to Appendices
LE TOURET	18/9/16		Lt Col Henderson assumed command of the new Left Group at 12 noon and took over 6 guns of A/165 - 4 guns of B/165 - 6 guns of C/165 - 4 guns of D/165 - and 2 guns of B/169. 50 firing by Group and Hostile artillery inactive. Police and rain all day.	
	19/9/16		6/165 - fired 9 rounds "A" on front line parapet with satisfactory result. D/165 - fired 8 rounds "B1" on trench junction S13 d 00.30 - Registration in case of firing at night. Two excellent bursts at trench. Enemy artillery quiet. Raining all day.	
	20/9/16		Fired 3 bursts in conjunction with 92nd Infantry Bde series on front line trenches S.6 a 75.20 and onto FERME du BOIS - There was no retaliation by the enemy artillery.	

WAR DIARY or INTELLIGENCE SUMMARY

Army Form C. 2118.

Place	Date	Hour	Summary of Events and Information	Remarks and references to Appendices
	20/9/16		Great earth thrown up by enemy at S.17.c.10.75. – Enemy machine guns active from 6pm to 10.30pm. – Heavy Trench Mortar activity from 11am to 5.30pm – Rifle Artillery only fired three times during day at 12.30pm 12.30 to 1.30pm & 6.10pm – all 77mm. No hostile artillery during night. – Weather dull and showery	
	21/9/16		Since parties of the enemy constantly walking about PER MEADOW BOIS and Trench running from S.16.d.25.of to S.16.d.35.0. Since parties of the Enemy walking westwards on road at A.a.30.35. Meenin two & three. funnels continuously in both directions along the LA BASSEE road. A Greenwear located at S.11.c.50.30 by enemy of our fires & refuses then moved further north presumably	

WAR DIARY or INTELLIGENCE SUMMARY

Army Form C. 2118.

Place	Date	Hour	Summary of Events and Information	Remarks and references to Appendices
	20/9/16		on a light railway. Considered retaliation with enfilading or heavy howitzer for which fired at 4-15 pm. 6 of the two howitzer shells with 4-5" How. von Field Battery - 8" How. also fired. At 6-15 pm. Placed howitzer again with same result. T.M's. Stokes and Rifle Grenadier Jerries front line for 15 minutes. At 7-30 pm howitzer fired again - seen by observer of 6/163" Bde. O.C. 6/163" Bde opened rapid fire and howitzer stopped. Col. Lt. Kent RHA dined on attachment.	M.B.
	21/9/16	9-10 9-30 pm	Very quiet day. Heavy H.T.M. active in evening. B/b's fired on LA BASSÉE at men seen moving stores. C/169 fired in conjunction with M.G. T.M's in evening as a covering fire. Very little firing on our front, as no more expenditure of ammunition is absolutely necessary is to take place.	

Army Form C. 2118.

WAR DIARY
or
INTELLIGENCE SUMMARY.
(Erase heading not required.)

Instructions regarding War Diaries and Intelligence Summaries are contained in F. S. Regs., Part II. and the Staff Manual respectively. Title pages will be prepared in manuscript.

Place	Date	Hour	Summary of Events and Information	Remarks and references to Appendices
	24-9-16		Quiet day. Our Heavy T.M. fired in answer of the Group Staff by 'in consequence'. Enemy retaliated to our T.M. fire with 5.9 & 8" on FACTORY O.P. (C/165)	
	25-9-16		A & C Batteries afforded covering fire to our T.M.s 9/69 retaliated on to T.M. which fired on our trenches. FACTORY O.P. (C/165) shelled with 8". No damage.	
	26-9-16		Orders received to cut down expenditure of A.X. & to fire no B.X. till further orders. This to establish a reserve for offensive questions or someone 9 accounts for little firing by this Group.	
	27-9-16		A/165 fired on enemy working parties at Tya 66 (Ropllings) from ROEBERG fire observed by C/169 by means of new O.P. Exchange just made. All Battery O.P.s can now communicate with others. Wires are also being connected to the Exchange, which is connected to Group H.Q. at X 16 D 68.	
	28-9-16		B/165 fired on LA BASSÉE road. Very little firing by Group on account of reduced allotment of ammunition.	
	29-9-16		Received orders that 5th Divisional Arty would relieve the 31st Divisl Arty very shortly, 9 that 31st Divl Arty would proceed to join 4th Army. Signed ____	

T2134. Wt. W708—776. 500000. 4/15. Sir J. C. & 8.

WAR DIARY
or
INTELLIGENCE SUMMARY.

Army Form C. 2118.

Place	Date	Hour	Summary of Events and Information	Remarks and references to Appendices
LE TOURET	30./X 16.		C/165 fired on working party, hipersing same - Considerable activity by other Group all day - B/165 tested fuzes (new) 101, 102, & 103 received per B.A.C. Report will follow - (AX.)	[signed]

[signed] C.J. Hibbothinson
Lieut & .... Adjutant,
165th (County Palatine) Brigade R.F.A.

VOL 8
31/10/16

Confidential

WAR DIARY

OF

165th BRIGADE R.F.A.

FROM 1st OCTOBER to 31st OCTOBER, 1916.

VOLUME X

165th RFA — October 1916

WAR DIARY or INTELLIGENCE SUMMARY
Army Form C. 2118.

Place	Date	Hour	Summary of Events and Information	Remarks and references to Appendices
LE TOURET	1.X.16	4.30	Arranged retaliation on Enemy H.T.M. at S11c50.25 at 4.30 p.m. Our trenches in line of fire cleared. Following guns & Mortars took part. 4.5 How, 8" How, H.T.M., Med T.M., Stokes & 18 pdr.	
	2.X.16		Lt Col G.P. Henderson took over command of 31st Div. Arty. forces night in absence of Lt Col G.B. Seward.	
	3.X.16		Raids arranged to take place by Rt & left Battalions. Artillery arrangements for left group prepared for use in case of emergency. 61st Div. Arty Batteries, & Centre Group 31st Div. Arty cooperated in these arrangements. Raid raids unsuccessful but no artillery assistance from this group called for.	
	4.X.16		Orders received for relief of Lt Com Groups 5 & Corporals Group of 5th Corporals Div. Arty consisting of batteries from 30th, 40th, 61st & 32nd Div. Arties. B/165 will be relieved by A/306, 61st Div Arty. & C/165 by B/306, 61st Div Arty. A/165 by C/169 & C/165, 30th Div Arty. Major Hills will command the group after departure of Lt Col Selle.	
	5.X.16		Major Hills came to Barracks in reconnaissance. B/165 & A/165 will not be relieved but will cover batteries arrival to begin times. Major Hills R.P.A. Col Henderson & self Reconnaissance for forward Batteries sent in.	

Army Form C. 2118.

WAR DIARY
or
INTELLIGENCE SUMMARY.
(Erase heading not required.)

Instructions regarding War Diaries and Intelligence Summaries are contained in F.S. Regs., Part II. and the Staff Manual respectively. Title pages will be prepared in manuscript.

Place	Date	Hour	Summary of Events and Information	Remarks and references to Appendices
LE TOURET.	5.X.16	11.5 a.m.	R/H's reported horses of 2.5 nm moving on road running N. & S. through T & S.9.C, & paid no attn. Moving to fire. Arty notified.	
	6.X.16		Relief started. A composite Bty of 61st Bde relieved R/H's in position. Relieved C/165. C/188 relieved C/169. Relays carried out under arrangements made by B.Cs concerned.	B/306
	7.X.16		Relief complete by 12 noon. All batteries of 15th & 61st Bde concentrated at their Wagon lines. Approval received for the following exchange of appointment on 5th inst: Lieut. O.L.B. Brisbane ranks 2nd command C/165 vice that from 27th Sept. 2/Lt E.R. Ch Vivian appointed Asst. 28th Sept. Captain R.H. Lynch R.E. Chaplain left to report War Office.	
	8.X.16		Brigade moved to ST LEGER entraining at VILLERS ST LEGER. Marched from DOULLENS and arrived ST LEGER morning of 6th Oct.	
	9.X.16	2 p.m.	Brigade Hdqrs Quartis moved into Battle Headquarters.	

Army Form C. 2118.

WAR DIARY
or
INTELLIGENCE SUMMARY.
(Erase heading not required.)

Instructions regarding War Diaries and Intelligence Summaries are contained in F. S. Regs., Part II. and the Staff Manual respectively. Title pages will be prepared in manuscript.

Place	Date	Hour	Summary of Events and Information	Remarks and references to Appendices
	10		Batteries moving into position.	
	11		and constructing emplacements.	
	12		" 1 O.R. Wounded.	
	13		Bringing up ammunition from D.A.C.	
	14		by hand from D.A.C. - Lt. Griffiths Wounded (at duty)	
			5. O.R. Wounded.	
	15		Registering points along the whole front from	
	16		Givenchy to the Divisional Front.	
	17		2nd Lieut. Lack. Henry Chief Off. the Strength on instructions	
	18		from D.A.C. 3rd Echelon. " 1 O.R. Killed - 2 O.R. Wounded.	
			Captain (T/Major) W.E. Fleming R.C. Chaplain joined for duty.	
	19		Wire cutting in front of third line. East battery to cut-	
			one or more gaps.	

WAR DIARY or INTELLIGENCE SUMMARY.

Army Form C. 2118.

Place	Date	Hour	Summary of Events and Information	Remarks and references to Appendices
	20.x		Wire cutting on the German third line as follows:- "A" Battery between POINT 63 K.24.a.60.25" and Trench Junction K.24.a.35.70. - "B" Battery between K.24.a.35.70 and Trench Junction K.25.b.95.99. - "C" Battery between K.25.b.95.99 and K.17.d.55.20. Trench firing as follows:- "A" Bty from 6pm to 10pm from BOX WOOD to K.20.a.29. "B" Bty 10pm to 2am from K.13.d.32 to K.14.c.0.15. "C" Bty- 2am to 5am from LA LOUVIERE FARM to K.15.d.95.45. - Capt. & 2 Liaison Officer Wounded - 1 OR Wounded.	
	21.x		18-pdr batteries cutting third line wire between K.18.a.1.3 and K.18.c.31 and were at K.18.d.30.95". House Battery bombards points 19.07 and 97 Register firing on railway - 2 OR Killed - 2 OR Wounded (gas shell) Capt R.G. Fitzgerald Sievers assumed command of "D" Battery.	

WAR DIARY
or
INTELLIGENCE SUMMARY.

Place	Date	Hour	Summary of Events and Information	Remarks and references to Appendices
	22-X		Batteries cutting wire between K.18.a.1.3. and K.18.c.8.7. Special bombardment and concentration on SERRE and PUISIEUX.	
	23-X		Special programme 6 to 6.75 am. Half the guns firing on front-line, and half on the support-line 7.15am to 6pm - all 18 pdr. Batteries cut-wire in the front; all others to their shooting on the support-line. Each battery having cut a lane in the support-line was prepared to cut a lane through the wire on the same front, then through the 4th "gap" when the 3rd is "gap" is cut. At night all 18 pdr. Batteries were to fire frequent bursts of fire throughout the night at the points on the enemy's wire at which they had been firing during the day.	

WAR DIARY
or
INTELLIGENCE SUMMARY.

Army Form C. 2118.

Place	Date	Hour	Summary of Events and Information	Remarks and references to Appendices
	23.x		How Battery from 6.0 to 6.15 am on Support Trench from point Sp.6 to point 33. 7.15 am to 6 pm the cuts were on "Lane" where it can be seen to the East of LA LOUVIERE FARM, also wire and defences of PUISYEUX between t.14.c.10.00 and t.14.c.03.60. At night How Battery will fire on Trench Junctions to be selected by Battery Commander. 3 O.P. Manned.	
	24.x		Firing as were on Front and Support Lines between K.23.B.5.2.2 and K.23.B.4½.6.1. Sight firing on wire cut during the day and on the Secondary approaches. K.18.C.14 to K.18.d.0.7. K.24.a.4.7 to "STARWOOD". K.1HA.5F.12 to L.m.C.40.38. How Battery to fire on Trench Junction at t.20.A.H.7.	

T2134. Wt. W708-776. 500000. 4/15. Sir J. C. & S.

WAR DIARY or INTELLIGENCE SUMMARY

Place	Date	Hour	Summary of Events and Information	Remarks and references to Appendices
	24-X		K.18.C.14 to I.18.d.07. and LA LOUVIERE FARM. Sgn Sh C.M.S. sam Wounded (gas).	
	25-X		15-pdrs continue were cutting as on previous day. Hows battery enfilading Fight-trench at point-60. with 2 guns. The other 2 guns cutting. 3-Farm were East of LA LOUVIERE FARM. Registering on wire cut during the day and on enfilading approaches. LM. g.o.5.12 to I.14.C. no.35. I.18 c.14 to K.18.d.o.7. K.18.C.14 to STAR WOOD from a.47	
	26-X		15-pdrs continue wire cutting as on previous day, 2 Hows battery also bombard the following points :- K.18.C.19 - K.18.C.3/2.5 and LA LOUVIERE FARM - 3 these East of LA LOUVIERE and front line trench at K.23.B.60.	

WAR DIARY or INTELLIGENCE SUMMARY

Army Form C. 2118.

(Erase heading not required.)

Instructions regarding War Diaries and Intelligence Summaries are contained in F.S. Regs., Part II. and the Staff Manual respectively. Title pages will be prepared in manuscript.

Place	Date	Hour	Summary of Events and Information	Remarks and references to Appendices
	26-x		Sight firing & wire cut during the day.	
	27-x		Programme as previous day - Slight firing & wire cut during today	
	28-x		Programme came as previous day. Slight firing & wire cut - during the day and the wire was cut between two special points - return wire up and F. hrs. Firing to take place West of the 3rd line after 8.0pm - Captain Lindsay founder "B" Bty. N.O.K. wounded.	
	29-x		"B" Battery engaged in destroying wire at- 17.23.a.50.20 to K.23.a.40.30. The second line wire will be cut as follows:-	

WAR DIARY
or
INTELLIGENCE SUMMARY.
(Erase heading not required.)

Army Form C. 2118.

Place	Date	Hour	Summary of Events and Information	Remarks and references to Appendices
	29.x		"A" Bty from K 23.a.99.30 to K 23.a.95.35 "B" Bty from K 23.a.90.40 to K 23.a.80.55 Sight-firing will be on the front-line Bank of Yser consisting of two Lewis gun fire at the following types: - 6.15 pm, 7 pm, 8 pm, E pm, 8.40 pm, 9.20 pm & 1.30 am. Lt Col E McEwan & Lt Q.G. Williams wounded - 10P Wounded Capt P.G. Walker R.A.M.C. reported for duty. Programme same as previous day with exception of the 6.0 am to 6.15 am programme which will not take place.	
	30.x		Enough firing bursts of fire at were cut-during day at the following times R.A. Bty 7 to 10 pm - "B" Bty 10 pm to 1 am "C" Bty 1 to 4 am. Each Battery to fire at irregular intervals on specially selected spots. Batteries to fire on front line every day from hours of early. B Capt H.D. Gourlay R.A.M.C.	

WAR DIARY
or
INTELLIGENCE SUMMARY.
(Erase heading not required.)

Army Form C. 2118.

Place	Date	Hour	Summary of Events and Information	Remarks and references to Appendices
	26-X		deported on instructions received from A.D.M.S. 62st DIVISION.	
	27-X		A Special Bombardment of communication trenches from 1-0pm to 2-40pm on K.17 & and also on various trench junctions. L.O.O.S to keep a sharp look-out on the gaps already cut and on the points to be bombarded, and report any movement observed or working parties seen, when Shop bursts of Shrapnel will be opened. Sight-firing as usual with exception of the following trenches in front or support line trenches or wire. 6 pm to 8 pm 1 and 9.5 pm to 1-40 pm. In addition to the usual programme there were to two bursts of fire by all Batteries	

WAR DIARY
or
INTELLIGENCE SUMMARY.
(Erase heading not required.)

Army Form C. 2118.

Place	Date	Hour	Summary of Events and Information	Remarks and references to Appendices
	31-	X	one at 5·30p.m, the other at 9·0a.m. 18 pdrs in front and support line were using Ruff Shrapnel fired half "H.E.", and H.E. shows ballot in the support trench within the zone.	

E.J. Gibbon 1/11/17
Adjutant,
100th (County Palatine) Brigade R.F.A.

CONFIDENTIAL.

WAR DIARY

OF

165 BRIGADE. R.F.A.

From November 1st 1916 to November 30th 1916.

(VOLUME XI)

165th Bde R.F.A
No 3/4

H.Q.
31st D.A.

Herewith War Diary
for the month of November,
1916.

2/11/16

L S Henderson
.... Lt. Col. R.F.A.
Commanding 165th (County Palatine) Brigade R.F.A.

165 Inf Bde H.Q. F.S. 30th Nov. 1916. Vol. XI.

Army Form C. 2118.

WAR DIARY
or
INTELLIGENCE SUMMARY.
(Erase heading not required.)

Instructions regarding War Diaries and Intelligence Summaries are contained in F.S. Regs., Part II. and the Staff Manual respectively. Title pages will be prepared in manuscript.

Place	Date	Hour	Summary of Events and Information	Remarks and references to Appendices
	1/11/16		Wire cutting. Cut gaps 30 yards wide at K.17.d.12.12. Other gaps cut 10 yards either side of THE POINT. Night firing carried out on approaches and front line wire except when patrols out. — Casualties Nil. —	
	2/11/16		Wire cutting continued, cleaning up gaps and cutting on support line. 4.5 hows opened two shoots by T.M. — Casualties Nil. — Usual night firing.	
	3/11/16		Wire cutting — cleaning up gaps and destroying apron. Usual night firing, also combined bursts on front line wire. — Casualties Nil. —	
	4/11/16		Wire cutting — gaps cut in front, support and 3rd line wire in connection with a raid by 13th Y&L. Concentration of 18pdrs & 4.5 thrown on Puisieux. Night firing as usual. One burst on m. gun line. — Casualty 1 O.R. —	
	5/11/16		Keeping gaps open. Usual night firing & bursts. — Casualties Nil.	

Army Form C. 2118.

WAR DIARY
or
INTELLIGENCE SUMMARY.
(Erase heading not required.)

Instructions regarding War Diaries and Intelligence Summaries are contained in F. S. Regs., Part II. and the Staff Manual respectively. Title pages will be prepared in manuscript.

Place	Date	Hour	Summary of Events and Information	Remarks and references to Appendices
	6/11/16		Wirecutting in connection with raid continued. 4·5" Hows destroying trench junction. Usual night firing, with bursts on front & support line wire. No firing after 11-0 pm on the wire. Casualties Nil.	
	7/11/16		Wirecutting — reopening gaps. 4·5 Hows bombarding trench junction. "C" Batty temporarily out of action owing to heavy rain, position flooded. Night firing & bursts as usual. Raid by 13th & 4th not a success. Liaison Officer of/to Beauchamp "B" Bty with raid commander. Capt. Halpin "B" Bty with raiders in fractive appear to have given considerable assistance. Casualties Nil.	
	8/11/16		Wire cutting on 3rd line, also cleaning up of gaps. Usual night firing with bursts on gaps in wire; also 2 bursts on La Louvrie Farm. Casualties Nil. "C" Bty still out of action.	
	9/11/16		On look out for working parties. Usual night firing, also 2 bursts on La Louvrie Farm. "C" Bty still out of action. Casualties Nil.	

Army Form C. 2118.

WAR DIARY
or
INTELLIGENCE SUMMARY.
(Erase heading not required.)

Instructions regarding War Diaries and Intelligence Summaries are contained in F.S. Regs., Part II. and the Staff Manual respectively. Title pages will be prepared in manuscript.

Place	Date	Hour	Summary of Events and Information	Remarks and references to Appendices
	10/11/16		"C" Battery in action again. Wirecutting on front & support line. Barrage on front & support lines from 5-45 am to 6.0 am. Usual night firing. — Casualties Nil. —	
	11/11/16		Wirecutting all day. H.E. Shrapnel destroys trench junction, also 2 points on LA LOUVIERE FARM. Usual night firing. — Casualties Nil. —	
	12/11/16		"Y" Day. Barrage on front and support lines from 5-45 am to 6-0 am. Wire cutting all day. Usual night firing. — Casualties. Capt E.R. Piper and 2/Lt. P. Earnshaw and 10 O.R. wounded.	
	13/11/16		"Z" Day. The day of attack. The Brigade took part in the General attack from a point just N. of Serre to a point S. of Beaucourt and Grandcourt. The Artillery barrage started at 5-45 am simultaneously with the infantry attack. The Brigade covered the 92nd & 93rd Infantry Brigades who were attacking on the extreme left of the front; the 92nd Inf Bde attained their objective with very few casualties, but were withdrawn at 2-0 pm owing to the failure of the	

T/134. Wt. W708—776. 50C000. 4/15. Sir J.C. & S.

Army Form C. 2118.

WAR DIARY
or
INTELLIGENCE SUMMARY.
(Erase heading not required.)

Instructions regarding War Diaries and Intelligence Summaries are contained in F. S. Regs., Part II. and the Staff Manual respectively. Title pages will be prepared in manuscript.

Place	Date	Hour	Summary of Events and Information	Remarks and references to Appendices
			3rd Division on their right. They lost considerably in the withdrawal. Enemy snipers used explosive bullets. Beaumont Hamel was captured early in the day and elsewhere along the front the attack was successful, except at Serre. A heavy fog made observation impossible all day, except for about half an hour about 4 p.m. Firing continued until 7 p.m. – Casualties NIL.	
	14/11/16		The Brigade reinforcing on the whole Divisional front, from John Copse to Sunken Road. Bursts of fire at night on Mortenwitz trenches. Casualties NIL.	
	15/11/16		Firing on Mortenwitz trenches. No rifle firing – Casualties NIL.	
	16/11/16		Very quiet day. Nothing to record. Casualties NIL.	
	17/11/16		Nothing to record.	
	18/11/16		Barrage on front + support line from 6.10 a.m. to 6.25 a.m. in connection with operations of 2nd + 5th Corps, further south. No rifle firing. Casualties NIL.	

T2134. Wt. W708–776. 500000. 4/15. Sir J. C. & S.

Army Form C. 2118.

WAR DIARY
or
INTELLIGENCE SUMMARY.
(Erase heading not required.)

Instructions regarding War Diaries and Intelligence Summaries are contained in F.S. Regs., Part II. and the Staff Manual respectively. Title pages will be prepared in manuscript.

Place	Date	Hour	Summary of Events and Information	Remarks and references to Appendices
	19/11/16		Destroying repairs to gaps in wire. Usual night firing. — Casualties Nil. Bde H.Q. moved from Battle H.Q. to Sailly.	
	20/11/16		Keeping gaps open, and firing on movement. Usual night firing. "C" Bty out of action while moving into new position. — Casualties Nil.	
	21/11/16		Nothing to record. Usual night firing. — Casualties Nil.	
	22/11/16		Ditto	
	23/11/16		Registering new zone, 3rd Battery Northwards to Naugelay Farm. Usual night firing. — Casualties Nil. Completion of registration.	
	24/11/16		Notice special to read. Ammunition allotment cut down to 25 rounds per 18 pdr and 30 rounds per 4.5 how per day. — Casualties Nil.	

WAR DIARY
or
INTELLIGENCE SUMMARY.
(Erase heading not required.)

Army Form C. 2118.

Place	Date	Hour	Summary of Events and Information	Remarks and references to Appendices
	25/11/16		Nothing special to record. Casualties Nil.	
	26/11/16		ditto	
	27/11/16		Lt.Col. S.I Hawkins O.C. 165 Bde. took command of Left Group, constituted as follows: A/165, B/165, D/165, B/170, C/170 and D/170. Group front extends from Sunken Road to Gommecourt Park. Front held by 9 & 2 Inf. Bde. and 93rd Inf. Bde.	
	28/11/16		Registering new zones. Special bombardment of Puisieux by 18pdrs and 4.5 Hows. in retaliation for enemy trenches in enemy shelling of HEBUTERNE. Wire unimportant.	
	29/11/16		Firing on small parties of men showing in enemy trenches. Trenches appear to be impassable in places. Night firing on approaches. Casualties nil.	
	30/11/16		Fired on a few working parties. Night firing as before.	

S.Hilton 2/Lt.
Offr. (Country Palatine) Brigade R.F.A
Adjutant

Vol 10

CONFIDENTIAL.

WAR DIARY

OF

165th BRIGADE R.F.A.

From 1st DECEMBER 1916 to 31st DECEMBER 1916.

VOLUME XII.

165th Bde R.F.A. Volume XII
1st to 31st Dec 1916.

WAR DIARY
or
INTELLIGENCE SUMMARY

Place	Date	Hour	Summary of Events and Information	Remarks and references to Appendices
	1/12/16		Bombardment of the trenches S. of Bonnecourt by H.A. 18 pdrs firing many movement resulting. Night firing carried out on main communication trenches. Orders for group retaliation and counter bombardments sent out.	
	2/12/16		Firing & movement as yesterday. Night firing in bursts on front line trenches and wire in combination with Infantry rifle & Machine Gun fire.	
	3/12/16		Nothing to record	
	4/12/16		Ammunition allotment. 18 pdrs 50 rounds per gun per day. 4.5 how 60 rounds per gun per day. Unlimited in case of attack. Only 25% to be shrapnel. Night firing, bursts on front line in conjunction with Infantry.	
	5/12/16		Selecting O.P.'s for new outfit. Burst of rifle arranged by Divl Arty on roads and communication trenches in vicinity of ROSSIGNOL WOOD.	

WAR DIARY or INTELLIGENCE SUMMARY

Army Form C. 2118.

Place	Date	Hour	Summary of Events and Information	Remarks and references to Appendices
	6/12/16		Firing on movement resulting from H.A. bombardment of trenches. Burst of fire at night in conjunction with Corps H.A. "A" & "B" Batteries moved into new position. Wire cutting positions selected for group batteries. Enemy communications sniped on intermittently throughout night.	
	7/12/16		Bursts of fire at night in conjunction with Corps H.A. on roads and railway near ROSSIGNOL WOOD. 100 rounds fired for each battery sniped on communications.	
	8/12/16		4.5 How retaliated on GOMMECOURT and ROSSIGNOL to shelling of Hebuterne. Night firing on communication trenches as well as official routine.	
	9/12/16		Expenditure of ammunition to be reduced to minimum except for retaliation and wire cutting.	
	10/12/16		Arrangements for 31st D.A. to cut gaps in wire under cover of a general bombardment in conjunction with operations by the French. 50 rounds a gun	

WAR DIARY or INTELLIGENCE SUMMARY

Army Form C. 2118.

Place	Date	Hour	Summary of Events and Information	Remarks and references to Appendices
	10/12/16 (contd)		for 18 pdrs to be changed at our positions. 4 gr/s allotted to Left Group, to be used afterwards for prep of Raid. Usual night firing. Casualties. 1 O.R.	
	11/12/16		Alterations in fronts held by Infantry. Only 2 Battalions in the line on Group front. French bombardment postponed. Usual night firing.	
	12/12/16		An O.P. manned at night for first time equipped with No.5 Director for spotting enemy flashes in conjunction with H.A. Counter Battery group. To be manned by an Officer. Lookout men rejoined us from 4.5" How Batteries.	
	13/12/16		Ammunition allotment 35 rounds a gun. Usual night firing.	
	14/12/16		Nothing to record. Bursts at night in conjunction with H.A.	
	15/12/16		Night firing on Communication Trenches by 18 pdrs. 4.5" hows on Railways. Also bursts as last night.	

WAR DIARY
or
INTELLIGENCE SUMMARY
(Erase heading not required.)

Army Form C. 2118.

Place	Date	Hour	Summary of Events and Information	Remarks and references to Appendices
	16/12/16		Wire cutting commenced in connection with raid to be made by Infantry shortly. 3 genuine S/Ps and 2 bogus ones started. Two S/Ps also started by Right Group. Whole Divisional front bombarded intermittently at night on front & support lines. Commenced working on new offensive positions.	
	17/12/16		Wire cutting continued. Night bombardment as yesterday. Very misty.	
	18/12/16		Wire cutting continued. 2 1/OC S/Ps still out quite clear. Bombardment at night as before.	
	19/12/16		Wire cutting continued. Raid by 18th Durham L.I., 93rd Inf Bde at point of Sonnecourt Salient. Very heavy bombardment carried out in conjunction with Corps H.A. XIII and VII Corps, also 4g= Div. Arty. Raiders entered without opposition to found trenches utterly demolished by the bombardment and deserted. Very little hostile retaliation from this bombardment a time f previous nights. Zero (time f entry) was 8-30 pm.	

WAR DIARY or INTELLIGENCE SUMMARY

Army Form C. 2118.

Place	Date	Hour	Summary of Events and Information	Remarks and references to Appendices
	20/12/16.		Wire cutting on gap for material continued by B/165. Thin gaps still being kept open. Work on defensive positions being continued daily with assistance of 30 men from D.A.C. No night firing. Casualties 2 O.R.	
	21/12/16.		Wire cutting continued. HEBUTERNE retaliated. Two How Batteries retaliated on Gommecourt and Puisieux. Counter Battery groups H.A. also retaliated. Brit field wrights on front support line also personal front.	
	22/12/16.		Wire cutting continued. A considerable amount of movement seen and fired on, chiefly small parties apparently working wet trenches. Night firing about as last night.	
	23/12/16.		Wire cutting completed. Bombardment (wire & so heavy as 19th) carried out by 11th E. Yorks, 9th & 2nd Inf. Bde., near NAMELESS FARM. Another raid being done by 94th & 2nd Inf. Bde. on our right. Time out 10.0 p.m. Both gaps were completely clear, but raiders found hand not another	

WAR DIARY or INTELLIGENCE SUMMARY

Army Form C. 2118.

(Erase heading not required.)

Instructions regarding War Diaries and Intelligence Summaries are contained in F.S. Regs., Part II. and the Staff Manual respectively. Title pages will be prepared in manuscript.

Place	Date	Hour	Summary of Events and Information	Remarks and references to Appendices
	23/12/16 (contd)		across both S/Ps. Dare to prevent enemy unable to get through. Bombs firing in turbulent group had tendency to form a protective round miles with certain fire in event of hostile barrage, but events more this unnecessary.	
	24/12/16		A good deal of movement seen and fired on. No firing at night except 3.0 a.m.	
	25/12/16		Christmas Day. Bursts fired refined firing between 3 a.m. and 6 a.m. in front and supporting and communications. Bursts fired intermittently throughout the day. A wagon, apparently containing Christmas presents, was knocked out and the resulting movement provided good targets throughout day. No night firing. Bursts were also fired by 3 I & 6 G Dirl Artilleries at the same time as ours.	
	26/12/16		Bombardment of Sommecourt Salient & trenches in the vicinity, in conjunction with Trench Mortars, one section of M/161 fired shrapnel into the trees. Night firing on roads and communication trenches.	

Army Form C. 2118.

WAR DIARY
or
INTELLIGENCE SUMMARY.
(Erase heading not required.)

Instructions regarding War Diaries and Intelligence Summaries are contained in F. S. Regs., Part II. and the Staff Manual respectively. Title pages will be prepared in manuscript.

Place	Date	Hour	Summary of Events and Information	Remarks and references to Appendices
	27/12/16		At noon to-day Lt Col. E. J. Henslow took over command of 31st Div. Arty, and command of Left Group passed to O.C. 170 Bde R.F.A. Temporary command of 165 Brigade taken over by Major W.L.Y. Rogers B/169 Bde R.F.A.	
	28-12-16		No batteries now under tactical control by O.C. 165 Brigade. Nothing to record.	
	29-12-16		Nothing to record.	
	30-12-16		Nothing to record.	
	31-12-16		Nothing to record.	

WLY Rogers
Major 165th (County Palatine) Brigade R.F.A.

Vol XI

CONFIDENTIAL.

WAR DIARY

OF

165th BRIGADE R.F.A.

FROM 1st JANUARY 1917 to 31st JANUARY 1917.

VOLUME XIII.

165th Bde. R.F.A.   Vol. XIII.

Army Form C. 2118.

WAR DIARY
or
INTELLIGENCE SUMMARY. 1st January 1917 to 31st January 1917.

(Erase heading not required.)

Place	Date	Hour	Summary of Events and Information	Remarks and references to Appendices
In the field	1/1/17 to 14/1/17		"A" "B" and "D" Batteries in Left Group, commanded by O.C. 170 Brigade R.F.A. "C" Battery in Right Group, commanded by O.C. 169 Brigade R.F.A. O.C. 165 Brigade R.F.A. having no Tactical control. There is nothing to record.	
	14/1/17		2nd Lieut. H.A. TOLSON, D/165 (attached A/165) wounded - shell shock.	
	15/1/17		All Batteries relieved by Batteries of 19th Division at 12. noon. and withdrew to wagon lines at COIGNEUX. H.Q. relieved by H.Q. 86th Brigade R.F.A. withdrew to COUIN.	
	16/1/17		31st Div. Arty moved into winter training quarters. 165 Brigade marched from COIGNEUX to OCCOCHES.	
	17/1/17 to 31/1/17		Brigade in winter Training Quarters at OCCOCHES.	
	26/1/17		On re-organization of Divisional Artillery one section of D/169 Bde. R.F.A. was absorbed by D/165 Bde R.F.A. the latter becoming a 6 gun battery. Surplus personnel and horses of B/169 D/169 absorbed by H.Q. 165 Bde. R.F.A.	

WAR DIARY
or
INTELLIGENCE SUMMARY.
(Erase heading not required.)

Army Form C. 2118.

Place	Date	Hour	Summary of Events and Information	Remarks and references to Appendices
	31/1/17		End of first period of winter training.	
	1/2/17		Divisional Artillery moved to ST. OUEN for second period of winter training. 165 Brigade marched from OCCOCHES to ST. OUEN.	

Vol 12

CONFIDENTIAL.

WAR DIARY

OF

165th BRIGADE R.F.A.

From 1st February 1917 to 28th February 1917.

VOLUME XIV.

Volume XIV

165th Brigade R.F.A.

WAR DIARY or INTELLIGENCE SUMMARY. Army Form C. 2118.

1st February 1917 to 28th February 1917

Place	Date	Hour	Summary of Events and Information	Remarks and references to Appendices
1st Area	1-9		Brigade engaged in 2nd part of Winter Training Programme	
	9		Orders received for Brigade to move up into the firing line to reinforce 18th Divl Artillery.	
	9		March to BEAUVAL. Various rear	
	10		March to BOUZINCOURT arrived 5 p.m. Execs & H.Q. Staff pushed on at once to neighbourhood of POZIERES into gun positions & Batt. H.Q.	
	11		2nd Bvy of "A" 5" mortally wounded. All batteries engage in cutting wire in front of S. Miraumont, Officers, etc & Bn trenches	
	12-16		Preliminary bombardment & preparations for attack on PETIT MIRAUMONT.	
	17		Attack on PETIT MIRAUMONT.	
	23		Execs pulled out early in the morning & Brigade marched back to Alpon lines between BOUZINCOURT & SENLIS.	
	24		Brigade march to Hebuterne Area. Bivwcd 88th Brigade on nights 24/25 & 25/26. H.Qrs at BAYENCOURT	

Army Form C. 2118.

WAR DIARY
or
INTELLIGENCE SUMMARY.

(Erase heading not required.)

Instructions regarding War Diaries and Intelligence Summaries are contained in F. S. Regs., Part II. and the Staff Manual respectively. Title pages will be prepared in manuscript.

Place	Date	Hour	Summary of Events and Information	Remarks and references to Appendices
Bayeneurt	26 to 28.		Enemy falls back from his front system of trenches via Hebuterne & Colincamps before action advance of our Infantry Brigade covering advance of 111 Brigade of this Division. H.H. Austin.	

CONFIDENTIAL.

WAR DIARY

OF

165th BRIGADE R.F.A.

From 1st March 1917 to 31st March 1917.

VOLUME XV.

165th Bde R.F.A. Confidential
N 23/4
H.Q.
 31st D.A.

Herewith War Diary
for the month of March,
1917.

2/4/17

G Henderson
Lt Col R.F.A
Comdg 165 Bde R.F.A.

165th Brigade RFA
1st March 1917 to 31st March 1917

WAR DIARY
or
INTELLIGENCE SUMMARY
(Erase heading not required.)

Army Form C. 2118.
Volume XV

Place	Date	Hour	Summary of Events and Information	Remarks and references to Appendices
BAYENCOURT	1/3/17		HQ's at BAYENCOURT – Batteries in action in advanced positions in HEBUTERNE PLAIN	
	6/3/17		Batteries advanced to occupy positions behind ROSSIGNOL WOOD	/5
HEBUTERNE	10/3/17		HQ moved to HEBUTERNE	/5
	11/3/17		HQ & Battery positions shelled – Casualties 2nd Lieut R.S. LOVETT-THOMAS & Battery fatally injured 1 OR wounded	/5
	12/3/17		Working parties supplied to establish light railway from STAR WOOD to Battery positions – Casualties 3 ORs killed	
	13/3/17		2 ORs wounded Attack in order defences of BUCQUOY	/5
	13/3/17			/5
	17/3/17		BUCQUOY occupied by Infantry and FOO's of Brigade wounded 1 OR	/5
	19/3/17		Batteries withdrawn from line to wagon lines at SAILLY AU BOIS	/1
	29/3/17		Brigade marched to billets in BON BERGES	/1

Army Form C. 2118.

WAR DIARY
or
INTELLIGENCE SUMMARY.

(Erase heading not required.)

Instructions regarding War Diaries and Intelligence Summaries are contained in F. S. Regs., Part II. and the Staff Manual respectively. Title pages will be prepared in manuscript.

Place	Date	Hour	Summary of Events and Information	Remarks and references to Appendices
	21/3/17		March to BOUBERS.	/.
	22/3/17		March to HEUCHIN.	/.
	24/3/17		March to RUITZ.	/.
	25/3/17		March to ECOIVRES attached to 1st Canadian Division	/.
	26/3/17		2nd Lieut R. Acheson wounded.	/.
	27/3/17		Batteries began to take up gun positions S.W. of NEUVILLE ST VAAST	/.
	30/3/17		Wounded 1 O.R.	/.
	31/3/17		Batteries in action.	/.

P J Henderson
Lt Col R.F.A
Comdg 165 Bde R.F.A.

Vol 14
31 Div

CONFIDENTIAL.

WAR DIARY

OF

165th BRIGADE R.F.A.

From 1st April 1917 to 30th April 1917.

VOLUME XVI.

Army Form C. 2118.

Volume XVI

165th Brigade R.F.A.

WAR DIARY
or
INTELLIGENCE SUMMARY.
(Erase heading not required.)

April 1917

Place	Date	Hour	Summary of Events and Information	Remarks and references to Appendices
Ecoivres	1st		Batteries in action S. of Neuville St Vaast just W. of Arras-Bethune Road, reinforcing the Batteries of C.F.A. covering 10th Battn Canadian Infantry, 1st Canadian Div.	
	2-8		Head Quarters established in dugouts at A.13.d.7.1. Preparation for pending operation	
	3rd		Casualties 1 O.R. "B" Batty (wounded)	
	4th		Casualties 3 O.R. "A" Batty, 1 O.R. "C" Batty (wounded)	
	9th		Attack on Thelus & Farbus. The Brigade took part in "rolling" barrage. All our guns out of range of enemy before evening	
La Fayette	11th		Batteries move forward to take up positions in or near Farbus outskirts of Pichincourt, covering infantry of 2nd Div.	
	14th		H.Q. moves to dugouts under the Arras-Bethune Cart run Madagascar Corner. Batteries move forward to positions near Maison de la Côte S. just West of Maison de la Côte. Casualties 2 O.R. accidentally wounded	
	15th		H.Q. move to cellars in Pichincourt. Batteries move forward to positions	

Army Form C. 2118.

WAR DIARY
or
INTELLIGENCE SUMMARY.
(Erase heading not required.)

April 1917.

Instructions regarding War Diaries and Intelligence Summaries are contained in F.S. Regs., Part II. and the Staff Manual respectively. Title pages will be prepared in manuscript.

Place	Date	Hour	Summary of Events and Information	Remarks and references to Appendices
Seducourt	16		Casualties 1 O.R. killed "D" Battery.	
	17		The Brigade came under direct command of C.R.A. 2nd Division.	
			2/Lt J. Cartridge "B" Batty wounded.	
	18th		Brigade transferred from command of 2nd Div. to that of C.R.A. 63rd (Royal Naval) Division. H.Q. moves to dugouts in Kadenyser ("B" Batty + H.Q.)	VS
	23rd		Casualties 2 O.R. wounded.	
			Attack on Gavrelle. Batteries took part in rolling barrage. Fire kept almost incessantly throughout the day and night. Two enemy counter attacks caught by barrage & dispersed. Casualties 6 O.R. wounded. "C" Battery again heavily shelled, two guns knocked out of action.	
	24		Two S.O.S. calls from in front of Gavrelle during the early hours of the morning.	
	25		S.O.S. call from our infantry in front of Gavrelle 3.50 a.m.	
	26th		Casualty 1 O.R. wounded. "D" Batty.	
	27th		do. 1 O.R. wounded "B" Batty. Batteries moved forward to positions between Bailleul and Oppy-Gavrelle road.	

WAR DIARY or **INTELLIGENCE SUMMARY**
(Erase heading not required.)

Army Form C. 2118.

2

April 1917.

Place	Date	Hour	Summary of Events and Information	Remarks and references to Appendices
	28		Forward Battle H.Q. established in old German gun-pits near our Batteries. Attack on Arleux-Oppy Line. Batteries took part in rolling barrage covering advance of 189th Inf Brigade. Casualties 1 O.R. killed ("B"Bty), 3 O.R. wounded	
	29		2/Lt. P. Scovill ("C"Bty) wounded, 6 O.R. "B"Bty killed	
	30			

C/Macdosm

Lt. Col. R.F.A.
Commanding 165th (County Palatine) Brigade R.F.A.

CONFIDENTIAL.

WAR DIARY

OF

165th BRIGADE R.F.A.

From 1st May 1917 to 31st May 1917.

VOLUME XVII.

160th Brigade. R.H.A.

Annex XVII

WAR DIARY or INTELLIGENCE SUMMARY. May 1917.

Army Form C. 2118.

Place	Date	Hour	Summary of Events and Information	Remarks and references to Appendices
Lucelle	May 1st		Batteries in action B28, S.W. of Lucelle. Brigade H.Q.s in old trench dugouts in H3a. Attached 63rd (R.N.) Division.	
	2nd		Casualties "A" Battery 3 O.R., "B" 1 O.R., "C" Batty 5 O.R. wounded. 4/- Casualties "A" Battery 10 O.R. killed. 31st Division relieve 63rd in the line.	
	3rd		Attack on Fresnoy trenches east of Gavrelle, Oppy & Fresnoy trench. Brigade took part in creeping barrage. Enemy counter attacked & retook Gavrelle. We then attacked to recover ground & gained night obj. Situation uncertain.	
			Casualties "A" Batty 1 O.R. killed, 1 O.R. wounded. "D" Batty 1 O.R. wounded.	4/-
Bailleul	4th		B.Q's moved to dugouts in Roclincourt Reg. Batteries moved back to positions in B26 just north of Lens – Arras Railway.	
			Casualties "B" Batty 2 O.R. wounded.	4/-
	6th		Casualties H.Q. 1 O.R. wounded.	
	7th		Casualties "A" Battery 4 O.R. killed, 2 O.R. wounded. "B" Batty Major H.C. Fitzgerald slightly wounded – at duty.	4/-

WAR DIARY or INTELLIGENCE SUMMARY

Army Form C. 2118.

Place	Date	Hour	Summary of Events and Information	Remarks and references to Appendices
Bailleul	May 8th		Casualties D" Battery 1 O.R. wounded	
	11th		"B" Battery fired in support of attack of XVII Corps on Lieven & the Chemical Works.	
			Casualties D" Battery 1 O.R. wounded (accidentally)	
	12th		Battery again called upon to support the attack of an attack by XVII Corps	
	13th		Casualties C Battery 1 O.R. wounded	
	14th		Lieut Colonel J.C. Anderson to Hospital. Lt.Col. A.B. Le Mercier assume command of the Brigade.	
	16th		One section of "A" & "B" Batteries moved into position N. of Lens-Arras railway.	
			Casualties "A" Battery 2" J.H. Roche wounded, "B" Batty 1 O.R. wounded. "C" Battery 2 O.R. wounded, D" Battery 2" R.B. Bartlett slightly wounded - at duty	
	18th		Battery fired in support of attack by 18 th D.L.9. on Lieven	

Army Form C. 2118.

WAR DIARY
or
INTELLIGENCE SUMMARY.
(Erase heading not required.)

Instructions regarding War Diaries and Intelligence Summaries are contained in F. S. Regs., Part II. and the Staff Manual respectively. Title pages will be prepared in manuscript.

3

Place	Date	Hour	Summary of Events and Information	Remarks and references to Appendices
Bailleul	18th		French Situation unchanged.	
	21st		Casualties "D" Battery 3 O.R. wounded.	16
	22nd		63rd Div. Infantry Relieve 32nd Div on the line	
			B.G. R.A. 63rd Div. Arty assumed control of R.F.A. covering Divn. front at 12 noon.	APMM
	26th		Casualties "B" Battery 2/Lt L.S Robertson wounded 12.30pm	APMM
	28th		Lt Col H.G. Lee-Warner D.S.O M.C. returned to 1st Army Artillery School	APMM
			Major H.R.S. Massey assumed command of Bde Brigade	APMM

J.H.Massey
Major
Comdg 158 Bde R.F.A

T.134. Wt. W708—776. 500000. 4/15. Sir J. C. & S.

CONFIDENTIAL.

WAR DIARY

OF

165th BRIGADE R.F.A.

From 1st June 1917 to 30th June 1917.

VOLUME XVIII.

165th Bde R.H.A
No 3/44
A.Q.
31st D.A.

Herewith War Diary
for the month of
June, 1917.

4/7/17

Leach

Heath Lockey
Comdg 165th Bde R.H.A.

June 1917.   165th Brigade   Army Form C. 2118.

WAR DIARY
or
INTELLIGENCE SUMMARY.
(Erase heading not required.)

Place	Date	Hour	Summary of Events and Information	Remarks and references to Appendices
Bailleul	1st		Batteries in action S.W. of Bailleul covering the "Drake" Bath. of 63rd (R.N.) Division Stabbing the line in the immediate vicinity of Gavrelle Windmill. Our policy of harassing the enemy by concentrated hurricane bombardments and point barrages produced considerable retaliation more especially on Battery positions. Casualties 1 O.R. wounded. Lieut J.A.Fes ("B" Batty) Killed. 1 O.R. ("C" Batty) wounded.	
	2nd		2" SJ Mason + 4 O.R. wounded. A + D. Batteries positions shelled heavy	
	6th		by 5.9 + 8" H.E., little damage done.	
			E.O.s established on Railway Bank with a view to cutting wire in front of Cadorna Trench.	
	12th		Lieut Col. C.R. Hackney D.S.O. assumes command of the Brigade.	
	17th		"D" Battery moved and section to forward position on the "Blue Line" 65	
			All Batts. actively engaged cutting wire on Cadorna trench. Marked	
	19th		decrease in activity of hostile batteries during last three days. Lethal bombardment each night introduced into nightly programme	

WAR DIARY or INTELLIGENCE SUMMARY

Army Form C. 2118.

Place	Date	Hour	Summary of Events and Information	Remarks and references to Appendices
Ingouville	20th		Police Garage. Bivouac Carette & Officer Miscutting on Colonca gangway staff.	
	21st		Hostile artillery activity increased. Carette Cond de fer & Cuan–Carette East heavily shelled.	B
	22nd		Successful raid on Colonca trench by 2nd Spanby Brigade. 2nd/B Wilson Liaison Officer. Enemy reply to our barrage was feeble & spasmodic.	
	23rd		106th Battery attached to this Brigade occupied portion of the detached section of "B" Battery West of Maison de la Côte. Enemy very active throughout day & night. Harassing bombardments "Communication" start "Lethal" bombardment.	15
	24th		Enemy guns unusually active against Battery positions. Railways (Cuan-Vins) & in vicinity of Totes & Ballent.	
	25th		One artillery wounded. Wood Alley & Madama	
	27th		Heavy Bombardment of our front & support line from Carette Mill to Optg." forming an adjunction for forward positions of 1st Army at BAILLEUL, covered by a smoke barrage.	B

T2134. Wt. W708—776. 500000. 4/15. Sir J. C. & S.

WAR DIARY
or
INTELLIGENCE SUMMARY.
(Erase heading not required.)

Army Form C. 2118.

Place	Date	Hour	Summary of Events and Information	Remarks and references to Appendices
	28th		"B" & "C" Batteries (accepting forward positions during the room of Gaillard, supported in the morning incurring intermittent shelling. Our cate on Cadorna trench put out during the night suddenly renewed before "Zero" hour. (over 6', 2'; respectively) Enemy again turned out and rushed times new fall of shrapnel awaiting hour to attack enemy on attack was quick affected. The XIII Corps attacked at 7:10pm. this signal covered advance of the Right Centre Battalion of 24th of Brigade (4th Liverpool Reg.) Liason Officer Lt. R. Carmichael. All objectives gained. Hostile barrage was not heavy, + the success was gained corresponding easy. Honesty + protective fire Lift 56 throughout the night.	15
	29th		Ammunition 10.5 (3" B.L.F.) received. "B" Batty bring rather lines. Gun pulled out of action before Zero hour. "A" Batty + "G" Batty pulled out of harness practice. Heavy shelling of ground captured by us yesterday.	
	30th		Hostile Batteries Hail Caliber active against Cadorna trench, Chemin des Dames and BIPA. B24 2nd. Our batteries replied on Vincennes, Effort trench + trench Moyet. 18	

(W) Mackenney Lt.Col. R.F.A.
Col. 165 Bde R.F.A.

No 17

CONFIDENTIAL.

WAR DIARY

OF

165th BRIGADE R.F.A.

From 1st July to 31st July, 1917.

VOLUME XIX.

Volume XIX.

165th Brigade
R.F.A.

July 1917.

WAR DIARY
or
INTELLIGENCE SUMMARY.
(Erase heading not required.)

Army Form C. 2118.

Place	Date	Hour	Summary of Events and Information	Remarks and references to Appendices
Bailleul	July 1st		Batteries in action in positions on W. slope of the ridge West of Bailleul, "C" & "B" in the village. Heavy shelling by enemy of Bailleul and our front system between Bty. & Pendle to which our Battns. replied vigorously. Enemy front counter-attacked & held up our attack. Battle Patrols still active against Bailleul.	
	2nd			
	3rd		"C" Battery pulls out of Bailleul to wagon line en route to line as Depot Battery at 1st Army Artillery school	15
	4th		Casualties "A" 1 O.R. severely wounded, B. 1 O.R. slightly wounded.	
	8th		O.C. 170th Bde. assumes tactical control of Batteries of the Bde. "A" Battery very severely shelled 8", 5.9 & a few 77mm Chocolate damage caused. 1 gun knocked out & several dugouts fallen in, including office. Moved to "C"s old position during 8pm. "A" again shelled at position when their one gun is. Casualties "A" 2 O.R. slightly wounded.	15
	9		His Majesty the King visits Army area. Brigade part turns out to see him pass along the road to Ernie.	16

Army Form C. 2118.

WAR DIARY
or
INTELLIGENCE SUMMARY.
(Erase heading not required.)

Instructions regarding War Diaries and Intelligence Summaries are contained in F. S. Regs., Part II. and the Staff Manual respectively. Title pages will be prepared in manuscript.

Place	Date	Hour	Summary of Events and Information	Remarks and references to Appendices
	11th		Colonel Hackney D.S.O. to D.A.H.Q. to act as C.R.A. in the absence of the General. Major H.B. Fitzgerald actg. O.C. Brigade. Heavy shelling during the evening of tracks near "D" Batty and observed 5.9 cm two inwards. There was no damage done. Little activity on either side	16
	13th		Railway cutting shelled intermittently all day, coming much further to H.Q. Enemy were being cut down after time. Casualties H.Q. 1 O.R. killed a/B"Ze, mortar wounded.	16
	14th		Quiet day. Little shelling by either side.	
	15th		Situation normal, very little activity on either side	
	16th			
	18th		Weather unsettled. Said times for night 18/19 for Brigade on recent front.	
	19th		Batteries fired in support of a raid by the Light Infantry Brigade in which 11 prisoners were taken	
	20th		Batteries pulled out of the line & march to Wagon lines	16
	21st		H.Q. also move back to W. line. "B" & "D" move up into "A" Batty & one section each of "B" & "D" more yet into	

WAR DIARY
OR
INTELLIGENCE SUMMARY.
(Erase heading not required.)

Army Form C. 2118.

Place	Date	Hour	Summary of Events and Information	Remarks and references to Appendices
	22.		Positions near Vimy Klurny Batty of 1st and Lancashire F.A. Bde.	
			Raid by 4th Canadian Div on our left in vicinity of Acor resulted in capture of 50 prisoners.	16
	23		Lt. Col. C.B. MacKay D.S.O. resumed the Brigade. Relief of Canadian F.A. Batteries by 165th, 170th & 2nd Bde R.F.A. completed. Controls of F.A. covering 1/30th Div Infantry assumed by Bde. 165th Bde 4 A/165. B/165/4guns, VB C. D)/170. 170th Bde (165 & 170 R/th Batteries form one group E. Battery. (A.Q. & 1 Dec. only) to	
Vimy.	24		Wagon Lines moves to vicinity of la Targette. Canadian bns attacked East Question div Artillery moves up into action on two fronts. We are now covering front from N. of Souchy to Mercicourt inclusive, div front of over 4000 yds.	
	25.		Situation remained. Little firing by day by our Batteries. There is the enemy will fifty to take holes runs & to to maintain more or two heavy harrassing fire on roads & tracks etc. by night.	

WAR DIARY
or
INTELLIGENCE SUMMARY.
(Erase heading not required.)

Army Form C. 2118.

Place	Date	Hour	Summary of Events and Information	Remarks and references to Appendices
	26th		Situation normal. Some counter battery work done today by D/165 & D/170.	17
	27th		Willerval & Vimy shelled D/165 & D/170 carried out shoots with aeroplane observation.	17
	28th		Vimy & Willerval again heavily shelled. "B" Battery pits cut & reigns to Bajus line for a rest. "E" Batty. taking their 4 guns	17
	29th		Vimy & Petit Vimy heavily shelled. Chinese Trench Artillery Zone "A"/165 withdrawn for Corps was inactive. Concentrated shot with gas shell on Bouvigny.	
	30		Vimy & Petit Vimy shelled intermittently throughout the day.	
	31st		Shelling of Vimy zero to lens became the worst day programme of North Batty. Zone to as Chart from that, they shod little activity. During the occupation of new position taken over from the Canadians, action long gradually pushed up to more advanced positions, a feeling of the	18

Army Form C. 2118.

WAR DIARY
or
INTELLIGENCE SUMMARY.
(Erase heading not required.)

Place	Date	Hour	Summary of Events and Information	Remarks and references to Appendices
			Operations was the use of "rifle" or "cover" vicinity at night to deceive the enemy as to disposition and to shorten range.	
			9.8.17.	C W Duckbury Lt Col C/165 Bde RFA

CONFIDENTIAL.

WAR DIARY

OF

165th BRIGADE R.F.A.

From 1st August to 31st August, 1917.

VOLUME XX.

165th Bde. R.F.a.

Volume XX

WAR DIARY
or
INTELLIGENCE SUMMARY.
(Erase heading not required.)

Army Form C. 2118.

1st Aug. 1917 to 31st Aug. 1917

Instructions regarding War Diaries and Intelligence Summaries are contained in F. S. Regs., Part II. and the Staff Manual respectively. Title pages will be prepared in manuscript.

Place	Date	Hour	Summary of Events and Information	Remarks and references to Appendices
S.S.E. of VIMY			165th Bde RFA	
	1-8-17		Concentrated night shoot on Bois BERNARD. Situation quiet.	ORMMW
	4-8-17		Combined artillery and M.G. bombardment of outskirts of MERICOURT 12 midnight.	ORMMW
	5-8-17		Concentrated night shoot on ACHEVILLE SUPPORT in T18.B	ORMMW
	6-8-17		Enemy opened heavy bombardment on L1 sector at 1.45 am mostly gas shells x HE. At 2 am our 4.5 Hows bombed dumps & dugouts at T6.D.85.35 with lethal shell & 18pdr fired creeping barrage of A & AX on tracks in the surrounding area.	ORMMW
	7-8-17		A combined A, AX, & gas shoot commencing at 9.45 pm was carried out on tracks in T6A & N36C to catch ration parties going to front line & ammunition carriers going to TX23 & TX30.	ORMMW
	9-8-17		Casualties 1 OR killed A 165. Situation quiet.	ORMMW
	11-8-17		B/w H.Q. & road between it and MONT FORET QUARRIES heavily shelled between 10 am & 12 noon with heavy armour piercing shell. Several dugouts damaged.	ORMMW
	12-8-17		An Albatross Scout brought down in T21A by one of our machines. The pilot, an officer, was taken prisoner. Casualties 1 OR killed D 165	ORMMW
	13-8-17		Casualties 2 OR A 165 wounded (1 since died)	ORMMW
	14-17-8-17		Situation quiet. Enemy activity normal. H.Q. 165 handed over Front to 1+9 170 and withdrew to WHITE HOUSE MONT ST ELOI. Continued.	ORMMW

WAR DIARY or INTELLIGENCE SUMMARY

Army Form C. 2118.

165th Bde. R.F.A.

Place	Date	Hour	Summary of Events and Information	Remarks and references to Appendices
Sr. H. of VIMY	16.5.17		Hostile artillery more active than usual. VIMY railway embankment in T12.B heavily shelled. Our trench line in T7.A.1.B heavily shelled in morning & afternoon.	
		19.5.17	We successfully discharged gas against enemy positions in T7.C.1.D & T13.B.2.D. Enemy retaliated by firing heavy bombardment of Bns. areas & of Bns. HQrs. Gibraltar & support system. Personnel reduced by B/165.	
		20.5.17	A/165 heavily shelled.	
		22.5.17	B/165 retaliated to enemy positions. Personnel reduced by D/165.	
		24.5.17	B/D/165 resumed control of Bde. & Bty of 16th Bde. HQ. at T30.A.5.1	
		26.5.17	Connecting & O.P. reconnoitred 16/165.	
			Cookhouse short on B/165 - 20 pdrs, 21 cm, 15 cm, 10.5 cm. front & rear. Enemy artillery also active on VIMY RIDGE.	
		21.30 h/	acc much. Retaliation normal	
		3.30 p/	Our trenches in T3 sector heavily shelled during day. Early morning	
		3.30 a.m	S.O.S. T3 received. Enemy attempted to raid on T.B. Battn. Left Bde. but was repulsed with heavy casualties. Our artillery stopped enemy & S.O.S. fire. We captured 1 prisoner & machine gun.	

Lt. Col. R.F.A.
Commanding 165th (County Palatine) Brigade R.F.A.

Army Form C. 2118.

WAR DIARY
or
INTELLIGENCE SUMMARY.
(Erase heading not required.)

Vol 19

CONFIDENTIAL.

WAR DIARY

OF

165 BRIGADE R.F.A.

From 1st Sept. to 30th Sept. 1917.

VOLUME XXI.

165th Bde R.F.A.
W 23/4

H.Q.
31st D——

[Stamp: 165th BRIGADE, R.F.A.]
[Stamp: HEADQUARTERS 31st DIVISIONAL ARTILLERY — 8 OCT. 1917]

Herewith War Diary for the Month of September 1917.

8/10/17

V. Elliott Capt & Lt Col R.F.A.
Comdg 165th Bde R.F.A.

September 1917 Volume XXI

WAR DIARY
or
INTELLIGENCE SUMMARY

Army Form C. 2118.

165th Brigade

Place	Date	Hour	Summary of Events and Information	Remarks and references to Appendices
2.S.E. of Vimy	1-9-17		Casualties 1 O.R. Wounded D.165. 4.5 Hows engaged 2 hostile batteries with god results. Hostile artillery very active in the afternoon against battery positions & dugouts in T.26.A.	OAM/N
	2-9-17		Casualties 1 O.R. Wounded. C.16.C. 3 hostile batteries were engaged by our 4.5 Hows and neutralised FARBUS was vigorously shelled throughout the day by 15 cm batteries. T.X.22 and U.W.93 were neutralised several times by the fire of our 4.5 Hows, but opened again soon afterwards. 18 pdr engaged several T.M. positions & M.Gs. At night, in view of projected German relief opposite our front, a special programme was carried out commencing from 10 p.m. 4.5 Hows using H.E. & Shrapnel shell blocked to half an hour the western ends of tracks known to be used by the enemy, later 18 pdr searched cross tracks & 4.5 Hows searched communication trenches & trail Ramps on selected areas, followed by bursts at irregular intervals through the hours of darkness.	OAM/N OAM/N

Continued

Army Form C. 2118.

WAR DIARY
or
INTELLIGENCE SUMMARY.
(Erase heading not required.)

Instructions regarding War Diaries and Intelligence
Summaries are contained in F.S. Regs., Part II.
and the Staff Manual respectively. Title pages
will be prepared in manuscript.

Place	Date	Hour	Summary of Events and Information	Remarks and references to Appendices
			Continued	
	3.9.17		Movement was engaged at intervals through the day by 18pr & 4.5 hows and dispersed. FARBUS was again shelled during most of the day. Vimy was shelled in the morning. At night patrols reported considerable movement and noise in the enemy trenches & in consequence a vigorous night firing programme was carried out, as it was thought that an enemy relief of the night before had prevented the enemy relief taking place. Casualties 1 O.R. B.165.	OMMN
	4.9.17		Several hostile batteries were engaged and neutralised during the day at movement was observed at several points by our guns. At 4.15pm a hostile aeroplane was brought down by one of our machines in T.15.B.55.5. Continued	OMMN

WAR DIARY
or
INTELLIGENCE SUMMARY.
(Erase heading not required.)

Army Form C. 2118.

Place	Date	Hour	Summary of Events and Information	Remarks and references to Appendices
			Continued	
	4.9.17		At 12 midnight an intense bombardment was opened on Vimy and roads and tracks leading to the forward area (the signal apparently being 3 red lights) with H.E. Shrapnel and gas shells in about the proportion of 1 H.E. to 3 gas shells. The rate of fire was approximately 50 per minute. This fire died down at 12.25 am. At 1.25 am 3 red lights were again seen and immediately a similar intense bombardment started which lasted till 2.20 am. The gas shell used was "Yellow Cross" 77 m.m. Many casualties were caused among our infantry and gunners, the worst were soft among batteries among the gunners. About 5000 gas shells were used. During this bombardment the 4.5 how carried out immers neutralising programme against active hostile batteries, viz HE & lachrymatory shell. Casualties resulting from these bombardments were B.165 2 OR gassed and 1 OR slightly wounded. D.165 2 OR gassed & 10 slightly wounded. None of the gassed cases proved fatal. They were all admitted to hospital. Continued	OMMM

WAR DIARY
or
INTELLIGENCE SUMMARY.

(Erase heading not required.)

Army Form C. 2118.

Place	Date	Hour	Summary of Events and Information	Remarks and references to Appendices
S.S.E. of Vimy			Continued	
	5.9.17		Several hostile batteries were again engaged by our 4.5 How. also 18 pr engaged movement & hostile MGs. The usual harassing fire on enemy tracks was kept up through the night.	OAFB.
	6.9.17		Vimy was steadily shelled throughout the afternoon with 77 mm & 10.5 cm guns. Hostile batteries were engaged by us.	OAFB
	7.9.17		The usual normal activity on both sides. This brigade was relieved by the 10" Canadian Bde CFA & our batteries moved into positions further south in B3, B8 & B13 taking over from 27th Bde RFA.	
FARBUS	8.9.17		Batteries were under tactical control of 27th Bde RFA. HQ at B13 c 35.30.	OAFB.
WILLERVAL	9.9.17		Took over the control of our batteries from 27th Bde RFA. at 12 noon. Casualties 1 O.R. D165 & 1 O.R. B165 wounded.	OAFB
			Continued	

Army Form C. 2118.

WAR DIARY
or
INTELLIGENCE SUMMARY.
(Erase heading not required.)

Instructions regarding War Diaries and Intelligence Summaries are contained in F. S. Regs., Part II. and the Staff Manual respectively. Title pages will be prepared in manuscript.

Place	Date	Hour	Summary of Events and Information	Remarks and references to Appendices
FARBUS & WILLERVAL			Continued	
	10-9-17		Enemy artillery much quieter than normal. He carried out a harassing fire programme at night in conjunction with M.Gs on enemy front line & wire. A good many extra lights were thrown up by the enemy but he did not retaliate.	BRNNN
	11-9-17		Hostile artillery fairly quiet during the day & doing very little firing during the night. On the day we were very active one Two trapped enemy trades with bursts of fire.	BRNNN
	12-9-17		We engaged and dispersed several working parties in the FRESNES - ROUVROY line, and some cavalry were seen to be interested at 11:35 pm our gun fired in support of a successful raid made by the 92nd Infantry Brigade, and also from 3:20 am in conjunction with a projection of gas.	BRNNN
			Continued	

WAR DIARY
or
INTELLIGENCE SUMMARY.
(Erase heading not required.)

Army Form C. 2118.

Place	Date	Hour	Summary of Events and Information	Remarks and references to Appendices
FARBUS & WILLERVAL			Continued	
	13.9.17		During the day we engaged working parties, active TMs and batteries. At night 18 pdrs x 4.5 hows took part in a bombardment in conjunction with another gas projection. Hostile artillery and TMs displayed more activity.	OMMN
	14.9.17		Enemy more active on our trenches, also ARLEUX and VIMY. A good deal of movement seen in enemy lines. Several parties engaged & dispersed. He did the usual night firing on tracks &c in fwd zone.	OMMN
	15.9.17		Hostile artillery active against our trenches. TMs becoming more active. We carried out a short retaliatory bombardment of the enemy trenches and soft spots during the afternoon.	OMMN
			Continued	

Army Form C. 2118.

WAR DIARY
or
INTELLIGENCE SUMMARY.
(Erase heading not required.)

Instructions regarding War Diaries and Intelligence Summaries are contained in F. S. Regs., Part II. and the Staff Manual respectively. Title pages will be prepared in manuscript.

Place	Date	Hour	Summary of Events and Information	Remarks and references to Appendices
FARBUS x WILLERVAL			Continued	
	16.9.17		Hostile artillery normal. Very little night firing.	
			Our 18 pr & 4.5 How engaged several TM emplacements. 4.5 Hows registered TM emplacements with aeroplane.	
			At 7.9 pm we co-operated with Stokes Mortars & M.Gs in a 5 minute intense bombardment of enemy's new trench in C.I.C. #	
	17.9.17		Hostile Art Mly normal. Our Cans were shelled w/t 10.15 a.m. Farbus also .... retaliation. The usual amount observed	
	18-9-17		Enemy Cal Mly carried out a destructive shoot on Farbus at 3.5 p.m. 60% of trgs were obtained in enemy's trench areas & dispersed. Enemy	
	19, 20, 21		Artillery normal. Red signals seen on the front. A marked increase	
	22, 23		in enemy's night firing. Usual work at M21 c 5.9. Willerval twice	
	24		shelled with 15 cm Hows -	

WAR DIARY
or
INTELLIGENCE SUMMARY.
(Erase heading not required.)

Army Form C. 2118.

Place	Date	Hour	Summary of Events and Information	Remarks and references to Appendices
St much	25.26		Fairly active on Vimy, Arleux and Lendelen	AAB
	27		15 cm Hows. were active, firing 12 noon to 2 pm A/16S. position at B.13.c.61.45 was registered. The first rounds	AAB
			were right to near lines and rounds dropped from a plane
			The position was heavily shelled between 6 & 7 pt.
			20 m 8.0 rds being expended.
			B/16S position at B.2.c.85.00 received a mixture of 4.2
			5.9 & 2" from 3.30 pm & 12 midnight about 400 rds in
			all.
	28 29		
	30th		Liff & Stormobile, Oderry & Montforet Quarries	
			received attention. Harassment directed at N.21.d. and	AAB
			N.21.c.75
			W.Mackay
			Mjr.
			6-10-17.	C/16S Bde RGA

Army Form C. 2118.

WAR DIARY
or
INTELLIGENCE SUMMARY.
(Erase heading not required.)

CONFIDENTIAL.

WAR DIARY

OF

165th BRIGADE R.F.A.

From 1st October to 31st October, 1917.

VOLUME XXII.

165th Bde RFA
A 23/14

165th BRIGADE,
R.F.A.

HEADQUARTERS
-5 NOV 1917
DIVISIONAL ARTILLERY

Herewith War
Diary for month
of October, 1917.

Elliott Capt
for Lt Col RFA

5/11/17

WAR DIARY
or
INTELLIGENCE SUMMARY.

Army Form C. 2118.

HEADQUARTERS 5 NOV 1917 XXII DIVISIONAL ARTILLERY

1/10/17 – 31/10/17   165 Bde   Volume

Place	Date	Hour	Summary of Events and Information	Remarks and references to Appendices
Nilland & Judea	1-10-17	18 hr	4.5 Hows and 18 pdr batteries registered by aeroplane on V4.57, V4.58. The batteries were silenced. Harassing fire on battr at night.	MRW
	2-10-17		Aeroplane registration. Active hostile batteries V4.56, V4.57 & V4.83 successfully neutralised as well as some active TMs. Battered shelled by 18 cm how in the evening.	MRW
	3-10-17		Aeroplane registration. At 9.36 pm gas was projected on our front, supported by 18 pr and 4.5 Hows, firing a creeping barrage over the gassed area. Enemy retaliated on our front line with a slow rate of fire. Enemy sent up "double green lights" followed by double red and yellow, with streamers. Enemy artly opened fire after double red rockets had been sent up.	MRW

WAR DIARY
or
INTELLIGENCE SUMMARY.

Army Form C. 2118.

165 Bde. RFA

Place	Date	Hour	Summary of Events and Information	Remarks and references to Appendices
Willerval & Farbus	4-10-17		Movement in FRESNES - ROUVROY Ln engaged and dispersed. Active T.M. engaged and silenced. Willerval shelled during the morning by CREST WOOD Battery. Casualties 1 O.R. C/165 wounded.	BMMN
	5-10-17		Hostile T.M's engaged and silenced. Aeroplane registration carried out. Willerval heavily shelled from early morning to 3-15 pm by 15 and 10.5 cm. Hostile T.M's active during night - early morning, a number of gas bombs being used.	BMMN
	6-10-17	12-15 am	Battery fired in support of raid by left Infantry Bde. Enemy reply very weak. Willerval, Arleux & Mont Foret shelled.	BMMN
	7-10-17	18pm	Engaged & dispersed working parties. Registered trench forwith aeroplane observation. Harassing fire on tracks at night. Willerval shelled by CREST WOOD Battery. 4.5 How.	BMMN

WAR DIARY
or
INTELLIGENCE SUMMARY.

(Erase heading not required.)

Army Form C. 2118.

165 Bde RFA

Place	Date	Hour	Summary of Events and Information	Remarks and references to Appendices
WILLERVAL & FARBUS	8.10.17		18 pdr engaged & dispersed enemy active trench Mortars. 4.5 Hows Harassing fire kept up during the night with machine gun bursts of fire in co-operation. Enemy seen bombarded by heavy artillery during the day. Willerval heavily shelled. ARLEUX & FARBUS lightly shelled.	BM
	9.10.17		Considerable movement observed and disturbed during the afternoon. 4.5 Hows carried out aeroplane registration. Harassing night firing programme carried out in view of unusual movement during the day. Willerval shelled.	BM
	10.10.17		Movement engaged & dispersed by day. Harassing fire carried out by night. Hostile artillery activity normal.	BM

WAR DIARY
or
INTELLIGENCE SUMMARY.

165 Bde RFA Army Form C. 2118.

(Erase heading not required.)

Place	Date	Hour	Summary of Events and Information	Remarks and references to Appendices
NEUVILLE X FARBUS	11-10-17		Made movement engaged and dispersed. Many targets successfully registered by aeroplane observation. During the night active TMs were engaged. Harassing fire maintained on enemy communications and tracks. Hostile artillery quiet.	BMMW
	12-10-17		Gas Projected at 10 am 2 minute barrage. Bombardment of all targets and trench lines carried out by all guns and Hows. No reply from enemy.	BMMW
	13/14-10-17		Movement and active TMs engaged, several large explosions caused. Hostile TMs more active	BMMW

WAR DIARY or INTELLIGENCE SUMMARY

165th Bde RFA   Army Form C. 2118.

Place	Date	Hour	Summary of Events and Information	Remarks and references to Appendices
WILLERVAL & FARBUS	14-10-17		Machinegun fire on TMs. with aeroplane observation. Our own trench mortars fired on during the night. Hostile artillery active on our front, especially TMs	
	15-10-17		Heavy bombardment of enemy trenches carried out in conjunction with trench 4.5 Hows engaged TMs with rifles and Lachrymatory shell. From midnight to 1-54 am heavy gas bombardment on WILLERVAL outskirts. A good deal of "Blue Cross" shell was used.	
	16-10-17		Enemy TMs very active. We carried out retaliatory bombardment of enemy trenches at OPs in C.13.	

Casualties. 2/Lt Charles Boyd Robertson killed (A/165)

WAR DIARY
or
INTELLIGENCE SUMMARY.
(Erase heading not required.)

Army Form C. 2118.

165 Bde RFA

Place	Date	Hour	Summary of Events and Information	Remarks and references to Appendices
NULLERVAL & FARBUS	17/10/17		Registration by aeroplane of three Brandt trench mortars. Heavy fire at night on tracks, men working and communication. NULLERVAL heavily shelled by CREST WOOD batteries and later by O418 and O423.	GAMMW
	18/10/17		Registration of T.Ms and trench points by aeroplane at 9.15 a.m. & 9.30 a.m. retaliatory bombardments of enemy trenches was carried out in reply to the hostile shelling of our trenches. Hostile artillery active.	GAMMW
	19/10/17		Hostile artillery active on B 5 c with 77 m.m and 9/10 shells during the night.	GAMMW

Army Form C. 2118.

WAR DIARY
or
INTELLIGENCE SUMMARY.   165th Bde RFA

(Erase heading not required.)

Instructions regarding War Diaries and Intelligence Summaries are contained in F. S. Regs., Part II and the Staff Manual respectively. Title pages will be prepared in manuscript.

Place	Date	Hour	Summary of Events and Information	Remarks and references to Appendices
NILLERVAL & FARBUS	19-10-17		Casualties 1 O.R. A.162 gassed	
	20-10-17		Movement - TMs & tanks engaged. Having fire on concentration ad tanks kept up throughout the day. Hostile activity below normal.	RMMWV
	21-10-17		Engagements with 18 pr incendiary shell were carried out against Bois VILAIN and some buildings in ASHEVILLE. One shell fire was caused.	RMMWV
	22-10-17		Shrapnel aeroplane registration carried out. Gas projected at 6.15 pm whilst 18pr and 4.5 Hows searched & swept tracks leading from the ground around the retaliation for to go's B13 c65.45 to B14 D30.40 Bde H.Q. moved from	RMMWV
	23-10-17		Batty position near NILLERVAL heavily bombarded all the morning. Some gas shell used.	RMMWV

Army Form C. 2118.

WAR DIARY
or
INTELLIGENCE SUMMARY.

16th Bde RFA

(Erase heading not required.)

Instructions regarding War Diaries and Intelligence Summaries are contained in F. S. Regs., Part II. and the Staff Manual respectively. Title pages will be prepared in manuscript.

Place	Date	Hour	Summary of Events and Information	Remarks and references to Appendices
MILLERVAL & FAMPOUX	24.10.17		No retaliation with "PUNISH" for shelling of Millerval. Harassing fire maintained throughout the night. Hostile battery quiet.	BAMPW
	25.10.17		Fired evening smoke screen for Newton TMs at night in field by enemy new track work out on [?] & cutting of retaining gaps. Hostile artillery quiet.	BAMPW
	26.10.17		Hostile batteries U4.64 & U4.61 engaged by 4.5 How & silenced. TMs engaged by 18pr & silenced. 4.5 How cutting wire with 106 fuze.	BAMPW
	27.10.17		Fired smoke screen for HTM & Newton TMs during the afternoon. At night shorts bursts were fired into enemy line at front line.	BAMPW

WAR DIARY
or
INTELLIGENCE SUMMARY.

Army Form C. 2118.

110 Bde RFA

Place	Date	Hour	Summary of Events and Information	Remarks and references to Appendices
WILLERVAL & FARBUS	28/10/17		Active hostile TMs in FRESNOY and ACHEVILLE area. WILLERVAL shelled during 4-5 hours. Enemy received a minute hurricane bombardment during the afternoon.	SAMMW
	29/10/17		Harassing fire during the day and at night with bursts on front line and support. WILLERVAL heavily shelled with about 280 15cm.	SAMMW
	30/10/17		Aeroplane registration & harassing fire by day. Hostile artillery moderately active. Harassing fire & bursts at night.	SAMMW
	31/10/17		Aeroplane registration. TMs not unusually engaged. Hostile artillery active on 18 pr positions in FARBUS. UW93. Registered by aeroplane. Casualties - B115 2 OR wounded.	SAMMW

Copies 16s 4 RA Div, 1 HQ Ra

H Weekley
Lt Col RA

Army Form C. 2118.

WAR DIARY
or
INTELLIGENCE SUMMARY.
(Erase heading not required.)

CONFIDENTIAL.

WAR DIARY

OF

165th BRIGADE R.F.A.

From 1st November to 30th November, 1917.

VOLUME XXIII.

165th Bde
N°23/10

H.Q.
31st D.A.

165th BRIGADE,
R.F.A.

SECRET

-4 DEC 1917

Herewith War Diary
for the month of
November, 1917.

4/12/17

O H McWilson Lt
for
Lt Col RFA
Cmdg 165 Bde RFA

WAR DIARY / INTELLIGENCE SUMMARY

Army Form C. 2118.
Vol XXIII

Place	Date	Hour	Summary of Events and Information	Remarks and references to Appendices
Bavin and Willerval	1-11-17		Wire cutting in preparation for raid D/165 cutting wire at T30 d 36. Wire to be cut along front of BRESNOY PARK	G.S
	2-11-17	4.15 p	Wire cutting by D-165. Several working parties engaged with good results. Practice barrage in preparation for raid. Retaliation very slight.	G.S
		4.30 p	Lt Col F.N. Mackenzie took over command of the Brigade from Lt Col E.B. Thackeray D.S.O	G.S
	5-11-17	4.18 pm	3 minute hurricane bombardment of FRESNOY — No retaliation. Wire cutting for raid still carried on (T30 D 5.7) Hostile artillery retaliated with about 30 rounds on T30 for our wire cutting. Quiet at night. Owing to foggy weather, raid arranged for 2-11-17 at a certain amount of "tog shooting" was carried out by us.	OMMN
	7-11-17		3 minute hurricane bombardment of FRESNOY at 4.20 pm — Drew no retaliation.	OMMN
	8-11-17		At 12 noon a daylight raid was carried out by the 92nd Inf Bde. Point of entry about T30 D 5.7. About 22 prisoners were captured and many casualties were inflicted on the enemy. Ten dugouts full of Germans were blown in by R.E.s. Our casualties were comparatively light. The hostile artillery reply was heavy and murderous at first, coming S. of OPPY and trickly battery death on a trench at ARLEUX and S. of FRESNOY, but this shelling was not very heavy. Then of the enemy who could get away tried to run to the FRESNES-ROUVROY Line and a number of them were caught by our fire. Infantry very keen with our shooting. Next day enemy shelled our trenches in T30 and T30 intermittently during the afternoon	OMMN

WAR DIARY
or
INTELLIGENCE SUMMARY.
(Erase heading not required.)

Army Form C. 2118.

Place	Date	Hour	Summary of Events and Information	Remarks and references to Appendices
Farbus & Willerval	10/11/17		We fired a 2 minute hurricane bombardment on new part of ULSTER Trench at 11 am. Enemy artillery did nothing unusual. Hostile Heavy and Medium Trench Mortars active at intervals.	BMMM
	11/11/17		Enemy has commenced to shell vicinity of ARLEUX, BAILLEUL and the ARLEUX–SUGAR FACTORY road much more frequently. About six MF. calls were received during the day and repeated 15p 4p & 5 Hour. Heaths cleaning a kit more and movement was seen to be normal.	BMMM
	13/11/17		We bombarded ULSTER Trench for one minute at intense rate at 4 pm, and engaged working parties with Shrapnel. FARBUS Shelled at an intense rate by 10.5 cm hows at 3 am.	BMMM
	14/11/17		Hostile artillery ministure during the day but continuous harassing fire on our trenches, roads & tracks was kept up during the night. Enemy fire was normal during the day except for a special bombardment of enemy trenches at 11 noon. Its whole night harassing fire.	BMMM
	15/11/17		Hostile artillery more active than usual on WILLERVAL during the afternoon with 77 mm & 10.5 cm, including gas shells.	BMMM
	16/11/17		In the afternoon some 10.5 cm & 15 cm How carried out a destructive shoot on the forward position of D1br (B'5'c 7.7). This direct hits on gun pits but comparatively little damage was done. No casualties.	BMMM

Army Form C. 2118.

WAR DIARY
or
INTELLIGENCE SUMMARY.
(Erase heading not required.)

Instructions regarding War Diaries and Intelligence Summaries are contained in F.S. Regs., Part II. and the Staff Manual respectively. Title pages will be prepared in manuscript.

Place	Date	Hour	Summary of Events and Information	Remarks and references to Appendices
FARBUS & WILLERVAL	17/4/17		He carried out a hurricane bombardment of FRESNOY Park at 11 a.m. Enemy retaliated at 3 p.m. with 5 minutes intense on T B & D	OWEN
	27/4/17		Hostile artillery more active again. Enemy fire on our trenches and a few gas shells on our trenches at Harmony Pit. WILLERVAL heavily shelled during the afternoon.	OWEN
	28/4/17			OWEN
	28/4/17 & 29/4/17		Hostile artillery becoming more active. Our trenches frequently shelled during the afternoon, probably to destroy T.M. emplacements. Sugar Factory, ARLEUX SUGAR FACTORY Road and FARBUS heavily shelled. More gas shells being used.	OWEN
	29/4/17		He carried out 2 minute bombardment on selected trench junctions at 2.5 e.m.t. He carried out a "Chinese attack" at 9 p.m. which drew a good deal of retaliation.	OWEN
	30/4/17		WILLERVAL was again heavily shelled from 11.35 p.m. to 2.55 a.m. at a return rate with HE and gas shells of all calibres. All batteries between RUNSOY and IZEL appeared to be firing. About 6000 rounds were fired in all. Casualties — Two swallowed by D 165. good. Material damage very slight.	OWEN

..............................Lt. Col. R.F.A.
Commanding 165th (County Palatine) Brigade R.F.A.

A5834   Wt. W4973 M687 750,000 8/16 D.D. & L. Ltd. Forms C.2118/13.

Army Form C. 2118

WAR DIARY
or
INTELLIGENCE SUMMARY
(Erase heading not required.)

Vol 22

CONFIDENTIAL.

WAR DIARY

OF

165th BRIGADE R.F.A.

From 1st December to 31st December 1917.

VOLUME XXIV.

165th Bde RFA
N 23/4

H.Q. 31 D.A.

Herewith War Diary
for the month of
December, 1917.

31/
/18.

[signature] Lieut & Adjt
Comdg 165 Bde RFA

Secret

WAR DIARY
or
INTELLIGENCE SUMMARY

Army Form C.2118.

165th BDE. R.F.A.

Place	Date	Hour	Summary of Events and Information	Remarks and references to Appendices
WILLERVAL and FARBUS	1st	6 pm	D/165 carried out shoots on tramway junctions during the afternoon. D/165 carried out a gas-bombardment of 13th HQ at V26d 9565	C.B.
"	2nd	2.25pm	"A" "B" "C" Batteries fired 140 rounds into RUPERT TRENCH in reply to the enemy's shelling O.BK. POST	C.B.
"	5th	5.10pm	The enemy heavily shelled our trenches in B.18 with 10.5 and 15 cm. How. Much activity against WILLERVAL SUGAR-FACTORY and FARBUS during the day. From 10 pm to 12 mn. about 2000 shells were fired against the ARLEUX VALLEY by guns of all calibres. About 50% of these were gas.	C.B.
"	7th	12.5 pm	All guns and hows fired 5 minute intense on the bunker tract in B7 instead in retaliation for the enemy shelling MARQUIS Trench	C.B.
"	8th	—	Hostile artillery slightly active against WILLERVAL	C.B.
"	10th	—	Enemy artillery very active against TIRED ALLEY in B10G. FARBUS received considerable attention	C.B.
"	12th	—	"A" "B" & "C" Batteries carried out harassing fire during the afternoon against the HENIN-LIETARD road. Slight enemy activity during the day on WILLERVAL and the Sugar Factory	C.B.
"	14th	—	All batteries carried out hurricane bombardments on NEUVIREUIL and on HQ at C1a51. "D" By. fired 32 rounds in hostile batteries V16R and OW341 in response to N.F. calls. Enemy active against our forward trench system.	C.B.
"	15th	—	D/165 carried out registration of HQ at C1a +510 by aeroplane	C.B.
"	16th	—	All batteries carried out hurricane bombardment of EAST COPSE	C.B.

Army Form C. 2118.

165th BDE. RFA

WAR DIARY
or
INTELLIGENCE SUMMARY.
(Erase heading not required.)

Place	Date	Hour	Summary of Events and Information	Remarks and references to Appendices
WILLERVAL and FARBUS	17th		A/B/C/D Batteries retaliated on the sunken road in C7c for hostile shelling of our forward tanks. Enemy artillery slightly active against our tanks.	C.B.
	18th	2.30pm	B/2 during the day. An unoccupied pit of D/165 damaged by hostile fire. All batteries carried out harass bombardment of the Sunken road in C3c.	C.B.
	19th	4pm	Enemy carried out a destructive shoot against A/165 position at B10c 4·3. Two pits were damaged, one gun badly damaged and another slightly damaged. No casualties to personnel. About 200 5.9" were fired. All batteries carried out harass bombardment of tramway road at C8c 90.	C.B.
	20th		Enemy carried out a heavy gas bombardment of B10c and B10a from 8pm to 10pm. About 2000 rounds were fired, chiefly from left batteries. 18 pdrs fired on personnel on roads in V26. All batteries carried out harass bombardments of the cross-roads and dumps at C3c 3575 and of the dump and track junctions at C22 & 3570.	C.B.
	22nd		BAILLEUL, WILLERVAL and ARLEUX were heavily shelled by 5·9 and 21 cm hows throughout the day. A destructive shoot was carried out against D/165 position at B3d 4·1. D/165 fired 250 rounds in trouble battery U.X119, U.X51 and U.X51.	C.B.
	24th		Special harassing fire carried out on enemy roads and tracks by all batteries during the night - 960 rounds fired in all. Enemy replied by scattering somewhat heavily	C.B.

Army Form C. 2118.

WAR DIARY
or
INTELLIGENCE SUMMARY.
(Erase heading not required.)

165th Bde. R.F.A.

Place	Date Dec.	Hour	Summary of Events and Information	Remarks and references to Appendices
WILLERVAL and FARBUS	25th		All batteries fired on FOOT-HILL, BOIS VILLAIN, and HENIN-LEITARD area at a slow rate as covering fire for T.M's from 12 noon to 12.15pm. Enemy retaliated on WILLERVAL and ARLEUX. Wagonn harassing fire carried out on enemy communications during the night.	O.B.
	26th		Hostile artillery very active against battery positions. Destructive shots carried out against C/165 and B/165. Battalion. Direct hits were obtained on two pits of C/165 at 13.9E 55F4, two guns were damaged. No damage was caused to equipment of B/165. No casualties to personnel in either case	O.B.
	27th		All batteries carried out hurricane bombardment of tracks in U2½e. Hostile artillery quiet	O.B.
	29th		Little activity on either side. Enemy carried out a slight harassing fire on roads in our zone	O.B.
	31st		C/165 Dispersed movement on the HENIN-LIETARD RD. Enemy carried out a few minutes bombardment of centre of activity in B2 and WILLERVAL at 11pm by 15 cm Hows and 77 mm guns	O.B.

[signatures]

Army Form C. 2118.

WAR DIARY
or
INTELLIGENCE SUMMARY.
(Erase heading not required.)

CONFIDENTIAL.

WAR DIARY

OF

165 BRIGADE R.F.A.

From 1st January to 31st January, 1918.

VOLUME XXV.

165th Bde RFA
No 3/H   Secret

H.Q.
31st D.A.

        -4 FEB. 1918   165th BRIGADE, R.F.A.

Herewith War Diary
for the month of January
1918.

                        Elliott Capt
                        for Lt Col RFA
31/2/18   Comdg 165 Bde RFA

165th Bde R.F.A.

WAR DIARY
INTELLIGENCE SUMMARY

Army Form C. 2118.

Place	Date	Hour	Summary of Events and Information	Remarks and references to Appendices
FARBUS & WILLERVAL	1-1-18		Commenced the New Year with a Brigade Salvo at midnight on CHEZ BONTEMPS. Enemy very quiet. In the evening about 6.30pm enemy put down a barrage on the trenches in the subsector on our left apparently with the idea of making a raid. The raid did not materialise owing to our fire.	OMMW
	2-1-18		Our fire Nil. Enemy more active than usual during the night. HE and gas shells fired at intervals on ARLEUX, WILLERVAL and FARBUS.	OMMW
	3-1-18		4.5 Howr registered trench junctions with aeroplane. Heavy positions near FARBUS and in BITS A heavily shelled with 15cm Howr.	OMMW
	4-1-18		Aeroplane registration of trench junctions by 4.5 Howr. Enemy fairly active on our roads and tracks during the night. Cont.	OMMW

165 Bde R.F.A.

Army Form C. 2118.

WAR DIARY
or
INTELLIGENCE SUMMARY.

(Erase heading not required.)

Place	Date	Hour	Summary of Events and Information	Remarks and references to Appendices
FARBUS & WILLERVAL	5.1.18		Our trench round ARLEUX were bombarded for a short period with 10.5cm and 15cm shell. We retaliated with shelling a "soft spot" in the enemy trenches. Usual light harassing fire on our roads & tracks during the night.	APPX IV
	6.1.18		Visitors and 18 pr attempted to register trench junction and dump with aeroplane observation, but were unsuccessful owing to mist. A hostile T.M. was engaged by both calibres at 9.20 pm, in retaliation which was asked for by the infantry. Hostile artillery fairly quiet.	APPX IV
	7.1.18		4.5 Hows registered T.M. emplacement with aeroplane observation. Our trenches in T30 were subjected to a two minute bombardment by 77 m.m. guns. We retaliated. Hostile artillery otherwise normal.	APPX IV
	8.1.18		Quiet day. 18 pr engaged occasional movement. Capt.	

165th Bde. RFA.

Army Form C. 2118.

WAR DIARY
or
INTELLIGENCE SUMMARY.
(Erase heading not required.)

Instructions regarding War Diaries and Intelligence Summaries are contained in F. S. Regs., Part II. and the Staff Manual respectively. Title pages will be prepared in manuscript.

Place	Date	Hour	Summary of Events and Information	Remarks and references to Appendices
FARBUS & WILLERVAL	9.1.18		4.5 Hows registered trench junction with aeroplane observation. 18p engaged movement, and fired for calibration. 15cm Hows shelled vicinity of Long Wood and Sugar Factory at intervals during the day. A few rounds from a 10 cm gun were fired into WILLERVAL during the night	OMMM
	10.1.18		18p fired on enemy dump with aeroplane registration. 4.5 Hows fired on six hostile batteries in response to NF call. Vicinity of Sugar Factory Road and Bailleul was heavily shelled with 15cm during the afternoon. Night firing on enemy roads and tracks was less than usual.	OMMM
	11.1.18		4.5 Hows fired on a trench junction with aeroplane observation during the morning. 18p engaged several working parties with success. At 9pm 4.5Hows fired 25 rounds of BNC on hostile battery U2 b.7, hostile battery vz b.7, of all calibres from 7.30 to 8.55 pm about 700 gas and HE shells of all calibres were fired into the FARBUS – WILLERVAL area. Later at 10.35pm and again at 1–1.30 am more gas shells were fired into the Same area. Cont'd	OMMM

165th Bde R.F.A.

WAR DIARY
INTELLIGENCE SUMMARY

Army Form C. 2118

Place	Date	Hour	Summary of Events and Information	Remarks and references to Appendices
FARBUS & WILLERVAL	12-1-18		4.5 Hows engaged two hostile Batteries in answer to N.F. call and fired on and dispersed hostile working parties. Hostile artillery normally active.	SAMPLE
	13-1-18		4.5 Hows engaged H.B's UW43 + UW93 + dispersed movement. H.A. carried out destructive about on heavy batteries in Farbus. 366 rds being fired. 2Pdrs also fired on Command. House Corner. H.A. generally above normal. Owing to good visibility considerable individual movement seen on several centres.	SAMPLE
	14-1-18		Bad visibility. 2 artillery on both sides quiet.	SAMPLE
	15-1-18		4.5 Hows engaged movement. H.A. kept up single harassing fire during the day. Slight individual movement seen.	SAMPLE
	16-1-18		Movement engaged by 4.5" Hows. Sugar Factory shelled with 250 rds 15" & 10.5cm. H.A otherwise quiet. Considerable individual movement + small parties seen.	SAMPLE
	17-1-18		H.B UW17 engaged. "2 organised shell fales regested by 4.5" hows with aeroplane observation. Hostile artillery quiet.	SAMPLE
	18-1-18		H.B's UW 93 twice engaged 4.5" Hows in answer to N.F. call. Movement in several places engaged. Reinforced by 4.5" Hows & 18 pdrs.	SAMPLE
			6" How parties in Farbus systematically shelled until 15.21 cm. H.A otherwise normal. Considerable individual movement, especially in Friancs - Rouvroy line. Smoke screen put up in C.21.c.	SAMPLE
	19-1-18		4.5" Hows engaged H.B. UW17 in answer to N.F. call. with aeroplane observation + also engaged movement at various points. H.A. exceptionally quiet. Working parties + individual movement above normal.	SAMPLE
	20-1-18		Movement + working parties engaged by 4.5" Hows + 18 Pdrs. Evening fire was below normal but a harassing nature.	SAMPLE

165th Bde R.F.A.

WAR DIARY
or
INTELLIGENCE SUMMARY.

Army Form C. 2118.

Place	Date	Hour	Summary of Events and Information	Remarks and references to Appendices
	20-1-18		Above normal movement at several points.	JMMMN
	21-1-18		Aeroplane registered 18 Pdrs on to Dumps and Mars, by 4.5" How on to T.M. above normal movement. Spasmodic fire on to QUERY-LA-MOTTE	JMMMN
	22-1-18		4.5" How engaged H.13, C.13.16, C.13 41, UX 53 & U.271 in answer to N.F. calls at dispersed movement. Heavy artillery position in B.15. Our batteries to a concentrated bombardment by hostile artillery. Sugar factory also shelled fairly heavily. Otherwise H.A activity below normal. Considerable movement seen chiefly in back areas.	JMMMN
	23-1-18		Mars T.M. were registered by 18 Pars & 2 by 4.5 Hows. 4.5 How engaged H.13 UY 56. 18 Pdrs dispersed movement a several points & carried out a hurricane bombardment. Hostile artillery very quiet. Visibility was bad & only a small amount of individual movement seen.	JMMMN
	24-1-18		H.13 UY57 engaged by 4.5" How. Track junction target registered by 18 Pars with aeroplane & movement dispersed by 4.5" How & 18 Pdrs. Hostile artillery exceptionally quiet. Enemy aircraft unusually active.	JMMMN
	25-1-18		4.5" How engaged H.13. UW 43. 18 Pdr registered track junction with aeroplane & dispersed movement at several places. 4.5" Hows & 18 Pdrs took part in a Hurricane bombardment. Hostile artillery fired 250 rounds 15 cms. on B.21.6 & BAILEUL & carried out a bombardment during daylight. Normal movement seen at visibility permitted.	JMMMN
	26-1-18		4.5" How fired on movement near CHEZ BONTEMPS T.H.Q. in BOIS VILBIM. Hostile artillery very quiet. Owing to very bad visibility very little movement seen.	JMMMN

165th Bde. R.F.A.

WAR DIARY or **INTELLIGENCE SUMMARY.**

Army Form C. 2118.

Place	Date	Hour	Summary of Events and Information	Remarks and references to Appendices
	27-1-18	12 mn 1 am 9.5 am 11.40 am	Hostile artillery very quiet, harassing fire only during night. About 50 MTM on trenches in B.18. About 120 rounds 15 & 21 cm fired on 6" How position in FORBUS. Some movement observed owing to mist. Some registration with aeroplane observation.	OAMPM
	28-1-18	12.30 to 3 pm	Hostile artillery active on FORBUS, about 70 rds 21 cm. otherwise quiet. Very little movement observed.	OAMPM
	29-1-18	11.30 to 11.32	4.5" Hows were registered & aeroplane on t. AB battery U×68, 18 Pdr were registered on to Dump in C.3 & railway junction in C.2 with aeroplane observation. 4.6 Hows 18 Pdr took part in hurricane bombardment.	OAMPM
	30-1-18	5.0 to 5.45 am 10.20 & 11.15	Hostile artillery kept up light but persistant harassing fire. Faint heavy bombardment of our trenches in OPPY. No movement seen owing to fog. 4.5 Hows were registered on to HB U/68 & engaged HB C345 in answer to MF call. Five minute intense bombardment of our trenches between ARLEUX HOPPY. Harassing fire on roads, tracks behind after dark. No movement seen owing to thick fog.	OAMPM
	31-1-18	7.44 to 7.57 12.45 & 3.20 am	155 Rounds were fired on S.O.S. U 1 & 2. 4.5 Hows & 18 Pdrs. 18 Pdrs fire 100 rds on tracks owing to report of unexpected relief. Hostile artillery very quiet. 4 + M.TM more active than usual on trenches round ARLEUX. Visibility very bad, no movement observed.	OAMPM

J. McKim Lt. Col. R.F.A.
Comdg. 165th (County Palatine) Brigade R.F.A.

Army Form C. 2118.

WAR DIARY
or
INTELLIGENCE SUMMARY.
(Erase heading not required.)

Vol 24

CONFIDENTIAL.

WAR DIARY

OF

165th BRIGADE R.F.A.

From 1st February to 28th February, 1918.

VOLUME XXVI.

165th Bde R.F.A.

WAR DIARY or INTELLIGENCE SUMMARY

Army Form C. 2118.

Place	Date	Hour	Summary of Events and Information	Remarks and references to Appendices
FARBUS & WILLERVAL	1-1-18		Our tie. 18 pr. fired 100 rounds on enemy tracks in C.1.A, C.2.A and C.3.A & 8 between 12.30 am and 3.30 am in view of suspected enemy relief. Prisoners information proved on by 92nd Inf. Bde. The weather was foggy nearly all day. Enemy did "fog shooting" on our tracks and roads. The usual amount of harassing fire was directed against our roads, tracks and trenches during the night. The trenches in T.7 and T.30 came in for more than their usual share from intermittent bursts.	SAMPLE
	2-1-18		C.165 fired 30 rounds on an experimental shoot. D.165 fired 32 rounds registering a T.M. emplacement at U.25 c 43.60 with aeroplane observation. A 15 cm Bttn and a 10.5 cm How battery combined in a destructive shoot on one of our heavy positions near the Sugar Factory, firing 166 rounds between 12 noon and 2 pm. Shelled by 15 cm Hows for a quarter of an hour at Bailleul was heavily — 1.10 pm. The Bois Bernard batteries fired small bursts on Willerval at intervals through the night. Some 77 mm gas shells were used against the Sugar Factory and Carman Rd during the night.	SAMPLE
	3-1-18		D.165 fired 43 8x on T.M. emplacement at C.1.C.6.7 with aeroplane observation. Hostile artillery quiet during the afternoon except for a few rounds 77mm on our tracks and roads. Sugar Factory, the T. road running from Arleux to the Sugar Factory was heavily shelled by 15cm hows from 6 to 8.30 pm. Light and medium T.Ms very active on our trenches opposite Oppy during the night.	SAMPLE

165 Bde R.F.A.

WAR DIARY or INTELLIGENCE SUMMARY

Army Form C. 2118.

Place	Date	Hour	Summary of Events and Information	Remarks and references to Appendices
FARBUS × WILLERVAL	4-2-18	4.5 Hours	fired 50 rounds B.N.E. on U.27.c at 8.28 pm. This battery was firing gas into an area result uncertain as more gas was fired afterwards. Hostile artillery carried out a destructive shoot during the afternoon on heavy positions near Bailleul (15cm hours). An unusually heavy harassing fire was kept up all night on the Arleux - Sugar Factory Road and the vicinity of Long Wood and the Sugar Factory. A certain amount of 77mm and 15cm shell was used.	W.P.W.
	5-2-18		In view of suspected enemy relief all calibres joined in a shoot on roads and tracks and railway terminus at Bois en T. Enemy bombarded Arleux loop in B5 c and D with 10.5 cm hows from 10.15 pm 16.12.3:00 am doing some damage to the trench. 77mm gas shell were fired in short bursts on our area during the night and early morning.	W.P.W.
	6-2-18	4.5 Hours	answered N.F. calls on UW73 and UN56. U26c. Hostile Artillery carried out a destructive shoot during the afternoon on a heavy position in B10d and another destructive shoot on Bailleul. A few rounds were fired on the Sugar Factory during the evening and the trenches in B12c were lightly shelled with gas. Hostile Artillery was very quiet during the night, although Hostile T.M.s were active on the West of Trenches in B12.	W.P.
	7-2-18		Our Operations were nil. Hostile Artillery was much quieter than usual. Bailleul was lightly shelled during the morning. The Scarpe-Arleux road was slightly harassed during the night. Hostile T.M.s were slightly active against our trenches in 73c Wood 13.6 a.a.d, &c.	W.P.
	8-2-18	4.5 Hours	engaged new work at U25c 15.55 with aeroplane observation. 18 OFS engaged & dispersed movement in c4f and U29d. Arleux was shelled during morning with 77mm R10.5cm. Ammunition of 7.2cc caliber there B15c. During afternoon Long Wood was heavily shelled with 15cm, and also shelled with 15cm Hows direction of Crestwood. Both targets were enemy positions.	W.P.

165 Bde. R.F.A.

Army Form C. 2118.

WAR DIARY
or
INTELLIGENCE SUMMARY.
(Erase heading not required.)

Instructions regarding War Diaries and Intelligence Summaries are contained in F. S. Regs., Part II. and the Staff Manual respectively. Title pages will be prepared in manuscript.

Place	Date	Hour	Summary of Events and Information	Remarks and references to Appendices
	9.2.18		4.5 Hows engaged a hostile T.M. at C7d 95.95 with Aeroplane Observation. 18pdrs engaged and dispersed movement. Hostile Artillery was very active on BAUVIN. Wind was still & bright during afternoon & by 15cm Hows.	HPL
	10.2.18		4.5 Hows engaged 2 hostile TMs at Y85.c.80.63 with Aeroplane Observation. 18pdrs engaged and dispersed movement. During the day 2 hostile artillery carried out destructive shoots of trenches with 10.5cm and 15cm against a heavy howitzer in BISC. TM shoot was fired in Grande Bois Z. Morning a 10cm gun. B3 registered 4th came of FORBES wood at B8a 85.25.	HPL
	11.2.18		4.5 Hows engaged new work at U25d 45.90 and 4 T.M. at T14d 80.25 with 2 Aeroplane Observation. 18pdrs engaged & dispersed movement. Hostile Artillery was unusually quiet the whole day.	HPL
	12.2.18		4.5 Hows engaged trench junction and dugouts at C15 55.00 with Aeroplane Observation. 18pdrs engaged & dispersed movement. Hostile Artillery was inactive during the day with a slight harassmt [?] was kept up to PROUVY-SORC-RF RY, FERIN WOOD and thereabouts. The Artillery on our left did a bombardment in Chiselar & lens slates at 3.50am & fusing at 3.45am. The enemy reply was feeble. 50m/m 7 M lights and green lights were sent up alternately for the enemy trenches as soon as the bombardment started.	HPL
	13.2.18		6.5 Hows fired 24 rds BX and 10 BNC & BW63 at 8.30pm. 18pdrs engaged and dispersed movement. Hostile Artillery was very quiet the whole day.	HPL
	14.2.18		18pdr enemy of and dispersed working parties. Hostile Artillery was very quiet during the whole day. Medium and Light TMs were registered on T30a and T17d during the whole day.	HPL

165 Bde R.F.A.

WAR DIARY
or
INTELLIGENCE SUMMARY.
(Erase heading not required.)

Army Form C. 2118.

Instructions regarding War Diaries and Intelligence Summaries are contained in F. S. Regs., Part II. and the Staff Manual respectively. Title pages will be prepared in manuscript.

Place	Date	Hour	Summary of Events and Information	Remarks and references to Appendices
	15.2.18		L.S Hows cut wires during the attempts at C1a 15.35. 18P² engaged and destroyed M.G at C9c. R1 at 9.30 p.m a 3/minute bombardment of RUPERT Trench U25660 & U25d 8.7 to 18P² & L.S Hows was carried out as a relation for a heavy shelling of our post. Hostile shelling was very quiet during the whole day. These used by L.F in vicinity of PRIEUX and T30.	L.P.
	16.2.18		L.S Hows cut wire during afternoon at C1a 15.35. At 7.55 Fig Pits at 39BX or U.X59 with Aeroplane observation & 5 upon a 3/minute bombardment of RUPERT front U25 8.6.06 – U25d 8.7 to 18P² and L.S Hows was carried out as retaliation for T.M activity in T.30. L.S Hows & 18P² engaged in harassing fire throughout the night on sunken road B6 & 57.40 & U25 <00 15. Hostile batteries were active during the afternoon in a heavy bombardment on B.I.K which was shelled until 15 cm. The PRIEUX – SUCRE road was subject of attempt by the enemy until 11 P.M. & 10.50. Tms was very active during whole day or T.30 a 57.2.0d	M.R.
	17.2.18		L.S Hows fired on HQ3 at C80 35 40 and C9C 80 35. Will Aeroplane observation. Harassing fire was kept up during the night. 18P² & L.S Hows & enemy tracks & were. Hostile Artillery kept a harassing fire in the PRIEUX – SUCRE road throughout the afternoon & night. Believe fire started with 15 cm shells in the afternoon. At 11.20 a.m. one of our balloons was observed to 3 hostile planes and was brought down in flames in T30. Several other of our balloons drifted over our own during the day.	L.P.
	18.2.18		L.S How fired on new work at C3d 90.57 with Aeroplane Observation 18P² engaged enemy trench & posts. Harassing fire was kept up through the night by 18P² which was shelled with 77mm Hostile Artillery was active in PRIEUX & T30 during the afternoon. In B2d was shelled with 10.5cm. & BOILLEUX also received a few 10.5 cm. Hostile T.Ms were active in T30 & T30.	M.R.

165 Bde R.F.A.

WAR DIARY
or
INTELLIGENCE SUMMARY
(Erase heading not required.)

Army Form C. 2118.

Place	Date	Hour	Summary of Events and Information	Remarks and references to Appendices
	19.2.18		6.5" Hows engaged CHEZ-BONTEMPS cross track junction at U14d 7.8 with Aeroplane Observation. Harassing fire was kept up through the night on tracks, crossings etc. Hostile Artillery was active on FARBUS mill 15 cm and 10.5 cm. Enemy slightly active between 7 & 9 PM on a mud road to the North of POELCAPPELLE and 390 R.9 ARLEUX POST. Dy railway during the night. At 6 PM. 469th IR The attack which was preceded by a heavy barrage between 1 & 6 PM. The vicinity of PRIEUR POST was completely repulsed, leaving 14 wounded prisoners and 5 dead. Four of our men were missing. The whole raid lasted just under an hour.	E.P.L.
	20.2.18		6.5" Hows - registered track junctions at U27a 2.8 and U20 6.8.5 with Aeroplane Observation. 18 P2's engaged a dispersed movement. Hostile Artillery was very quiet throughout the whole 24 hours.	E.P.L.
	21.2.18		4.5" Hows engaged junction of UNENDING & FRESNES ROUGES Lane U27a 6.1 & new work C8c 28.69 with aeroplane observation. 18 P2's engaged and dispersed movement. FARBUS was heavily shelled between 15 cm and 10.5 cm throughout the whole 24 hours. Movement was much above normal during the day.	A.P.L.
	22.2.18		Our Operations were Nil. Hostile Artillery very quiet during the whole 24 hours.	A.P.L.
	23.2.18		4.5" Hows engaged Dugouts in NEW SWITCH C8a 4.4 & Crossroads at U20 d 70.35 with Aeroplane Observation. 18 P2's Dispersed movement. Hostile Artillery very quiet.	E.P.L.
	24.2.18		4.5" Hows engaged H.Q. at U25 d 37.58 & rifle track junction C2d 63.86 with Aeroplane Observation. 18 P2's engaged & dispersed movement. Hostile Artillery carried out a destructive shoot with 10.5 cm & 8.15 cm on FARBUS during the afternoon. The offending battery was U.N.65 & U.W.56. Movement was very quiet above normal during the afternoon.	G.P.L.
	25.2.18		4.5" Hows engaged Dug outs at U25 a 81.76 and track junction U26 a 3.9 with Aeroplane Observation. 18 P2's engaged & dispersed movement. Hostile Artillery quiet throughout the whole 24 hours.	E.P.L.

165 Bde R.F.A.

Army Form C. 2118.

WAR DIARY
or
INTELLIGENCE SUMMARY.
(Erase heading not required.)

Instructions regarding War Diaries and Intelligence Summaries are contained in F. S. Regs., Part II. and the Staff Manual respectively. Title pages will be prepared in manuscript.

Place	Date	Hour	Summary of Events and Information	Remarks and references to Appendices
	26.2.18		4.5 How's engaged hostile T.M's at C10.35.80 and U.25.a.25.30 with Aeroplane Observation. 18Pdrs engaged hostile movement. Mostly the others were quiet. Except for a shelling of B15c with 15cm about 180 rds. were fired.	W.P.R
	27.2.18		4.5 How's engaged Dug-outs at U.25.d.27.37 and Track junction at U.26.d.05.22 with Aeroplane Observation. 18Pdrs Distracted movement. BAILLEUL was heavily shelled during the afternoon with 15cm. One of our R.E. 8's was brought down in B15d by hostile A.A fire.	E.P.R
	28.2.18		4.5 How's engaged H.Q at C.d.50.05 with and track junction at C.3.c.3.8 with Aeroplane Observation. 18Pdr dispersed movement. MILLERVAL was shut down in the afternoon with about 200 rds 10.5cm & 15cm and BAILLEUL was shelled with about 80 rds 10.5cm. A.H.V. fire was active in the woods behind FER.1803 during the night from the direction of QUIERY-LA-MOTTE	E.P.R

F.W. Mackenzie Lieut Col
Comdg. 165th Bde.
R.F.A.

31st Divisional Artillery

WAR DIARY

165th BRIGADE R. F. A.

MARCH 1918

CONFIDENTIAL.

WAR DIARY

OF

165th BRIGADE R.F.A.

From 1st March 1918 to 31st March 1918.

VOLUME XXVII.

WAR DIARY
or
INTELLIGENCE SUMMARY.

Army Form C. 2118

Place	Date	Hour	Summary of Events and Information	Remarks and references to Appendices
Douchy	25.3.18		In action in Douchy Valley. Infantry in front of Ayette and Aerodrome. All German attacks repulsed. Casualties 2 officers Yorkeley injured and 3 O.R. (slightly wounded)	OMMM
	26.3.18		Infantry withdrew to Ayette line. Brigade took up positions in Valley in Wd N.E. of Moneny au Bois. Got out of Douchy Valley by road on S.W. side of Adinfer Wood with only four casualties – 2 killed & 2 wounded by shellfire – Casualties Colonel 1 O.R. Wounded 3 O.R.	OMMM
	27.3.18		Batteries moved into new forward positions near Rabbit Wood behind Adinfer Wood in the evening.	OMMM
	28.3.18		In action near Rabbit Wood X.19.	OMMM

31st Divisional Artillery.

165th BRIGADE R.F.A. ::: APRIL 1918.

CONFIDENTIAL.

WAR DIARY

OF

165th BRIGADE R.F.A.

From 1st April to 30th April, 1918.

VOLUME XXVIII

165th Bde R.F.A. Volume VIII
1st to 30th April 1918
Army Form C. 2118.

WAR DIARY
INTELLIGENCE SUMMARY.
(Erase heading not required.)

Place	Date	Hour	Summary of Events and Information	Remarks and references to Appendices
DOUVEY VALLEY	1/4/18		Our batteries subjected to a good deal of gas shelling (mustard gas) from 77mm and 4.2's.	OTMMM
	3/4/18		Ayette captured by 32nd Division at 2am. Front line now runs just on F. edge of the village.	OTMMM
	4/4/18		Hostile artillery very active. Ayette heavily shelled at 11.15am. Douvey Valley, Quesnoy Farm and Monchy au Bois heavily shelled with HE & gas (mustard)	OTMMM
	6/4/18		Douvey Valley again shelled with mustard gas during the night.	OTMMM
	7/4/18		Hostile artillery active in Ayette area, Adinfer Wood, Douchy, Douvey Valley shelled during the night & early. Very little movement seen.	OTMMM
	8/4/18		Very heavy bombardment of Douvey Valley with 77mm & mustard gas shell between 5.30 and 8am. 15cm howrs also shelled the valley all the morning.	OTMMM
	10/4/18		The most harassing fire was maintained on our area. Batteries were manned to the last. The enemy engaged a good deal of movement in 405 Howrs engaged hostile batteries within range.	OTMMM
	15/4/18		Douvey Valley again bombarded with about 500 mustard gas shell in the early morning. Our 4.5 Hows engaged new work, dugouts, batteries. 18pdr engaged movement.	OTMMM
			CmdT	

WAR DIARY or INTELLIGENCE SUMMARY

Army Form C. 2118.

165th Bde. R.F.A.

Place	Date	Hour	Summary of Events and Information	Remarks and references to Appendices
Douchy Valley	15/4/18		Enemy artillery active at intervals. Normal harassing fire on our area. Also several heavy bursts.	OMMN
	16/4/18		He engaged special targets with organised harassing fire as well as annoying movement and centres of activity. Intense hostile artillery much quieter.	OMMN
	17/4/18		Enemy much more normal harassing fire with occasional heavy bursts.	OMMN
	18/4/18		18 pdrs were used against Douchy Valley. Captured 18 pdr battery suspected in a position just North of Courcelles.	OMMN
	20/4/18		He directed several intense bursts against hostile centres of activity & the enemy artillery retaliated on our lines with short intense bursts of about the same duration as our own.	OMMN
			On previous nights the Douchy Valley was heavily shelled by 4.2s during the morning of 21st and again on the evening of 22nd with by 15 cm Hows. Hostile movement normal.	
			Most of the enemy fire on Douchy Valley comes from the direction of the COURCELLES Group.	
			Enemy seems to be doing work on forts & MG emplacements, but no continuous line is being dug.	
	23/4/18		Quesnoy FARM & vicinity subjected to 5 minute intense bombardment by batteries in direction of LogEAST WOOD about 10:30 am with aeroplane observation.	OMMN

Army Form C. 2118.

WAR DIARY
or
INTELLIGENCE SUMMARY. 165th Bde R.F.A
(Erase heading not required.)

Instructions regarding War Diaries and Intelligence Summaries are contained in F. S. Regs., Part II. and the Staff Manual respectively. Title pages will be prepared in manuscript.

Place	Date	Hour	Summary of Events and Information	Remarks and references to Appendices
DOUAI VALLEY	24/4/18		Hostile harassing fire manual. Its engaged selected targets when new work and movement had been seen. 4.5 How engaged several hostile batteries within range.	OMMM
	26/4/18 27/4/18 28/4/18		Hostile artillery much quieter. Units then moved. Some guns from then south for use further North. Its carried out harassing fire at engaged movement when seen.	OMMM
	29/4/18		Hostile artillery quiet during the night & morning. At 3.30 p.m. there was a 3 minute hurricane bombardment directed on our battery positions in the Douai Valley and ADINFER WOOD.	OMMM
	30/4/18		Hostile artillery fairly quiet. At intervals small bits of hurricane fire pants on our front, but no continuous line is being done by the enemy on our front. Casualties for April —	OMMM

	Officers			Other Ranks		
	Killed	Wounded	Gassed	Killed	Wounded	Gassed
	1	3	7	8	51	115

FJWalkinger
Lt. Col.
Comdg 165th Bde R.F.A

Vol 27.

CONFIDENTIAL.

WAR DIARY

OF

165 BRIGADE R.F.A.

From 1st May to 31st May, 1918.

VOLUME XXIX.

165th Bde R.F.A
W 23/4

H.Q.
31 D.A.

[stamp: 165th BRIGADE. R.F.A.]

Herewith War Diary
for the month of May
1918.

5/6/18

Major R.F.A.
Comdg 165 Bde R.F.A.

165 S. Bde R.F.A. Vol XXIX

WAR DIARY
INTELLIGENCE SUMMARY.

1st–31st May 1918

165 Bde R.F.A.

Army Form C.-2118.

Place	Date	Hour	Summary of Events and Information	Remarks and references to Appendices
Douchy Valley	1/5/18		Normal harassing fire on Douchy Valley, Adinfer Wood & district, hostile batteries near Courcelles-le-Comte and harassing fire directed against S.W. corner of Adinfer Wood. 4.5 Hows x 18 pdr engaged enemy artillery directed a heavy bombardment against them during the day.	OMWW
	2/5/18		10.10 a.m. to 10.35 a.m. Continuous and heavy harassing fire directed against our battery positions in Douchy Valley all morning, and during the day. A T.M. experiment was engaged. Enemy movement was engaged by 4.5 Hows and dispersed. A red propaganda balloon floated over into our lines.	OMWW
	3/5/18		Hostile fire continues round Douchy Valley with heavy bursts at intervals. We engaged a good deal of movement round Courcelles – also several hostile batteries were harassed by 18 pdr at intervals.	OMWW
	4/5/18		Hostile artillery a little quieter. We engaged all movement seen.	OMWW
	5/5/18		Hostile artillery normal harassing fire – 2 short hurricane bombardments of Douchy Valley at 2 pm. We engaged movement, inflicting several casualties. On harassing fire kept up every day & night.	OMWW
	6/5/18		Hostile fire heavier during afternoon and night. Several short intense bursts directed against Douchy Valley. We engaged movement during the night.	OMWW
	7/5/18		A vigorous harassing fire on both sides – nothing unusual.	OMWW

WAR DIARY or INTELLIGENCE SUMMARY.

Army Form C. 2118.

165 Bde R.F.A

Place	Date	Hour	Summary of Events and Information	Remarks and references to Appendices
DOUCHY VALLEY	8/5/18		Fairly heavy harassing fire on Douchy Valley. A heavy burst fired down on road & track in F9c at 10 am. 77mm 10cm. HE & gas. Gas concentration at 3.30 am.	AMMN
	9/5/18		4.5 How fired gas in the early morning. "Counter Preparation". 4.5 How destroyed a hostile T.M. in the morning.	AMMN
	10/5/18		Hostile fire normal. We maintained usual harassing fire by night and day.	AMMN
	13/5/18		Hostile fire normal. Nothing unusual.	AMMN
	14/5/18		Hostile artillery more active. Heavy destructive fire directed against Road — F13.B, x15c (Ely points), and against battery positions in F8c during morning and afternoon. In the evening at 7-15 pm a 15 minute intense bombardment was directed against battery area in F9c. Hostile Batteries in direction of LOGEAST WOOD. We carried out a gas shoot on a LUNEAU bombardment in the early morning. Hostile fire normal except to destructive fire by 15cm How on battery positions at N.E. end of ADINFER WOOD and one 9cm positions in DOUCHY VALLEY (c.165). 4.5 How engaged for hostile batteries in answer to NF calls. In addition to the usual harassing fire 4.5 How fired 300 rds of BNC gas at artillery dugouts in A15A.	AMMN
	15/5/18			AMMN
	16/5/18		Douchy Valley received a lot more than the normal attention at intervals. Five hostile batteries were engaged by our 4.5 Hows.	AMMN

WAR DIARY or INTELLIGENCE SUMMARY

Army Form C. 2118.

165th Bde R.F.A.

Place	Date	Hour	Summary of Events and Information	Remarks and references to Appendices
Douchy Valley	17/5/18		Hostile more active than usual. Mainly on Douchy Valley & vicinity. ADINFER WOOD. 4.5 Hows engaged two hostile batteries & sent carried out a successful shoot on hostile battery ANS with aeroplane observation.	OAMMN
	18/5/18		Two hostile batteries engaged with good results in answer to NF calls, also Hostile artillery less than usual on Douchy Valley. The RANSART - ADINFER Rd & XISE received normal attention from 10.55 hrs.	OAMMN
	19/5/18		Normal harassing fire	OAMMN
	20/5/18		HQ 165 Bde held an entire & Right front K HQ 170 Bde RFA.	
	26/5/18		Usual harassing fire carried out by night and day the last few days. Hostile fire slightly decreased during this period.	OAMMN
			HQ. 165 moved command to Right Group. Hostile artillery put down heavy barrages on our front & support lines at 10.30 pm and 2.10 am. He replied by firing for 10 minutes on areas S.O.S lines. Also salvos fired on "Annihilate" fire zones.	OAMMN
	27/5/18		Hostile artillery became very active against batteries protection than N. end of ADINFER WOOD and behind the WOOD 10.5 x 15 cm. Douchy Valley heavily fired on during the afternoon by 77 mm & 10 cm. A heavy barrage was put down on our front at support lines from ABIAINZEVELLE to MOYENNEVILLE from 4.25 am to 4.35 am.	OAMMN
	28/5/18		Very heavy fire 10.5 cm & 15 cm was directed against the M. end of ADINFER WOOD at intervals—sending the areas to batteries & OPs at 10.35 pm. Another heavy barrage was put down on our front & support line from 10.55 pm (ABIAINZEVELLE - MOYENNEVILLE)	OAMMN

WAR DIARY
or
INTELLIGENCE SUMMARY.   165 Bde RFA

Army Form C. 2118.

Place	Date	Hour	Summary of Events and Information	Remarks and references to Appendices
Doseuy Valley	29/5/18		Hostile Artillery a bit quieter. We maintained an active harassing fire by day & night on areas of enemy activity. Movement in engaged during the day. Six hostile Batteries were engaged by 18 pr & How. Enemy heavy minnies engaged on lines after dark pm towards back areas.	STAMP
	30/5/18		Relieved by 40th Div Artillery. 178th Bde RFA relieving 165th Bde RFA.	STAMP
Humbercourt	31/5/18		In Mobile Reserve at Humbercourt.	STAMP
			31st Div Artillery under control of Guards Div during May /18.	
			Casualties May 1918. Officers Nil.	
			Killed OR 5 Wounded OR 17	

G Brand Capt.

for Comdg 165th Bde R.F.A.

CONFIDENTIAL.

WAR DIARY

OF

165th BRIGADE R. F. A.

From 1st June to 30th June, 1918.

VOLUME XXX.

165th Brigade RFA
WA23/4
31st Div Arty.

165th BRIGADE,
Secret

Herewith War Diary
for June

3 JUL 1918
HEADQUARTERS
51st DIVISIONAL ARTILLERY

2/7/18

A/B Hand Cpt
to Lt Col RHA
Comdg 165th Brigade RFA

Vol XXX
Army Form C. 2118.

WAR DIARY
or
INTELLIGENCE SUMMARY.

165 Bde RFA   JUNE 1918

(Erase heading not required)

Place	Date	Hour	Summary of Events and Information	Remarks and references to Appendices
HUMBERCOURT	1-6-18 / 15-6-18		In mobile Reserve. Normal training carried out.	@MWW
Vicinity of RABBIT WOOD Sheet 51c X.19	16-6-18		Relieved 14th A.H.A. Bde.	@MWW
			A.B. & C. positions silent. 2 guns each of A & B Bys found the "Composite" By and carried out all the 18 pdr harassing fire. "D" By had a found section S.E. of ADINFER WOOD. The Composite 18 pdr & the 4.5 Hows carried out normal harassing fire by day and night. None of the Bdes were fired upon. Enemy artillery much quieter on the sector. Nothing unusual occurred.	@MWW
	26-6-18		Relieved by 14th A.H.A. Bde. Brigade marched to Doullens stopped the night, & marched to BERGUETTE next day entraining there for BERGUETTE. Marched from BERGUETTE by way of AIRE to LA BELLE HOSTESSE to relieve 17th Bde RFA. at E.19 & E.20 Sheet 36A, About to take place about 2/7/18.	@MWW
	30-6-18		Casualties for month 1 OR slightly wounded.	@MWW

J W Mastermann
Comdg. 165 Bde RFA

165th Bde R.F.A.
No. W 23/4

A.Q.
31 D.A.

SECRET

165th BRIGADE,
R.F.A.

- 3 AUG 1918

Herewith War
Diary for the month
of July, 1918.

3/8
   AMWilson Lt
18   Lieut. Col. R.F.A.
   Commanding 165th Bde RFA

CONFIDENTIAL.

WAR DIARY

OF

165th BRIGADE R.F.A.

From 1st July to 31st July, 1918.

VOLUME XXXI.

Vol. XXXI

WAR DIARY
INTELLIGENCE SUMMARY

1st - 31st July 1918

165 Bde R.F.A.

Army Form C. 2118.

Place	Date	Hour	Summary of Events and Information	Remarks and references to Appendices
C.22.A Sheet 36A	1-7-18		In camp at LA BELLE HOTESSE	OAMMN
E.19 & E.20 Sheet 36 A	2-7-18		Relieved 17th Bde R.F.A. 29th Divn. E.19 & E.20. Right Battery front. Normal fairly quiet	OAMMN
	3-7-18		Taking over. Centre of Right Battery front. Harassing fire on both sides.	OAMMN
	9-7-18		28th Bde A.F.A assumed control of Right artillery group. H.Q. 165 Bde to magazine	OAMMN
	10-7-18		Lt Batt 94th Inf Bde raided enemy evidence at E.30.A.06.40. D.165 fired in support of this. Enemy found to be very strong held + no identifications were obtained. 93rd Inf Bde relieved 94th Bde in Right sector night 10/11.	OAMMN
	12-7-18		Left by Bde 31st Divn carried out a minor operation & captured about 70 prisoners near TERN FARM & advanced the line about 400 yds on a front of about 1000 yds in E.17 (about 36A)	OAMMN
	19-7-18		At 7am the 93rd Inf Bde attempted to advance the outpost line to R. PLATE BECQUE. Lt met with strong opposition, and finally withdrew to the original front line. During the operation Right Group Batteries put down a protective barrage beyond R. BECQUE and at 9.10am fired in response to SOS RJ	OAMMN
	30-7-18		Harassing fire normal 100% during night.	OAMMN
	31-7-18		11.30pm all Batteries fired 50 rounds in conjunction with a gas projector bombardment of LA COURONNE	OAMMN

Army Form C. 2118.

WAR DIARY
or
INTELLIGENCE SUMMARY.   165 Bde RFA

(Erase heading not required.)

Instructions regarding War Diaries and Intelligence Summaries are contained in F. S. Regs., Part II. and the Staff Manual respectively. Title pages will be prepared in manuscript.

Place	Date	Hour	Summary of Events and Information	Remarks and references to Appendices
E19 c E20 Sh 51 A	23-7-18	2.15 & 3.30am	Battery fired "Barrett" Preparation in reply to heavy shelling of R front line.	OMMM/1
	27.7.18		Command of Right Group passed to now to OC 165 Bde RFA	OMMM
	30.7.18 31.7.18		Three hostile battery positions engaged by 18pr & 4.5 Hows.	OMMM
			Harassing fire carried out every day & night on enemy occupied areas, roads, tracks &c. Enemy artillery activity normal during the week.	OMMM

Total casualties for July, 1918

Killed		Wounded		Gas	
Officers	OR	Officers	OR	Officers	OR
	1	1	8		2

A. P. Boxall
Lt Col
Comdg 165th Bde RFA

Vol 30

CONFIDENTIAL

WAR DIARY

OF

165th BRIGADE R.F.A.

From 1st August to 31st August, 1918.

VOLUME XXXII.

HQ 165 Bde RFA   1-31 Aug 1918   Vol xxii

WAR DIARY
or
INTELLIGENCE SUMMARY.
(Erase heading not required).

Army Form C. 2118.

165 Bde R.F.A.

Place	Date	Hour	Summary of Events and Information	Remarks and references to Appendices
NIEPPE FOREST	1-8-18		Vigorous harassing fire carried out by night and day on enemy's area. Hostile batteries engaged with usual satisfactory results. In addition to harassing fire a hostile battery position was put out of action & silenced.	Appx IV
	3-8-18		Harassing fire and counter-battery work. Enemy's movement considerably curtailed in area by 9.2 H Bde & our harassing fire. Enemy active.	Appx IV
	4-8-18		Several hostile batteries engaged by 18pr & H.S. Harassing mg posts & road communication.	Appx IV
	5-8-18		An eventful and busy day. Enemy shelled our area, also put down a ten minute hurricane bombardment on VIEUX RUE. Several hostile batteries engaged and day by day by 18pr & 4.5 HH. Enemy active against hostile positions & front system. Held in enemy positions by 18 pdrs & 4 5H.	Appx IV
	7-8-18		At 11pm enemy put down a sparse barrage - completed a gas projection on sp. 15 d. The hostile batteries were engaged by air observation 15 batteries.	Appx IV
	8-8-18		In the course of the day 26 prisoners and two machine guns were captured. Our batteries engaged. Enemy fire normal.	Appx IV
	9-8-18		harassing fire on hostile batteries engaged by 15pr & H. Shoots also in retaliation to enemy. Normal enemy harassing fire.	Appx IV
	11-8-18		At 10.30 am hostile shot down our observation balloon on enemy front. Enemy machine guns & aerial activity and distribution fire on enemy forces. Many fires seen to be burning in enemy line at night.	Appx IV

WAR DIARY or INTELLIGENCE SUMMARY

Army Form C. 2118.

16th Bn RFA

Place	Date	Hour	Summary of Events and Information	Remarks and references to Appendices
Nieppe Forest	13-8-18		Our batteries carried out counter battery shoots on hostile batteries also harassing bombardment on enemy forward areas and known tracks by night and BEAULENSAIS and VERTE RUE, GRUYETTE FARM. Enemy guns of the heavier calibre shelled PLATE BECQUE, MORT artillery active in afternoon an expressive harassing fire at BATAVIA SQUARE, PONT DU PIERRE and to E and W of MERVILLE. He all night of enemy harrassing fire at burg Levis every even just near many wounded and gas shell on A105 Bate portion of END 05.57.90 Damage about 1735 hours on A105 Bate portion of END 05.57.90 Damage	Appx I
	17-8-18		A.C.T.D. batteries co-operating with 29th Inf Brigade on left 13 Corps westwards. Smoke barrier barrage	Appx II
	18-8-18	19-8-18	Brigade fired barrage in support of attack by 94" Infantry Brigade who advanced their line to LE OUTTERSTEENE — VIEUX BERQUIN ROAD LYNDE FARM and LEBIS FARM also taken	Appx III
	20-8-18		Z patrolling few infantry reserves of Infantry Patrols house west kill enemy on BIEU HULLEBERG FARM houses at F20C 17 33. COMET CORNER GEMET CORNER "ODD" CEMETERY	Appx IV
	21-8-18		Owing to little infantry owing apportion of guns were moved forward to positions in front line	Appx V
	22-8-18		During nights 22/23rd 1st Bde occupied U COMET CORNER - F215 59 - F21E 11 - F27a - 1 - 7 - BROUET CORNER - ROOSTEN FARM - KEW CROSS - PONT RONDIN - SCCHIEN CORNER 9/1 v5 a 05" Li. Bty showed were to L2E

Army Form C. 2118.

WAR DIARY
or
INTELLIGENCE SUMMARY.
(Erase heading not required.)

165th Bde RFA

Instructions regarding War Diaries and Intelligence Summaries are contained in F. S. Regs., Part II. and the Staff Manual respectively. Title pages will be prepared in manuscript.

Place	Date	Hour	Summary of Events and Information	Remarks and references to Appendices
NIPPE FORREST	25-8-18		Our infantry took Neuve Eglise 31 Bgde ordered up to selected M.G. positions between BISHOPS CORNER + FAUVOE. 140 rounds in night.	Appx IV
	27-8-18	10am	165 Bde RFA. Fire attacked across BECKET CORNER - BISHOPS CORNER ROAD, covered by creeping barrage put up by all batteries. 210 rounds 2/- batteries + MG sections.	Appx IV
	31-8-18	7:30pm	Bde RFA Infantry pushed forward under cover of fire to line DENVER - BISHOP CORNER - RUE PROVOST and BOUNDY COTTAGES - 280 rds.	Appx IV
	- do -		Infantry pushed advanced line to GAVE FARM - ACTON CROSS 4.5 How Battery advanced across A.22.A.21.B missing barrage in front.	Appx IV
	31-8-18		Enemy Guns moved advanced Limbers at dawn on 1-9-18 result of enemy retirement DOULIEN +	Appx IV

Casualties for August 1918.

Killed   Wounded   Accidentally injured   Sick
O.R.   O.R.   O.R.   O.R.
3   7   3   4

Y. Hitchmann Lt Col

Comdg 165th Bde RFA

CONFIDENTIAL.

WAR DIARY

OF

165th BRIGADE R. F. A.

From 1st September to 30th September, 1918.

VOLUME XXXIII.

165th Brigade Headquarters
H.Q. 31st D.T.A. 18

Herewith copy of War Diary
for the month of Sept

1/10/18   Grn Hutchinson
                 Lt Col R.F.A.
                 Comdg. 165th Bde R.F.A.

WAR DIARY

OF

HEADQUARTERS 31st DIVISIONAL ARTILLERY.

From 1st. October to 31st. October, 1918.

VOLUME XXXIV

CONFIDENTIAL.

WAR DIARY

OF

165th. BRIGADE, R.F.A.

From 1st. October to 31st. October, 1918.

VOLUME XXXX

165th Bde. R.F.A.

H.Q.,
    31st Div Art.

Herewith War Diary for the month of October, 1918.

9-11-18.

Lieut Col. R.F.A.
Commanding 165th Bde. R.F.A.

165th Bde. R.F.A. / W.D. 31st Oct 1918   Vol. XXXIV   Army Form C.2118.

WAR DIARY or INTELLIGENCE SUMMARY

(Erase heading not required.)

HEADQUARTERS 165th BRIGADE, R.F.A.

Place	Date	Hour	Summary of Events and Information	Remarks and references to Appendices
Ploegsteert	1/10/18		H.Q. 28/T 12 a 43 Batteries in action in U.7. Enemy holding line of LYS river.	43.
"	5/10/18		Brigade moved forward to PLOEGSTEERT WOOD. Batteries in action U.20 & U.26.	43.
"	6th to 15/10/18		Usual harassing fire carried out.	43.
"	15/10/18		Enemy retired from line of LYS RIVER.	43.
"	17/10/18		Brigade moved to wagon lines in vicinity of NEUVE EGLISE (sheet 29)	43.
"	18/10/18		" " " " " rest billets at CAESTRE.	43.
CAESTRE	18th to 24/10/18		Training and recreational training carried out.	43.
"	24/10/18		Brigade marched to QUESNOY.	43.
"	25/10/18		" " HARLEBECKE.	43.
VICHTE	27/10/18		Brigade moved into action at INGOYHEM (sheet 29). HQ at VICHTE CHAU.	43.
"	27th to 30/10/18		Harassing fire carried out on enemy communications and works east of BERCHWIJK and TIEGHEM.	43.
"	31/10/18		Brigade action fired creeping in two phases in conjunction with attack by 94 Inf. Bde. Batteries advanced to positions in vicinity of KLEINBERG (29/J.34) during pause between first and second phases. One gun per battery worked with attacking infantry. Operation entirely successful, objectives gained, 700 prisoners and 12 guns captured by 94 Inf. Bde. Casualties – Rated 1 O.R. Wounded 3 O.R.	43.

Signed [signature] Lt Col R.A.
Comdg 165 Bde R.F.A.

165th Brigade R.F.A.

H.Q.,
31st Div. Arty.

Herewith War Diary for month of November, 1918.

15.12.18.

J. E. Hibbert
Major R.F.A.
Commanding 165th Bde RFA.

CONFIDENTIAL.

WAR DIARY

OF

165th BRIGADE. R.F.A.

From 1st November to 30th November, 1918.

VOLUME XXXV.

Army Form C. 2118.

Vol. XXXV

WAR DIARY 1st November 1918 – 30th November 1918
or
INTELLIGENCE SUMMARY. 165 Bde RFA

Place	Date	Hour	Summary of Events and Information	Remarks and references to Appendices
AVELGHEM – GOTINGHEM Area	1-11-18		Batteries in position in Avelghem–Gotingham Area. No firing done.	OAMMW
	2-11-18		Brigade marched from above area to Harlebeke.	OAMMW
BOUSBECQUE	3-11-18		Marched to Bousbecke.	OAMMW
	7-11-18		Marched to Lauwe.	OAMMW
AVELGHEM	8-11-18		Marched to Avelghem to take part in attack which did not take place owing to German retirement.	OAMMW
	10-11-18		Crossed River Scheldt near Orroir	OAMMW
RUSSIGNIES	11-11-18		Prepared to move forward from Russignies in support of 93rd Inf Bde. when further advance was cancelled by orders re Armistice, which commenced at 11.00 hours.	OAMMW
	16-11-18		Marched to Sneveghem	OAMMW
	17-11-18		Marched to Gulleghem	OAMMW
	26-11-18		Marched from Gulleghem to Menin	OAMMW
	27-11-18		Marched from Menin to Vlamertinghe.	OAMMW
	28-11-18		Marched from Steenvoorde.	OAMMW
	29-11-18		Marched to Staple	OAMMW
WIZERNES near ST.OMER	30-11-18		Marched to Wizernes, and took up billets there	OAMMW

J.J. Hubbock

J. Gregson RFA
Comdg 165 Bde RFA

CONFIDENTIAL.

WAR DIARY

OF

165th BRIGADE R. F. A.

From 1st December to 31st December, 1918.

VOLUME XXXVI.

165th Bde R.F.A.
W 23/4

H.Q.
21. D.A.

165th BRIGADE.
R.F.A.

Herewith War Diary
for the month of December
1918.

6/1
1/19

S Bandran
for Lt Col R.H.A.
Comdg 165 Bde R.F.A.

WAR DIARY or **INTELLIGENCE SUMMARY.**

1st–31st December 1918   Vol. XXXVI   165 Bde R.F.A.

Army Form C. 2118

Place	Date	Hour	Summary of Events and Information	Remarks and references to Appendices
WIZERNES near STOMER	1-12-18 to 31-12-18		Training and recreation. Education. Bullery have standings.	

Jas Hutchinson Lt Col.
Comdg 165 Bde R.F.A.

Vol 35

CONFIDENTIAL.

WAR DIARY

OF

165 BRIGADE R. F. A.

From 1st January to 31st January, 1919.

VOLUME XXXVII.

165th Bde R.F.A.
W 93/44

H.Q.
31

185th BRIGADE, R.F.A.
HEADQUARTERS
No.
-4 FEB 1919
Date
31ST DIVISIONAL ARTILLERY

Herewith War Diary
for the month of January
1919.

Franklin
O.C. 165 Bde R.F.A.

4/1/19

165 Bde R.F.A. D/

Army Form C. 2118.

WAR DIARY
or
INTELLIGENCE SUMMARY. 1st–31st January 1919. Vol. XXXVII
165 Brigade R.F.A.

(Erase heading not required.)

Place	Date	Hour	Summary of Events and Information	Remarks and references to Appendices
WIZERNES near ST OMER	1/1	9k	Training and Recreation	
	3/1/19		Supervising billets and Horse Standings	

J. G. Hibbert
Major R.F.A.
Comdg. 165 Bde R.F.A.

Vol 36

CONFIDENTIAL.

WAR DIARY

OF

165th BRIGADE R. F. A.

From 1st February to 28th February, 1919.

VOLUME XXXVIII.

165th Bde. R.F.A.
W.23/4

SECRET

H.Q.
   31st D.A

Herewith War Diary for the month of February, 1919.

5-3-19.
                                            Lieut Col. R.F.A.
                              Commanding 165th Brigade   R.F.A.

Vol. XXXVIII

Army Form C. 2118.

WAR DIARY
or
INTELLIGENCE SUMMARY.
(Erase heading not required.)

165th Brigade. R.F.A.

Place	Date	Hour	Summary of Events and Information	Remarks and references to Appendices
WIZERNES FRANCE	1st Feb to 28th Feb		Training and Recreation; Education; Improving Billets and Horse Standings.	

[signed]
Lieut Col. R.F.A.
Commanding 165th Brigade R.F.A.

CONFIDENTIAL.

WAR DIARY

OF

165th BRIGADE R. F. A.

From 1st March to 31st March, 1919.

VOLUME XXXIX.

165th Bde. R.F.A.

H.Q.
    31st Div Art.

Secret

Herewith War Diary for the month of March, 1919.

6-4-19.

                                          Lieut Col R.F.A.
                               Commanding 165th Bde. R.F.A.

WAR DIARY or INTELLIGENCE SUMMARY

Army Form C. 2118.

Place	Date	Hour	Summary of Events and Information	Remarks and references to Appendices
WIZERNES, FRANCE	1st March 1919 to 31st March 1919.		Training and Recreation ; Education ; Improving Billets. The following is a resume of movements of Officers and Other Ranks since 11th November, 1918:-	

Officers serving on 11th Nov, 1918.

Rank.	Name.	Unit	Remarks.
Lieut. Col.	C.B.Grice-Hutchinson, D.S.O.	H.Q.	
Captain.	G.Brand.	H.Q.	
Lieut.	F.J.Vann.	H.Q.	
Lieut.	O.A.McL.Wilson.	H.Q.	
Captain.	B.E.Gunns, M.C.	A/165.	Posted to A/165 12-2-18.
Lieut.	E.W.Walker.	A/165.	Posted to 170 Bde. 21-12-18.
Lieut.	G.L.Young.	A/165.	Demobilized 9-2-19.
2nd Lieut.	E.P.Lewns.	A/165.	Demobilized 26-1-19.
2nd Lieut.	E.L.Chandler.	A/165.	Demobilized 11-1-19.
2nd Lieut.	E.E.Rice.	A/165.	Posted to 2nd Army. 9-1-19.
			Posted to 5th Army Animal Collecting Camp. 10-3-19.
Major.	R.C.Bartlett, M.C.	B/165.	
Captain	F.E.Harrison, M.C.	B/165.	
2nd Lieut.	W.M.McDonald.	B/165.	To 5th Army A.C.C. 10-3-19.
2nd Lieut.	R.C.Kerr, M.C.	B/165.	-do-
2nd Lieut.	D.W.Du Buisson	B/165.	
Lieut.	C.Clarke.	B/165.	
2nd Lieut.	C.E.Bulpitt	B/165.	Posted to D/165. 16-2-18.
Major.	D.Mackay, D.S.O., M.C.	C/165.	Demobilized 18-3-19.
Captain.	F.E.Charter.	C/165.	
2nd Lieut.	J.T.Rose.	C/165.	
2nd Lieut.	E.V.Mackey	C/165.	Demobilized 9-2-19.
2nd Lieut.	W.G.H.Bromet	C/165.	To 5th Army A.C.C. 10-3-19.
2nd Lieut.	F.G.Thompson.	C/165.	Demobilized 7-1-19.
Major.	S.B.L.Jacks, M.C.	D/165.	
Captain.	R.Kirby, M.C.	D/165.	Posted to 5th A.A.C.C. 10-3-19.

Army Form C. 2118.

WAR DIARY
or
INTELLIGENCE SUMMARY.
(Erase heading not required.)

Instructions regarding War Diaries and Intelligence Summaries are contained in F. S. Regs., Part II. and the Staff Manual respectively. Title pages will be prepared in manuscript.

Place	Date	Hour	Summary of Events and Information	Remarks and references to Appendices
WIZERNES, France.	continued.			18-3-19.

Rank.	Name.	Unit.	Remarks.
Major.	S.E.Hibbert.	A/165.	Joined 16-12-18. Posted 31 D.A. 26-1-19.
2nd Lieut.	J.D.Close, M.C.	D/165.	Demobilized. 26-1-19.
2nd Lieut.	H.G.Close.	D/165.	Demobilized. 10-2-19.
2nd Lieut.	A.Campbell,M.C.	D/165.	Demobilized. 1-2-19
2nd Lieut.	S.J.Kelly.	A/165.	Rejoined from Base. 21-1-19.
	ATTACHED.		
Captain.	C.E.Meryon. (R.A.M.C.)	H.Q.	To 93rd Field Ambulance 6-1-19.
Captain.	S.G.Bright. (R.A.V.C.)	H.Q.	Demobilized. 5-4-19.
Captain.	H.Clayton. (3/1st Notts Yeo)	H.Q.	To 19th Corps Animal Collecting Camp 7-3-19.
Captain.	W.Tonge (C.F.)	H.Q.	

Total number of Other Ranks on the strength of Unit on 11-11-18.

712.

The Brigade has been gradually reduced to Cadre "A", the largest number of Officers and Other Ranks going in one batch, being -

Officers.	Other Ranks.
5.	192.

10-3-19. The above party was posted to 5th Army Animal Collecting Camp, with effect from

[signature]
Lieut. Col. R.F.A
Commanding 165th Brigade R.F.A.

CONFIDENTIAL.

WAR DIARY

OF

165th BRIGADE R. F. A.

From 1st April to 30th April, 1919.

VOLUME XL.
_____

165th Bde. R.F.A.
W.23/4.

H.Q.
   31st D.A.

SECRET

Herewith War Diary for the month of April, 1919.

3-5-19.

                                            Lieut Col. R.F.A.
                                 Commanding 165th Brigade R.F.A.

165 Bde R.F.A. 1st – 30th April 1919
Vol. XL

Army Form G. 2118.

WAR DIARY
or
INTELLIGENCE SUMMARY.

(Erase heading not required.)

Instructions regarding War Diaries and Intelligence Summaries are contained in F. S. Regs., Part II. and the Staff Manual respectively. Title pages will be prepared in manuscript.

Place	Date	Hour	Summary of Events and Information	Remarks and references to Appendices
WIZERNES. France.	1st April to 30th April 1919.		Training and Recreation; Education.	

Lieut Col. R.F.A.
Commanding 165th Brigade. R.F.A.

165 Bde RFA 31

WAR DIARY
INTELLIGENCE SUMMARY

Army Form C. 2118.

App 39

Place	Date	Hour	Summary of Events and Information	Remarks and references to Appendices
Witheries	1/5/19		Out Training & Recreation; Education. Cadre entrained on 13th May, 1919 for Dunkirk to proceed to Ripon; Embarked on S/S "Mobile" for Remainder being demob.	Cancelled
	17/5/19			

Lt Col NG
O.C 165 Bde RFA

WD95 / 2349(4)

WD95 / 2349(4)

31ST DIVISION
DIVL ARTILLERY

169TH BRIGADE R.F.A.

MAR 1916 - JAN 1917

Broken up

Army Form C. 2118.

WAR DIARY
of
INTELLIGENCE SUMMARY.
(Erase heading not required.)

161st Bde RFA
Part of VIIIth I (not M.E.F.)

Mar 16
Jan 17

Instructions regarding War Diaries and Intelligence Summaries are contained in F.S. Regs., Part II. and the Staff Manual respectively. Title pages will be prepared in manuscript.

Hour, Date, Place		Summary of Events and Information	Remarks and references to Appendices
9.0 am	1-3-16 ALEXANDRIA	H.M.T. "EBOE" left, also H.M.T. "KNIGHT TEMPLAR"	A.S.2
	6-3-16 MARSEILLES	Advance party arrived and proceeded by rail to "ABBEVILLE" reaching ABBEVILLE 8-3-16 for the purpose of taking over wagons & horses behind to replace those left in EGYPT.	A.S.2
	7-3-16 do.	H.M.T. "EBOE" arrived MARSEILLES, disembarkation began.	A.S.2
2.30am	8-3-16. do.	Party landed from H.M.T. "EBOE" + entrained.	A.S.2
	8-3-16 do.	H.M.T. "KNIGHT TEMPLAR" arrived	A.S.2
	9-3-16 do.	"A" "B" + "C" Batteries disembarked + entrained	A.S.2
4.0 am	10-3-16 PONT REMY	"D" Battery, "B" A.C. + Headquarters Staff detrained and marched to Billets at FRUCOURT. ("B.A.C." to WOIREL)	A.S.2
	11-3-16 FRUCOURT	Advance party rejoined Brigade, marching from ABBEVILLE.	A.S.2
	12-3-16 do.	"A" "B" + "C" Batteries arrived @ PONT REMY detrained and marched to Billets at FRUCOURT.	A.S.2

Army Form C. 2118.

WAR DIARY
INTELLIGENCE SUMMARY.
(Erase heading not required.)

Instructions regarding War Diaries and Intelligence Summaries are contained in F.S. Regs., Part II. and the Staff Manual respectively. Title pages will be prepared in manuscript.

Hour, Date, Place		Summary of Events and Information	Remarks and references to Appendices
19-3-16	FRUCOURT	Lieut B.K. Portenus A.V.C. left for no 14 Vety. Hospital ABBEVILLE	AR
20-3-16	do.	Lieut B.A. Brown assumed duties of Veterinary Officer VC.	
		Sick horses were evacuated to ABBEVILLE and Remounts obtained from R. Depot, ABBEVILLE to fill up to complete establishment.	AR
		Men earmarked for Trench Mortar Battery.	
27-3-16	do.	The Brigade left for AMPLIER. Billeted en route at YSEUX – BELLOY – LA CHAUSÉE night of 27/28.	AR
28-3-16	BELLOY.	Left for NAOURS. Billeted night of 28/29	AR
29-3-16	NAOURS.	Left for AMPLIER. Arrived at AMPLIER 10-30 am	AR
31-3-16	AMPLIER	'A' Battery + 1 Section each of 'B' C+D Batteries attached to 4th Division temporarily for tactical purposes, went into action. Remaining sections of these Batteries proceeded on 1st + 2nd April. COLINCAMPS stello. Trench Mortar Battery left for course of instruction at VALHEUREUX. AR	

169 R.F.A
vol 2

31 Div.

<u>Confidential</u>

War Dairy.

of

169th Bde R.F.A

from 1st April 1916 to 30th April 1916

Army Form C. 2118.

WAR DIARY
or
INTELLIGENCE SUMMARY
(Erase heading not required.)

169 A Bde. RFA

Place	Date	Hour	Summary of Events and Information	Remarks and references to Appendices
AMPLIER	1.4.16		1 Section "B" Battery + 1 Section "D" Battery attached to 40th Div for tactical purposes, going into action the same day	TBR
do	2.4.16		1 Section "C" Battery attached to 40th Div for tactical purposes. Went into action the same day	TBR
COLINCAMPS	6.4.16		"A" & "B" Battery taken took from 40th Div & with 1 Sect of "C" Batty 171st Bde (How) formed the Left Group under command of MAJOR W. L. Y. ROGERS	TBR
do	7.4.16		H.Q. Staff moved into billets at COLINCAMPS from AMPLIER. COLONEL H.C. WILSON took over command of Left Group. Wagon Lines of "A" + "B" Batteries moved up from AMPLIER to BERTRANCOURT	TBR
do	9.4.16		COLONEL H.C. WILSON proceeded to FLIXECOURT on a Course for Senior Officers. MAJOR W. L. Y. ROGERS assuming command of the Left Group from that date. The Right Section of "C" Battery 171st Bde RFA (How) came under command of Left Group	TBR
do	10.4.16		Great difficulty being experienced in obtaining water in the village	TBR
do	11.4.16		H.Q. Staff Horse removed to BERTRANCOURT. 1 Off. + 40 men of the PIONEER BATTN K.O.Y.L.I. arrived in consolidating gun positions for the LEFT GROUP	TBR
do	13.4.16		B.A.C. moved from THIEVRES to AUTHIE	
do	28.4.16		LT COL W.S.D. CRAVEN assumed command of the Brigade vice TEMP. LT. COL. T. HON. COL. H.C. WILSON	TBR (Auth. A.G. D/1155 dated 27/4/16)

W. R. Rogers Major
ADJT. 169th BDE, R.F.A.

169 RFA Vol 3

Confidential.

War Diary
of
169th Bde RFA

from May 1st 1916   to May 31st 1916

(Sheet 7)

Army Form C. 2118.

169th Bde RFA

WAR DIARY
or
INTELLIGENCE SUMMARY
(Erase heading not required.)

Instructions regarding War Diaries and Intelligence Summaries are contained in F. S. Regs., Part II. and the Staff Manual respectively. Title Pages will be prepared in manuscript.

Place	Date	Hour	Summary of Events and Information	Remarks and references to Appendices
COLINCAMPS	3.5.16		Rt. Sect. of "D" Battery relieved by Rt. Sect. "D" Batty. 165th Bde R.F.A. Major Sir R.V.C.W. Nixon posted to command "D" Batty, 165th Bde R.F.A. with effect from that date.	T.O.R.
do	4.5.16	12 am	"D" Battery travelled and posted in to "D" Batty 165th Bde R.F.A.	T.O.R.
			Left section exchanged dummy enemy of the "D" Battery wagon line removed to ORVILLE	
do	5.5.16		"D" Battery emplacer trolled in ORVILLE	T.O.R. T.O.R.
do	11.5.16		Handed over gun pits etc in course of construction to 4th Division.	T.O.R.
do	15.5.16	12.30	Heavy bombardment of trenches between John Copse + Mathew Copse.	T.O.R. map sheet 57D.
do	16.5.16	12 noon	"C" Battery 165th Bde R.F.A. took over from "D" Batty 169th Bde (the latter going into the Heavy group still)	T.O.R. T.O.R.
do	19.5.16		Experiments carried out with portable bridges	T.O.R.
do	19.5.16 12.15 pm		The B.a.c's of the Divl Artill. were merged in the D.A.C.	T.O.R.
do	22.5.16 12 noon		Reorganisation of Brigade "D" Batty 169th Bde became "B/(17)1st Bde," & "B/(17)1st Bde (How.) became "D"/169th Bde R.F.A.	T.O.R.
do	23.5.16	3 pm	COLINCAMPS shelled by 5.9 am How.	T.O.R.
do	27.5.16	3.30 pm	COLINCAMPS shelled by v. 9 am How.	T.O.R.

Original

Confidential

WAR DIARY

of

169th BRIGADE R.F.A.

from 6 June 1916 to 30 June 1916

Volume I. Sheets 8 + 9

WAR DIARY or INTELLIGENCE SUMMARY

Army Form C. 2118.

Page 8

Place	Date	Hour	Summary of Events and Information	Remarks and references to Appendices
COLINCAMPS	3/4 June 1916	MN	31st Divn made a raid on enemy lines. For 10 minutes there was an intense Bombardment of the German front line, & at 12.10 am the infantry fired a Bangalore torpedo, successfully cut the enemy's artillery wire, & entered the German trenches. At 12.40 am the artillery fire was directed back to the front line (after the raiding party had left the enemy's trenches) & continued till 1.30 am when the fire ceased. The Germans retaliated on our front line during the Bombardment, but put in barrages on villages & approaches behind the line.	
COLINCAMPS	10/11	11.25pm to 12.15am	Enemy bombarded 1st & 15th lines of Pacte Battalion. Trenches retaliated on selected points, & enemy fire eventually ceased at 12.15am.	
	17th	6pm	"B" Battery shelled with 15 cm in Avenue - 4 killed 3 wounded	
	23rd		Bde Hdqrs moved into CHALK.PIT. There was a terrific wind, with rain and continuous heavy thunder in the afternoon.	
	24th	6am	"U" Day. Bombardment of SERRE, and wirecutting, began by 10 pdr 14.5" How.	
		3pm	Enemy fired salvos of 15cm diagonally across the Avenue - now your Batteries lit.	
	25th		"V" Day. Rain in the morning delayed COLINCAMPS shells for 20min from noon and again in afternoon. Projected gas attack 10pm not carried out owing to heavy wind. Artillery honour, carried out bombardment programme from 10 & 70.10 pm. 4 h Divn let off gas by mistake & gassed some of our men in trenches.	

2449 Wt. W14957/M90 750,000 1/16 I.B.C. & A. Form/C.2118/12.

Army Form C. 2118.

Page 9

WAR DIARY
or
INTELLIGENCE SUMMARY
(Erase heading not required.)

Place	Date June	Hour	Summary of Events and Information	Remarks and references to Appendices
COLINCAMPS	25th (con.)		9 German observation balloons brought down on British front by aeroplanes firing flaghting bullets from pistol.	
	26		"W" Day. Heavies joined in bombardment programme. Gas discharge arranged for 10 pm. Artillery again bombarded hard from 10.10 to 10.20 though gas was not discharged owing to slack wind. COLINCAMPS shelled in afternoon. Raid into German lines failed owing to uncut wire. (4 killed 3 off + 75 R wounded).	
	27		"X" Day. Gas discharged with artillery bombardment at 2.45 pm. Front line wire still uncut - trench mortars appear to have been a failure in this respect. Heavies bombarded more energetically today - reply practically nil. BUS & COLINCAMPS shelled. Artillery most unsuccessful. B/171 moved into forward position near HITTITE lodge on X/Y night.	
	28		"Y" Day. Day of attack ("Z" day) postponed 48 hours from 7.30 29th inst. Wire cutting. Raid by E.Yorks on Point 10 failed. A/169 should have gone up into forward position at LEGEND ST on night of Y/Z but - were kept back.	
	29		Y₁ Day - original "Z" Day. Wire cutting all day. Raid at night failed.	
	30		Y₂ Day - wire cutting - another raid failed. The bombardments for these raids had been spread over all the front the concentration on point of entry was marked as our only persons laid on night of 3/4 June. Gunners merely authorised to fire on gently	

31st Division.

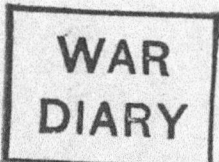

169th BRIGADE R. F. A.

1st to 31st JULY 1916.

Vol #2/5

Confidential

War Diary
of
169th Bde R.F.A.

July 1st to 31st 1916

169 Bde A/Sh. · Volume VIII. July 1916.

169 Bde A/Sh Army Form C. 2118.
X Corps. 31st Army
Page 10

WAR DIARY
or
INTELLIGENCE SUMMARY
(Erase heading not required.)

Place	Date	Hour	Summary of Events and Information	Remarks and references to Appendices
COLINCAMPS	July 1		2ⁿᵈ Day of the Attack. A very misty early morning; so that visibility was impaired for a/169 and 3/171 in their forward position.	
		6.30 am	Bombardment began and continued till 7.30. The last 10 mins being very intense. The enemy's lines and our front lines were completely hidden in a dense cloud of smoke.	
		7.26	Previous to assault enemy put up heavy barrage on our front line causing us heavy casualties. 94th Brigade started some 4 mins before time. Consequently they followed close up to our Barrage & so apparently escaped the casualties due to German machine guns which were mounted on parapet as soon as our fire lifted. After our left, heavy rifle machine gun fire slows from the enemy. 94th Bde – 1st · 12th wave appears to have reached SERRE without considerable lines of trenches as they took them, but no supports followed and consequently the men who reached SERRE were probably cut off and never seen again. 93rd Bde – held up at 2ⁿᵈ line wire (C) and enfiladed from QUADRILATERAL which the 4th Div had not captured (excepting front line).	
		8.40	German Barrage still on front line – progress unascertainable.	
		9.10	Barrage extended heavy on his (enemy's) own support line. 4th Div who was said to be in MUNICH TRENCH enfiladed by M.G.s in turn from direction of Wd PUISIEUX.	
		11.30	Quieter.	
		1 pm	Learnt that 93rd Bde had had 3 Battns (13ᵗʰ 16ᵗʰ + 1ˢᵗ W Yorks) broken in attempting to	
		3.30	One silent. Hardly a man seen could be seen anywhere.	

Army Form C. 2118.

Page 11

WAR DIARY
or
INTELLIGENCE SUMMARY
(Erase heading not required.)

Place	Date	Hour	Summary of Events and Information	Remarks and references to Appendices
	July 1st (contd)		A/169, above line in the afternoon, were firing in action on Germans advancing from pt 25 to counterattack (open sights - 700 yds range). Germans counterattack said to be counterattacking as far as DUNTON Trench - this rumour never confirmed. Major STRABENZEE (A Batt) wounded at Cheapside O.P. - 2nd Lieut POLLITT (A Batt) sustained severe shell shock in his main load attempting to lay forward wire with after infantry. A/169 withdrawn from forward to old position night of 1st/2nd with casualty or mishap. B/171 withdrawn from forward position to wagon line. Guns lent out (1 to A/165 - 1 to B/169, 1 to C/169, 1 to 90m.) night g/169/2nd quiet.	
	2nd		Some bombardment with bursts of 7.9 how in afternoon & evening.	
	3rd		Very quiet day.	
	4		Certain amount of enemy Thaw fire in region of CHALK PIT	
	5		Hdq Groups relieved at noon by 241 Bde (41st Div) They took over all guns except A/165 Batt. Bde remained in wagon line at BUS for night of 5/6	
	6		Bde marched at 11.30 am. via DOULLENS to AUTHEUX. Hdq A,C,D Batts billetted very comfortably in AUTHEUX - B Batt in BOIS BERGUES	
	7		All Batts watered in BOIS BERGUES. Div Arty established at MONT PLAISIR. Received order that we to move on 9th.	

Army Form C. 2118.

PAGE 12

WAR DIARY or INTELLIGENCE SUMMARY

Place	Date	Hour	Summary of Events and Information	Remarks and references to Appendices
AUTHEUX	July 9		Battries marched independently, starting of 3 hrs beyond AUXI LE CHATEAU where Hq entrained. Train due to leave at 3.30 p, 6.30, 9.30, 12.30 a.m. (C & D batts about 3 hrs late in moving (thro' rain). Detrained at THIENNES. Marched on to billets in HAVERSKERKE. Hdqrs at LA BRASSERIE. Div Arty Hdqrs at ST VENANT.	
HAVERSKERKE	10	10 pm	Village bombed from aeroplane 10 p.m. - about 300 x from Bde Hdqrs.	
	13	10 am	Inspection of Brigade dismounted by G.O.C. 31st Division.	
		11 am	D.D.R. 1st Army inspected horses.	
		2 pm	I.O.M. looked over guns of the Brigade.	
	14	8 am	O.C. Bdes went to SAILLY to reconnoitre zone we are to take over. On arriving there found that Division was not relieving as detailed.	
		6 pm	Fresh Orders received to take over from part of 61st Division. Colonel & C.O.'s went up to see positions - Batteries followed, leaving guns at 6/51 Div wagon lines and taking personnel up to relieve 61st Batteries as follows. A/169 relieves A/305 B/169 " C/305 C/169 " B/306 D/169 " C/306 Zone was from FAUQISSART - TRIVELET road southwards to just N. of N. CHAPELLE.	
	15	7 am	Hdqrs moved to L'AVENTIE. Arranged to share hdqrs with O.C. 305 Bde. Later Col. NEVINSON (8th Div Arty) also reported & stayed with O.C. 305 Bde.	

WAR DIARY
INTELLIGENCE SUMMARY

PAGE 13

Place	Date	Hour	Summary of Events and Information	Remarks and references to Appendices
LAVENTIE	July 15 (contd)		169 Bde HQrs established at PONT DU HEM (M14b) and communication established from there to all batteries by 12 M.N. B Batty very unfortunate in matter of guns taken over — all had the teeth taken down and overhauled in Battery.	
	16		C/169 moved out of position occupied by 13/356 into alternative position.	
	17		5th Australian & 61st Div attack postponed.	
	18		Wire cutting at points of projected raid by 92 Bde on night after attack.	
	19	11 – 11.30 am	18 pdrs & How (4.5) registered on wire to be cut.	
		11.30 – 1 pm	Heavies alone registered. 18 pdrs silent.	
		1 – 3	18 pdrs wire cutting.	
		3 – 6	18 pdrs continue wire cutting with bombardment by Heavies.	
		6 pm	5th Aus Div & 61st Div attacks German 1st & 2nd line. 61st Div right obtained footing in Gr 2nd line but relieved own 6 Bde Stokes & St Oliphalon. attack quite successful but afr holding heavily throughout the night they had to withdraw owing to danger on flanks.	
		12.42	4 raids by 92 2/Bde. 1 (only) successful – 2/5 Wen covered gnd gap in wire cut by us – raid met by strong German wiring party so withdrew.	

Army Form C. 2118.

PAGE 14

WAR DIARY
or
INTELLIGENCE SUMMARY

(Erase heading not required.)

Place	Date	Hour	Summary of Events and Information	Remarks and references to Appendices
LAVENTIE (PONT DUHEM)	July 20, 21, 22		Quiet. Nothing to report.	
	23		Our Battery just North of road PONT-DU-HEM — LAVENTIE shelled w/some steady all day afternoon. Half of Batteries relieved by 61st Div in night 23/24 as follows A/169 by A/306. B/169 by C/305, C/169 by B/306, D/169 by D/306.	
	24		Relief of Batteries completed in evening and control handed over to OC 305 Bde at 10pm. Held in all lines laid down to Batteries. Batteries remained at their wagon lines at night — Hdqrs at PONT-DU-HEM.	
	25		Bde Hdqrs moved into Billets at QUENTIN + PACAUT (A + C Batts) (Hq. + D) B Batty informed they were not c/305 (in wagon lines) who had case of GLANDERS.	
	29 2 pm		A Batty moved into billets at LA PIERRE AU BUETRE & their lead Rein 4 guns b B/170. Maken one gun of this Batty with join.	
	30 9 am		B + C Batts moved into billets at LA PIERRE AU BUETRE and ran BACQUEROLLES FARM. Last B + C Batt each lent 1 gun to A/170 & took one gun of Batts being replaced of 30th. BETHUNE	

Army Form C. 2118.

PAGE 75

WAR DIARY or INTELLIGENCE SUMMARY

(Erase heading not required.)

Place	Date	Hour	Summary of Events and Information	Remarks and references to Appendices
QUENTIN	July 31		OC's B & C Batteries went up to reconnoitre positions to reinforce Left Group. As no guns were left in Brigade, going into action was delayed.	

Vol 6

CONFIDENTIAL.

WAR DIARY.

of

169th BRIGADE R.F.A.

From AUGUST 1st, 1916   to   AUGUST 31st, 1916.

VOLUME. VIII

169th B.F.A.

ORIGINAL
August 1918
Volume VIII.
PAGE 16

Army Form C. 2118.

WAR DIARY
or
INTELLIGENCE SUMMARY
(Erase heading not required.)

Place	Date	Hour	Summary of Events and Information	Remarks and references to Appendices
QUENTIN	Aug 3/4		B/169 moved into action to reinforce L/h Group. B/169 took 2 guns into action at S.14.a.5.7. Wagon lines at R.16.c.8.1. C/169 " 3 guns into action at M.26.a.8.8. Wagon Lines at R.22.a.8.6	EMD
do	7		Recon. of this Bde. were ordered to reconnoitre the Village line position in area occupied by 31st Divn. This was completed and report forwarded to 31st D.A. on 12th inst. (copy of report given in Appendix A). Practically all these reserve positions would require complete rebuilding as they are in very delapidated condition. O.P's have had no work done on them at all. C/169 (along with B/170) handed over tactical control to 61st D.A. on reorganization of southern 169 Bdes were ordered to reconnoitre fire positions for were cutting Batteries in event of an advance in this area. These (with alternative positions) were	EMD Apx A
do	12.8p 21		reconnoitred on 21st and following positions were chosen — Work was to be completed by 17th September. Six other positions were being made by the Bde R.A. parties from A → D Batteries (4 strong, 3 rank and a officer) commenced work on two positions where some work had already been done viz	EMD
	22		The work which was to be done was to sink the gun pit floor and prepare & make a necessary brick platform for taken wheels; also to prepare ammn. dumps for 600 rds pr gun.	EMD
	23.		Orders received for Hqrs, "A" → D Batts with C/306 & C/307 from 61st Divn. to proceed to 40th Divl area as a group under L/Col. E.B. Crane R.F.A.	EMD

Army Form C. 2118.

Page 17.

WAR DIARY
or
INTELLIGENCE SUMMARY
(Erase heading not required.)

Instructions regarding War Diaries and Intelligence Summaries are contained in F. S. Regs., Part II. and the Staff Manual respectively. Title Pages will be prepared in manuscript.

Place	Date	Hour	Summary of Events and Information	Remarks and references to Appendices
QUENTIN	Aug 23	11 a.m.	Lt.Col. Crewe with four Battery Commdrs (on advance +2 NCOs each) went over to NOEUX le MINES to 40th D.A. to reconnoitre positions. 16th Division were to be withdrawn into rear area and their front taken over by 40th Div pending arrival of 3rd Division. The 40th Div was reinforced on the left ("14 BIS Group") by 112th Infy Bde covered by this group of artillery.	
do	24	9 a.m.	Hqrs. 'A' & 'D' Batteries moved via LOCON and BETHUNE to NOEUX les MINES arriving about 2 p.m., and assembled in temporary wagon lines (very crowded) at K 24 b 87 (sheet BETHUNE, combined, 1/40,000). C/316 and C/307 marched here independently and assembled in wagon lines close by, also. An Offrs and 3 telephonists from Hqrs reach battery went forward to new positions around FOSSE No 7d BETHUNE.	
MAZINGARBE	24	9.30 p.m.	MAZINGARBE shelled (6 — 10.5 mm) 10R. A/169 wounded also a hut & Pltonner, 2 horses killed.	
do	25/26	9.30 to 11 p.m.	A section relieving batteries were bivy'lints position. — batteries keeping their own guns. A/169 relieved D/80 C/316 relieved A/17 D/169 " " C/307 " " B/17	
	26/27	9.30 to 10.30 p.m.	Remaining section were relieved (in very heavy rain).	
	26	noon	Ammunition and telephone communication taken over from Army Group 16th D.A.	

249 Wt. W14957/Mgo 750,000 1/16 J.B.C. & A. Forms/C.2118/12.

Army Form C. 2118.

WAR DIARY
or
INTELLIGENCE SUMMARY
(Erase heading not required.)

PAGE 18

Place	Date	Hour	Summary of Events and Information	Remarks and references to Appendices
MAZINGARBE	26		The position occupied by C/177 (who moved out night of 26/27) was not taken over by this group. Ammunition dumps there and telephone system of the battery were handed on to B/169 to be guarded and kept in working order.	
	"	3pm	Control taken over from Centre Group 10th D.A. The sector (held by 112th Inf Bde - and designate 14 BIS group) was covered as in Appendix B attached	Appendix B
	28		A/169 and D/169 required one gun each on HARRISON'S CRATER (M6c 2.6.) in case assistance required by LOOS group. Support by LOOS group to 14 BIS group arranged as per appendix D	Appendix C Appendix D
	30		Barrage ("LOOP and "CHALK PIT") attack to L Flank group arranged a/c appendix E	appendix E
		12noon	Maj. Gen. Hon. Mr. Arlington R.F.A. (from 171 Bde R.F.A.) assumed command of this Brigade, consequent on reorganisation of Divnl Artillery, having that taken up. 171 Bde R.F.A. C/169 split up - half to A/169 and half to B/169. Guns transferred as follows - C/169 — 2 guns to B/170 (now 161st D.A.). 1 gun to B/169 1 gun to A/170	

Army Form C. 2118.

WAR DIARY
or
INTELLIGENCE SUMMARY

PAGE. 19

(Erase heading not required.)

Place	Date	Hour	Summary of Events and Information	Remarks and references to Appendices
MAZINGARBE and FOSSE	August 30		A/169 received 2 guns from A/165 to be kept in line at x 9c 4.5 (known as HAYSTACK POST) and battery to 3rd D.A. B/169 received 1 gun from B/165 (kept gun at HAYSTACK POST) and 1 gun c/169 (to be kept in reserve). A/169 received 4 wagons from c/169; and B/169 4 wagons from c/171.	[initials]
MAZINGARBE			Personnel gotten from A/169 remain at x 9c 4.5. Heavy Trench How 169 R.F.A. remain attached 169 R.F.A. to carry on 161S GROUP (right group of Composite Artillery, 3rd Division).	

[signature] Major R.F.A
Comd/ 169 R.F. B.D.

Original

Mr Deavy
for B de Rhr

APPENDIX A

DEFENCE SCHEME NEUVE CHAPELLE & FERME DU BOIS SECTIONS
VILLAGE – ST VAAST – CROIX BARBEE SYSTEM.

UNIT.	ZONE.	BATTERY POSITION.		O. P.		MATERIAL AVAILABLE ON SPOT.
		LOCATION.	DESCRIPTION.	LOCATION.	DESCRIPTION.	
1.R.	M 27 c 3.3 to M 32 b 5.3	R 23 c 28	4 old gun platforms of slate & rubble. Overgrown sandbag emplacements and ammunition troughs. Lateral trench would need pulling down & rebuilding.	M 20 d 6.2½ Tree	fair view	Some old timber in old dug-outs & epaulments.
2.R.	Cross Roads ROUGE CROIX to M 27 c 3.3	R 23 b 9.4		R 30 a 5.2 House	Better view would be obtained from House R 30 b 59 or from tall trees R 30 a 72	
5 R	Cross Roads ROUGE CROIX to S 3 a 1.0	R 17 c 31	6 gun pits & epaulments. Trench behind. Ammn. dump to each gun pit - dugout in rear to 5 guns. All overgrown.	M 25 b 26 House	View indifferent	nil
9 R	Cross Roads ROUGE CROIX to S 13 d 3.3	R 26 d 13	4 small epaulments 2' to 3' high each under large tree.	R 36 c 29 Tree	Moderate view	Several large logs of timber on road from Port. to Vielle Chapelle.
15 R	M 32 c 5.2 to S 13 d 3.3	X 8 d 4.2.5	4 prepared platforms that covered with rectangular roof 10'×10'×25'	X 10 d 3.4	Impossible to see from house at present. Better view from tall trees in hedge E. of House.	
12 R	S 2 a 7.10 to S 13 d 3.3	X 3 b 25.7	4 overgrown sandbag epaulments 5' high.	X 4 d 5.2 House	Good. Also large high tree on S. of house.	
18 R	Cross Roads ROUGE CROIX to S 13 d 3.3	X 10 c 5.6	4 overgrown circular breastworks 4-5 ft high all way round - 15' diameter. Lateral trench. Thick hedge in front requires cutting.	X 19 c 4.3 Tree	moderate view	

DEFENCE SCHEME NEUVE CHAPELLE & FERME du BOIS SECTIONS

VILLAGE - ST. VAAST - CROIX BARBEE SYSTEM.

UNIT	ZONE	BATTERY POSITION		O.P.		MATERIAL AVAILABLE ON SPOT
		LOCATION	DESCRIPTION	LOCATION	DESCRIPTION	
14 R	S 13 d 3.3 to S 2 c 5.1	X 9 c 65	4 good built up gun pits - 2 Sandbags thick - hardly any cover on top - 1 dugout of sandbags	X 9 c 46 House	Suitable	
7 R	Cross Roads, ROUGE CROIX to M 32 c 6.2	R 22 b 87	6 gun position - epaulements, dugdown 2 feet. Small Ammn dumps. Trench lateral and to rear. Delapidated gun pit in rear of No. 4 gun.	R 36 c 29 Tree	Moderate view	
3 R	M 32 b 6.3 to M 32 c 6.0	R 27 b 5.5	Nil	M 25 b 7.9 Tree	Fair View	
11 R	M 32 c 5.2 to S 2 c 5.1	X 4 d 14	at present being used by Heavy Artillery.	X 5 a 3.1 House	House not suitable. Better from tree left front of House	
4 R	S 2 b 9.5 to S 8 b 27	R 23 b 2.1	5 low Sandbag epaulements. Ammn dumps for each gun situated Trench lateral into rear. Delapidated dug out in rear of No 4 gun			
6 R	S 3 a 3.1 to S 13 d 3.3	R 26 b 2.8	Nil Very little cover in Winter	R 29 c 2.8 Tree	Moderate View	
17 R	Cross Roads, ROUGE CROIX to S 13 d 5.3	R 34 c 9.1	6 low overgrown epaulements	X 16 d 2.8 Tree	Good.	

Note
All O.P's - to each whether has been chosen. Pits require deep traverse against holein roof which cannot be done here as they are all inhabited.

Appendix B

14 BIS. GROUP.

DAY ZONES

C/307 covers Right Battalion
    H31 c 9.1 to H 25 d 0 2

C/306 covers Left Battalion
    H 25 d 0 2 to H 19 d 4.1

A/169 }
B/169 } covers Group Front
(How)

NIGHT LINES

C/307
    H 31 c 9.1
    d 1. 3¼
    d 1½. 8
    b ½. 9½

C/306
    H 25 d 0.2 to H 25 b 6½.2

A/169
    H 25 b 6½.2 to H 19 d 4.1

D/169
    H 31 d 6.5
    25 d 3.4
    d 9½. 9½
    b 9 4½

GROUP CONCENTRATIONS.

CAT   H 31 d 6.5
DOG   H 32 a 5.8
COW   H 26 b 2.0
RABBIT   H 25 d 9½.9½

(sd) W.S.D Craven /Lt Col
Comdg 14 BIS Group

28.8.16

APPENDIX C.

Support to LOOS. GROUP.   [Code word - LOOS]

A/16q can fire 1 gun on   M6c 2.6 (Harrison's Crater)
C/307   "   " 1   "   "   M6a 2.8
D/16q   "   " 1   "   "   M6c 2.6 (Harrison's Crater)
(How)

No other guns can reach this point.

                                          (sd.) W.S.D. Craven, Lt Col. R.F.A.
29.8.16   Comdg 14 BIS group

APPENDIX D

Support from LOOS. Group.   [Code word - 14 BIS]

B/181	A/181	A/185	D/181.
Barrage Wire from	Barrage Wire from	Barrage Wire from	(1) H31c 9.1
H31 a 2.5	H31 c 8.0	H31 b 2.2	(2) H31 a 1.3
to	to	H25 d 2.5	(3) H31 d 2.6
H31 b 2.5	H31 d 2.6		(4) H31 b 2.0

APPENDIX E

"LOOP BARRAGES"

- A/169 — NIGHT LINES
- C/306 — from H19d 09.35 to H19d 21.17
- C/307 — " H19d 21.17 to H19d 30.00
- D/169 — Trench Junction H19d 13.59
  - H19d 18.80
  - H19d 40.88
  - H19d 50.27

"CHALK-PIT BARRAGE"

- A/169 — NIGHT LINES
- C/306 — NIGHT LINES
- C/307 — H25b 47.55 to H25b 55.30
- D/169 — Trench Junction H19d 48.25
  - H25b 82.46
  - H25b 68.40
  - H25b 83.15

Code calls as given in 'inverted commas.

30. 8. 16

Vol 7

CONFIDENTIAL.

WAR DIARY

OF

169th Bde. R.F.A.

From 1st September 1916 to 30th September 1916.

(VOLUME IX)

WAR DIARY or INTELLIGENCE SUMMARY

Army Form C. 2118

VOLUME # 9
PAGE 20

HQ Brigade R.F.A.
3rd Division
XI Corps
FIRST ARMY

Place	Date	Hour	Summary of Events and Information	Remarks and references to Appendices
LE TOURET	1/9/16	—	Dispositions of 169" Brigade after reorganisation had been effected. Brigade Head Quarters, Brigade Commander (Col Hostle MM. ADDINGTON) and the time in tactical command of Right Group 31st Divisional Arty. Group H.Q. situated at LE TOURET — map reference — (X.16.d.8.8. Sheet 36ᴬ S.E. 1/20000). C Battery (late B/171 Batt.) in action in same Group at X.17.d.9.7. with wagon line at X.8.b.4.2. (Ref Sheet 36ᴬ S.E. 1/20000). "B" Battery now a 6 gun Battery having been reinforced by a section of late "C" Battery, in action in LEFT Group 31st Divl Arty. A & D Battery's temporarily detached from the Division. (See previous Volume). For further detail concerning reorganisation see appropriate correspondence.	See A1. A.1.
LE TOURET	2/9/16	11:30 AM to 12 NOON	A minor organised bombardment of 100ft of enemy's front line from S.16.a.6.5.5 to S.16.a.7.0.2.5. carried out by C.165 Batt. (18 lbs) — C.169 (How) 1 Battery of 2" Trench Mortars and 1 Heavy Trench Mortar.	W. W

WAR DIARY or INTELLIGENCE SUMMARY

Army Form C. 2118

Volume 7 Part 21

69 Brigade R.F.A.
3rd Division
XI Corps
FIRST ARMY

Original

Place	Date	Hour	Summary of Events and Information	Remarks and references to Appendices
LE TOURET	2nd	5 pm to 5:30 pm	The dose was repeated at 5pm. Same afternoon. Much damage was done to the enemy's parapets. Their bursts drew very heavy retaliation from T.M.S — Enemy replied with his T.M.S. 77 mm and 5.9 How.s.	WS
LE TOURET	3rd	10 am to 11:30 am	A/165 Bde shelled enemy front line from S.10.d.00.05 to S.16.d.60.75 in co-operation with T.M.S — effect good — enemy retaliated with about 20 rounds of 15 cm on C.9.d.65.70 and the Rue du Bois.	
		9:55 am	C/169 fired 16 rounds of H.E. on support line from S.10.d.15.00 to S.16.d.40.70. Several of these rounds were observed to drop plumb into the trench.	
		10:35 am		
		4 pm to 4:30 pm	A/165 and C/169 in conjunction with 2" T.M.S repeated the 10 am programme. Enemy retaliated on the Rue du Bois with his 4.2 & 5.9 How.s in the O.P.s	WS
LE TOURET	4th	—	Very quiet day on our front — weather very unsettled and against clear observation.	WS
	5	—	LIEUT. H.E. McC INCE ordered to report to FOURTH ARMY to take over command of a Battery.	WF

VOLUME 1
PAGE 22

169 Brigade RFA
/ 31 Division
XI Corps
FOURTH ARMY

Army Form C. 2118

WAR DIARY or INTELLIGENCE SUMMARY

(Erase heading not required.)

Place	Date	Hour	Summary of Events and Information	Remarks and references to Appendices
LE TOURET	5.		2/Lieut. J.P. WHITLEY patrol and primed A169 Bde R.F.A. A.165 expended 117 rounds wire cutting at S.16.c.80.62. Slightly. Batt. report attached, appendix. B.G. R.A. XI Corps visited Right Group H.Q. afterwards. Together with Group Commander inspected Battery positions.	Appendix
LE TOURET	6.		Quiet day on our front. Two organised bursts of fire by all Batteries of the Group in co-operation with T.M.S. and infantry on our front to catch enemy's working parties and patrols. 1st burst at 12.5 am. 2nd at 1.30 am.	
LE			The three 18 pr Batteries continued to cut gaps in the enemy's wire at various points. Progress very good.	
LE TOURET	7.	11.30AM to 1.30AM	Enemy shelled The OVEN O.P. badly which caused the operations of B.165 to cease temporarily whilst Sky Crash wire-cutting. Selected another point for observation. 1 telephonist was slightly wounded. O.P. badly damaged by several direct hits from 15 cm Howitzer.	

PAGE 7
VOLUME 23

169th Brigade RFA
XI Corps 3rd Division
FIRST ARMY.

WAR DIARY or INTELLIGENCE SUMMARY

Army Form C. 2118

(Erase heading not required.)

Place	Date	Hour	Summary of Events and Information	Remarks and references to Appendices
LE TOURET	8th Sept	12.30 A.M.	An Infantry raid was carried out on the night 7-8 Sept on the enemy's trenches. Bombardment commenced at 12.27 am. The raiders being in position in NOMAN'S LAND. At 12.30 am. the raiders entered the enemy trenches at point S/6.c.80.53. (Refsheet 36.S.N.) The result of raid being 12 casualties to our raiding party and the capture of one prisoner who died shortly after being brought in. Germans suffered about 1.30 am. All our raiders returned to join the 1st Division. Lieut. B.C. RICHARDS of A Battery left the Brigade to join the 1st Division cutting by the 3.18prs of the Group continued. The existing gaps being widened and fresh gaps commenced. During the afternoon a 4.5 How of C/169 placed well forward about 12 or yards from the enemy's front line carried out registration from an enfilading position with excellent results. Three bands of fire were made on our front from all natures to catch enemy working parties, at 9.4.45 pm. 11.30 pm and 2.15 am.	

PAGE 7
VOLUME 24

169 Brigade R.F.A.
3rd Division
XI Corps
FIRST ARMY

WAR DIARY or INTELLIGENCE SUMMARY

Army Form C. 2118

Place	Date	Hour	Summary of Events and Information	Remarks and references to Appendices
LE TOURET	10.	1.28 AM	In support of 9th Infantry Brigade raid on this Divisional left sector. An intense bombardment was opened on our front line closed down a/c 1.35 am on right Coy's front and continued till 2.30 am on left Coy's, on whose front the raid took place reported the raiders to have entered enemy's trenches and inflicted several casualties. On casualties were slight. Nothing unusual occurred during the day.	W.S. W.S.
LE TOURET	11.		A Battery arrive in this area from 14 B.S Group	W.S.
LE TOURET	15.		A169 at K.Q.C.4.4. D Battery & BHQ at QUENTIN (Q22 Ref BETHUNE Map 1/40000) W.S Orders received to the effect that the 31 Division would be relieving their line further South - the 30th Division being withdrawn from our right and put into ARMY reserve.	
LE TOURET	night 16-17		1 Section of A & B Batteries take over section in action of A150 Bde & C149 Bde respectively. B169 relieve a section of B149.	W.S W.S

PAGE 7
VOLUME 25

169 Bde R.F.A.
31st Division
XI Corps
FIRST ARMY

WAR DIARY or INTELLIGENCE SUMMARY

Place	Date	Hour	Summary of Events and Information	Remarks and references to Appendices
LE TOURET	16.		LIEUT. J.N. GRAY hands over the Adjutancy to LIEUT. H. BRITTAN and is posted to HQ Battery. B/170	
	17.	12 noon	Colonel H.M. ADDINGTON Commanding Right Group 31st Division resumes duties of G.O.C. R.A. during temporary absence of Brig Gen Lambert G.O.C. R.A. Brigade Groups taken over by Maj. H.S.D. CRAVEN Comdg D Battery.	
	Sept 16. - 17.6		No relief took place according to instructions received.	
		noon	Remaining sections of A + B Batteries completed relief. The detachments were relieved by noon.	
LOISNES			169 Bde HQ took over command of Groups from 30th Div at noon. Also Group of Batteries at LOISNES (6 18pdrs) also in Indian command	
			The group consists of A/169. (6 18pdr); B/169 (6 18pdr); C/169 (2 4.5 How) ; D/169 (4 4.5 How) (2 Brigade 15 pdrs) Appx 2	
	20th 21st 27th		Very wet and cold days.	
	28th	5p	Lieut Col. D. Craven R.A. assumed command of 4th Bde Reece toward to relieve Tony An organised Bombardment of German wire and trenches in S22c was carried out by 8" How – 4.5 How – 2¾" T.M's & Stoke Guns. (see Appendix 3)	Appendix 3

WAR DIARY or INTELLIGENCE SUMMARY

Army Form C. 2118
Page 26
Volume 7

Place	Date	Hour	Summary of Events and Information	Remarks and references to Appendices
LOISNES	29th (cont'd)	9 pm 6.9.17 pm	A further bombardment of trenches was carried out 3.15pm joined in, for slight barrage purposes. The intention of the operation was to prepare for a dummy raid & so induce the enemy to man his parapets and disclose the intensity of his barrage, if any. Enemy reply was very weak. At 5.12 pm he fired about 15 rds. 7mm at S31d,1 falling beyond blued on front line. At 5.45 pm 3 salvos of 3 rds each 15 cm. were fired further S., in the same area, badly aimed damage was done. This reply to the evening bombardment was given here — 6 rds 4.2 How. on S22c at 7.38 pm	H. H.
	30th		Orders received to prepare for move to 4th Army area. On this group front from 12h 6.30h inst. the enemy has been singularly inactive and practically no aggressive artillery or T.M. activity on his part whatever.	H.D. H.P.

M. Rowe
Lt. Col. R.F.A.
Comdg. 169th Bde., R.F.A.

SECRET.   R.A. No. 270.   Appendix

RE-ORGANIZATION, 31st DIVISIONAL ARTILLERY.

1. The 31st Divisional Artillery will be re-organized according to attached instructions.

   171st Brigade will be split up, and three Brigades formed as follows:-

   165th Bde. - Lieut.Col.G.J.Henderson R.F.A.
   A, B, & C/165 - 3, 18pdr Batteries, each of 6 guns.
   D/165 - 1 How. Battery of 4 Hows.

   169th Bde. - Col.Hon.H.W. Addington R.F.A.
   A & B/169 - 2 18.pdr Batteries, each of 6 guns.
   C/169 (late D/171) & D/169 - 2 How. Batteries, each of 4 Hows.

   170th Bde. - Lieut.Col. C.B.Simonds, R.F.A.
   A, B, & C/170 - 3 - 18.pdr Batteries, each of 6 guns.
   D/170 - 1 How Battery, of 4 Hows.

165th BRIGADE R.F.A. -

Existing Battery.	Addition.	Battery Commander.	Second in Command.
A/165 4 guns.	& ½ A/171	Capt. Jude.	
B/165 4 guns	& ½ A/171	Major Staveley	Capt. Roper from C/169.
C/165 4 guns.	& ½ B/171	Capt. Benson.	
D/165 4 Hows.	& Major Nixon.	Major Nixon.	Capt. Fletcher.

169th BRIGADE R.F.A. -

Existing Battery.	Addition.	Battery Commander.	Second in Command.
A/169 4 guns.	& ½ C/169	Capt. Ryan.	Lt. Ince.
B/169. 4 guns.	& ½ C/169	Major Rogers.	
D/171 complete becomes C/169. 4 Hows.	Capt. Fitzgerald.	Capt. Fitzgerald.	Capt. Hussy
D/169. 4 Hows.	Major Craven.	Major Craven.	Capt. Williams.

170th BRIGADE R.F.A.

Existing Battery.	Addition.	Battery Commander.	Second in Command.
A/170 4 guns.	& ½ C/171	Major Strover	Lt. McKay.
B/170 4 guns.	& ½ C/171	Capt. Pickard.	
C/170 4 guns.	& ½ B/171	Capt. Massy.	
D/170 4 guns.		Capt. Featherstonhaugh.	

(Continued.)

As details of the establishment of six-gun batteries have not yet been received, batteries transferred will be divided as equally as possible, and the surplus ⌐ in the Brigade as reformed will be reported without delay to D.A.H.Q. Nominal rolls of subalterns surplus, shewing to which Batteries attached, to be forwarded separately.

O.C. Brigades will select a second in command for each Battery, where one has not already been nominated, and forward their names to D.A.H.Q. as soon as possible.

The second in command will perform duties as such, and not those of a Section commander.

NOTE. - ALL TRANSFERS TO BE COMPLETED BY 12 NOON, WEDNESDAY 30TH INSTANT.
ALL TRANSFERS OF AMMUNITION TO BE REPORTED AND TAKE EFFECT FROM SAME DATE AND TIME.

2. GROUPS, ZONES, ETC.

The two Groups will remain covering their present sections, but some alteration of positions and control is necessary to conform to the 6 gun-Battery formation as detailed below.

ZONES.

LEFT GROUP: - Lt.Col. C.B.Simonds, R.F.A. 170th Bde. R.F.A.

Extent - present boundaries -
To be covered by 18.pdrs, A/170 (6 guns) C/170 (6 guns) B/169 (5 guns)
(Hows:- D/165 (4 Hows.) and D/170 (4 Hows.)

B/170 (6 guns) will be attached to 61st Div. R.A. to cover the present zone of B/170, and 2 guns of C/169.

RIGHT GROUP. Col.Hon. H.W. Addington, R.F.A. 169 Bde. R.F.A.

Extent - present boundaries.
To be covered by -
18.pdrs, C/165 (6 guns) A/165 (6 guns) B/165 (6 guns).
Hows: C/165, (4 Hows)

3. 18.PDR. GUNS.

The guns themselves remain in their present positions with the following exceptions :-

2 of B/171 guns, to be taken out and handed over to O.C. C/165.
2 of B/171 guns to be taken out and handed over to:-
1 to C/170. and
1 to A/165.

Note. - O.C. C/170 takes over both guns at PONT LOGY.

2 of B/165's guns to be taken out and handed over to A/170.
2 of B/165's guns to be taken out and placed in C/171's alternative position, taken over by O.C. B/165.
Note O.C.
Note. - O.C. B/169 takes over 1 gun from B/165 in single gun position near HAYSTACK POST.

⌐ Figures showing the total establishment for each Brigade will be found on attached list, but no allowance has been made for cycles in lieu of horses

(Continued.)

- 3 -

        1 of C/169's guns to be taken out and handed over to A/170.
        1 of C/169's guns to be taken out and handed over to O.C. B/169 and placed in reserve.

        2 guns from A/165 to be handed over to A/169; at present to go to wagon line at X.9.c.4.5.

4. DETACHMENTS.

        Batteries will man the extra guns allotted to them with the personnel of the half battery transferred in each case.

5. VACATED POSITIONS.

        Vacated positions will be occupied by 3 caretakers and communications from these positions will be left as they stand, except for wires to the Infantry which should be picked up.
        These positions will again be occupied later for an offensive action.

6. WAGON LINES.

        A/171 wagon line at R.27.b.4.4. will be occupied by A/165.   A/165 wagon line at R.27.d.6.3. to be vacated.
B/171, at R.20.c.7.2. to be vacated.
C/171 at X.9.c.4.5. will be reoccupied by A/169.
D/171 remains as C/169.
Present wagon line of C/169 at R.22.a.8.6. to be occupied by D/169 (on return).
Pending return of "A" & "D" 169, 1 section of C/169 (now transferred to B/169) to remain at R.22.a.8.6.; and 1 section to be transferred to the present C/171's wagon line at X.9.c.4.5.

D.A.H.Q.   *H.O.Hutchinson*   Captain R.A.

27.8.16.   Brigade Major 31st Divisional Artillery.

        Copies to H.Q. 165th Bde. R.F.A.
                      169th Bde. R.F.A.
                      170th Bde. R.F.A.
                      171st Bde. R.F.A.
                      31st D.A.C.

Appendix 1

CENTRE GROUP

Battery	Gun Position	Alternative Gun Position	Wagon Line	Zone of Fire (True Bearing)	Barrage Zone	Forward OP's	M.G. line of fire Zone	No. of Position	Infantry Concerned
A/169 (4 guns)	X23a9.2	X22d7.8	X9c4.5	98° – 131°	A9b63.8 to S27d61.5½	GUN HOUSE (S20d1.1)		21	Right Battalion
B/165 (2 guns)	S14c2.6		R31d2.7	132° – 154°				34	
B/169 (4 guns 2 guns)	F5t.61.2½ X30c7.2	X30e7.2	X25b0.0 "	54° – 94° 61° – 101°	S27d61.5½ to S22c6.7	BREWERY (S20d41.2½)		(unnumbered) 24	Left Battalion
C/169 (2 guns)	X19d9.7	X18a2½.0	X8b4.3	70° – 106°	S22c6.7 to S28a6.2½	See over INDIAN VILLAGE (S2b7½.2½)	S22c9.1 S28a8.2	23	Left Company Left Battalion
D/169 (4 guns)	F5c0.9	X30c5.5	W30b8.2	63° – 117°	S28a6.2½ to A9b63.8	GIRLS SCHOOL (A9b6.9) No 39 (S25d5.5)	A3d6½.2 A3c2.5 S27d6.2½ S28c4.4½	26	Right Battalion Right Company Right Battalion

* Battery reported to flank section

27.9.16

W/ Gowen

OBJECTIVE. Appendix 8

TIME.	NATURE OF FIRE.	GUNS.	PLACE.	MAP LOCATION.	RATE OF FIRE PER GUN PER MIN.	ESTIMATED EXPENDITURE OF AMMUNITION.	REMARKS.
9-10½ to 9-15	BARRAGE	FOUR 4·5" HOW?	TRENCHES.	S 28 a 7.4 S 28 a 5.2 S 22 d 2.3½ S 22 c 7.9	1	20	
	do.	ONE 8" HOW?	AS AT 5 P.M.		¾	4	
		2" T.M. STOKES	} DO NOT FIRE				
	do.	THREE 18 PR. (IF AVAILABLE)	TRENCHES	MARRAIS ALLEY. EITEL ALLEY SOUTH EITEL ALLEY NORTH. ADALBERT ALLEY	1½	24	
9-15 to 9-17	BOMBARDMENT	FOUR 4·5" HOW?	FRONT & SUPPORT LINE.	S 28 A 7.4 to S22 c 6.6½	4	32	
	do.	ONE 8" HOW?	AS AT 5 PM		ANY ROUNDS	UNEXPENDED	
	do.	TWO 2" T.M.	FRONT LINE	RIGHT & LEFT OF WHERE WIRE IS CUT	1	4	
	do.	L.T.M.	do.	AS AT 5 PM.	?	?	
	do.	THREE 18 PR (IF AVAILABLE)	do.	S28 A 7.4 to S22 d 6.6½	4	24	

ALL BATTERIES CENTRE GROUP WILL STAND BY UNTIL 10 P.M. TO DEAL WITH ANY POSSIBLE RETALIATION.

TIME	NATURE OF FIRE	GUNS	PLACE	MAP LOCATION	RATE OF FIRE PER GUN PER MINUTE	ESTIMATED EXPENDITURE OF AMMUNITION	REMARKS
5 PM TO 5:20 PM	BOMBARDMENT	Four 4·5 Hows.	Machine Gun Emplot	S28A 7.4. S22c 9.3. 6.6½. 9½.5½.	1/3	28.	
	REGISTRATION.	One 8" How.	Strong Point.	S28B 6½.8.	1	4.	
	WIRE CUTTING	Two 2-in T.M.	Wire	S22c 8.4 TO S22c 6½.6.	½	20.	
	BOMBARDMENT.	L.T.M.	Front Line	S28A 9½.7 TO S22c 9.4	?	?	
9 PM TO 9:10 PM	BOMBARDMENT	Four 4·5 in Hows One 8 in How		As at 5 PM.	1 3/4	40. 8.	
9:10 PM	do	Two 2-in T.M.	Front Line	S22c 8.4 to 6½.6	1	20	
	do	L.T.M.	As at 5 PM.		?	?	
9.10. TO 9.10½.			SILENCE.				

Vol 8 3/ Bum

Confidential

WAR DIARY

OF

169th BRIGADE R.F.A.

FROM 1st OCTOBER to 31st OCTOBER, 1916.

VOLUME X

CONFIDENTIAL

WAR DIARY
of
161 Brigade. R.F.A.   Vol 810

pages 27 - 35

from 1 - 31 October 1916.

169 H Bde R.F.A.   October 1916.   Army Form C. 2118
Page 27
Volume V / 10

WAR DIARY
or
INTELLIGENCE SUMMARY

Place	Date	Hour	Summary of Events and Information	Remarks and references to Appendices
LOISNES	3		Emergent on orders for 3rd Div. to join XIII Corps (4th COVIN), 94th Inf Bde (which had been covered by his Bde) were relieved in the line by 13th Inf Bde (5th Div.) 2 raids were planned for night 3/4. Both were abortive owing to Bangalore torpedoes being non-effective — in the 1st case by being blown up by enemy, 2nd case by being damped.	(KB)
	5		G.O.C. 132 Inf Bde took over command of FESTUBERT Section	
	5/6	night	Relief of 3rd DA'ty by Corps Arty began. B/149 4 guns at F5b 41.2½ by B/161 — A/169 6 guns at X23 a 9.2 by B/155 D/169 4 hows F5c O.8 by D/161 — C/169 4 hows at X17 c 9.7 by C/148. B/169 withdrew two guns from X30 c 7.2 to wagon line. Incoming batteries handed over their guns at wagon line.	(KB)
	6	9a.m.	G.O.C. 5th Div. took on command (divisional front)	(KB)
	6/7	night	Arty relief completed. Batterie concentrated in Wision.	(KB)
	7	noon	This group relieved by corps arty group as above under Major Westhole D/161 forms Right group — D/188 forms Left group.	(KB)

WAR DIARY or INTELLIGENCE SUMMARY

Army Form C. 2118
Page 28
Vol 8

Place	Date	Hour	Summary of Events and Information	Remarks and references to Appendices
LOISNES	7	—	OC: Bde proceeded to BUS & AUTHIE. Hq to be attached 51st Div — 165 and 170 to 19th Div — all XIII Corps. 31st DAHQ hremain at MARIEUX MM 31st Div Hq. (on infantry MM being in line). (NB)	
LOISNES	8		Advance party of BCiv proceeded to BUS (51st DAHQ). Billets for night at LOUVENCOURT, where Wago line for Bde was found. (NB)	
MERVILLE	9	4.20am	A/169 enhanced for CANDAS & arrives LOUVENCOURT 10pm	
		7.20am	B/169 ,, ,, ,, ,, 1am, 10th	
		9.20	C/169 ,, ,, ,, ,, 5am	
		1.20	Hq. & D/169 ,, ,, ,, ,, 5pm (having stayed night at CANDAS).	
			Great shortage of billets for men. Eventually 92 hrs shelters obtained. (NB)	
COURCELLES	10		Hq Bde Holges at COURCELLES MM 256 Bde RFA (51st Div). (NB)	
	10/11		15 pdr Batteries moved into action made camouflage { A/169 K20 d 1¼ 2 / B/169 K26 b 2¾ 9½ (NB)	
	12		4.5 How Bath moved into action { C/169 K30c 5¼ 5¼ / D/169 (2)- K30C 3½ 1½ & 3m K20C 2½ b.	
			D/260 attached for tactical purpose to this group at K30a 5.0.	
			The group carried no further defence zone, but covered whole of 51st (Divl)	

WAR DIARY or INTELLIGENCE SUMMARY

Army Form C. 2118
Page 29
Vol 8

Place	Date	Hour	Summary of Events and Information	Remarks and references to Appendices
COURCELLES	12	Cont'd	Dual front from K23d 3.1 K23a 9.4. Guns ordered not to fire except for Registration. (MB)	
"	13		"Wire demonstration" barrage projected approach of tanks. B/169 in STAR WOOD (60 RX). D/160 on Western edge of PUISIEUX (60 RX) (MB)	
"	14		Staps moved into huts in bank of Sunken Road at K19c 6½.½. (MB)	
COLINCAMPS K19c 6½.2	16		92nd Inf Bde relieves R.N. Batt. 5th Div in the line, consequent on withdrawal of 5th Div to BEAUMONT HAMEL. (MB)	
	16/17	night	5th Div Arty withdrawn and 169 Bde. (with A/251 left behind for myMB 16/17 for liaison purposes). Defence front (N Batt) K17d 0.½ to K23d 7.1. 92nd Inf Bde also 106th and 19th Divisional on its left & relief part (covered by 170 Bde Arty.). 1105 Reinforces whole front. (MB)	
	17		All amn in dumps left behind by 237, 256, + 266 Bdes (57th Div) taken in charge by this Bde. Bde total then approx: {15000 A 7000 RX } {7000 BX 1100 2 gas}	
	16/17	nightW	Raid planned by 4th Gordons (51st Div) proved abortive. Apps /169 pros Shrapnel barrage at K23b N of point of entry. (KH)	

WAR DIARY or INTELLIGENCE SUMMARY

Army Form C. 2118
Page 30
Vol 8

Place	Date	Hour	Summary of Events and Information	Remarks and references to Appendices
COLINCAMPS K19c 6.2.	17		Trench mortars of 9th & 15th Divn attacked this front. Their programme generally was to fire intensively for 1 hour during the day on support line of this Bdes Defence Zone; during the remainder of the day their detachments with-drew. At first their fire was covered by special fire for but as the daily bombardment increased this became unnecessary. During the night 15 pdrs fired on support line & deepening zone to stop any work that the enemy might try to do to his damaged trench mines. (JR)	
do	18		C/116g & D/116g were told off as Antigas Batteries. (JR)	
do	19		Very wet day. Advance posts B/firs new line in COIGNEUX (JR)	
do	19/20	night	33rd Div Left moved in and took over certain [dumps] ammn on charge of this Bde (1st & 11st. 162 & 166 Bdes). Iron artillery in action solely for use with purpose on the defence zone of Neg M.A. 11cg 11aa mine cutters gone from front to 300° north g.i.l. (JR)	
do	20		Bde wagon lines moved to COIGNEUX (JR)	

Army Form C. 2118

Page 31
Vol 8

WAR DIARY
or
INTELLIGENCE SUMMARY
(Erase heading not required.)

Place	Date	Hour	Summary of Events and Information	Remarks and references to Appendices
COLINCAMPS Kpt c 6.4.1.	21	12.6 pm	Artillery fired in the front in connection with Operation of II Corps. 10 min intense bombardment of front, support & third line trenches in turn. The enemy retaliation began on 2nd & 3rd line (NY)	
"	21/22 night		Hos & 179 Battn in hollow S. of HEBUTERNE shelled with lethal gas shells - 36 casualties in all (JN)	
"	22		Arty Concentration (FdArty & Heavy How) on Village. PUISIEUX 3.20 – 3.50 pm SERRE 4 – 4.20 pm. All 15 pdr Guns 3rd gun fire into PUISIEUX at 4.15 pm to catch any enemy who might have come out to watch bombardment of SERRE. 92nd Inf Bde ordered relieved in line as they are to make an attack on 2 days on left flank of I Corps (opposite SERRE). Projects. Raid & gas discharge consequently abandoned. The R.F. Battn has only 4 slight casualties in line since 16th. High Explosive – Hans exploded FRITZ ALLEY – 1 pdr a support (magazine) KB	
"	23	5 am	General Bombardment began (X day) Heavier fire from 5.67 am when (Tie as)	

WAR DIARY
or
INTELLIGENCE SUMMARY.

Army Form C. 2118.
Page 32
Vol 8.

(Erase heading not required.)

Instructions regarding War Diaries and Intelligence Summaries are contained in F.S. Regs., Part II. and the Staff Manual respectively. Title pages will be prepared in manuscript.

Hour, Date, Place	Date	Summary of Events and Information	Remarks and references to Appendices
COLINCAMPS. K.19.c.6½.½ (O.P.)	23	Our Artillery opens fire. 50% & 18pdr barrage fire support line – 2 mins intense zone. (2nd heavy guns). ½ of 50% of 18pdrs on support line (1 – 2 hy pr minute), ½ of the guns of front line then on that support line. 6.15 – 7.15 Pause. Then 7.15 a onwards fell wire cutting programme was continued (same guns being now fired from 50' N of found down to 60.) 4.5 Hows fired on quadrilateral & trenches between POINT and 31 (HD) Thick mist unsuitable for observation for shells fired shallo JD	
	23/24	Enemy shelled JIFFA with about 60 gas shells from 10.45 to 11.20 p.m. Bursts giving - - - - - on LOUVIERE FARM and STAR ALLEY (HD)	
	24	B/160 to cut wire opposite JOHN COPSE. Enemy to Zero being halfway thro. Wire is now ½ day thick mist rendered observation for accurate impossible.	

Army Form C. 2118.

WAR DIARY
or
INTELLIGENCE SUMMARY.
(Erase heading not required.)

Page 33.
Vol 2.

Hour, Date, Place		Summary of Events and Information	Remarks and references to Appendices
COLINCAMPS K19c 63½	24/25	No night firing by 4.5 Hows. 50 rds fired upon Battn or Support Trench (Auburn Lane) (MR)	
	25.	Annual allotment regimental reserves. Rain and mist again hindered observation. (MR)	
	27.	Early morning bombardment on mil. Postponed if for day. 6.27 h. B/169 authorise Bayart support line behind CRATER at K23d 6.2. Fighting patrol of 15½ W/Yorks to enter German trenches at POINT. Found wire well cut but wire spotted when firing firing up to enter trench. Were fired on and retired. Enemy appeared the hold it in strong widely [points]. (MR)	
	28	6.5-6.15 Bombardment half previous rate of fire. B/169 on wire as for 27 h. (6 prs 92" Ts of 17" of 20 GR. 11p of fighting patrols and 1 pr 93rd Bde of 20ft + 40 mm) bomb German trench at various points. There are no [artily]	

WAR DIARY
or
INTELLIGENCE SUMMARY.
(Erase heading not required.)

Army Form C. 2118.

Page 34
VOL. 8

Hour, Date, Place	Summary of Events and Information	Remarks and references to Appendices
COLINCAMPS K19c6.1. Oct. 28th (contd)	artillery preparation or barrage. The 93rd Bde patrol was through wire from true south and knocked out recognition. On searching from gap & up through second line there were gaps (presumably) by division on our right.) Returns under rifle fire; There was no machine gun or artillery. Enemy produced by effect sup. gone then away. JB.	
29th	Quiet morning bombardment on 29th. J. Barrage to 2 day. from 3.39 to 6 3.42 h had aeroplane have attention in observing it & parameters were all observation. Burst of fire on front line (12 pdr) and heard (45 yards) between POINT 60 at 6.15 t.7.0, 8.0, 6.40, 7.20, 1.30 am. Patrol went out between 9.20 and 7.30 to scout front and wounded German with preparent of X day. JB.	
31st	C.O. Batt. shells communication trenches in K17d Corps. H.Q. bombard trench junction in K17, 19, 23, 24. (Cr.10)	

Army Form C. 2118.
Page 35
Vol 8

WAR DIARY
or
INTELLIGENCE SUMMARY.
(Erase heading not required.)

Hour, Date, Place	Summary of Events and Information	Remarks and references to Appendices
COLINCAMPS: Oct. 31st (cont.)	At night — 5.30 and 9.0 p.m. — bursts of fire from all Howrs (front line wire) and 18 pdrs (front line wire). Antigas gas from 6 p.m. C/169, K.7.d.0.1 to D/169, K.17.d.1.58. Reserves K.17.d.1.55 to K.17.b.0.2. Oks	

1.11.16

W. Cowen
Lt. Col. R.F.A.
COMDG. 169TH BDE., R.F.A.

CONFIDENTIAL.

WAR DIARY

OF

169 BRIGADE. R.F.A.

From November 1st 1916 to November 30th 1916.

(VOLUME XI)

Army Form C. 2118

WAR DIARY
or
INTELLIGENCE SUMMARY
(Erase heading not required.)

Place	Date	Hour	Summary of Events and Information	Remarks and references to Appendices
COLINCAMPS K19 c 6½ ½	Nov. 1		18 Pdrs wire cutting. Hows bombarding trench junctions at K17 d 40.65. At night, bursts of fire by 18 Pdrs at enemy front line wire at 8.10 P.M. 11.20 P.M. and 5.15 A.M	
	Nov 2		Concentrated bursts by Hows on trench junctions. 18 Pdrs actively firing at gaps in enemy wire. Normal night firing until 10 P.M. At 11 P.M., acting on pre-arranged rocket signals we bombarded enemy trenches for 1 hour.	
	Nov 3		18 Pdrs Wire-cutting. B/169 assisting 33rd Div. with wire behind CRATER. Hows on K23 b 7.6 and PIG TRENCH. At night - bursts of fire on enemy front-line wire at 8 P.M and 11.30 P.M. Hostile Aircraft very active during the afternoon - repeatedly driven off by our A.A. guns.	

169 Bde. R.F.A.

Page 376 30th Nov/16
1st Nov/16 — 30th Nov/16
Army Form C. 2118

WAR DIARY
or
INTELLIGENCE SUMMARY
(Erase heading not required.)

Place	Date	Hour	Summary of Events and Information	Remarks and references to Appendices
COLINCAMPS K19c 6.2.	Nov 4		B/169 continue to assist 33rd Div. 18 Pdrs wire-cutting during day. 4.5 Hows on communication trenches & trench junctions.	
		4.35 P.M.	HEBUTERNE shelled with 5.9's.	
	Nov 5		Wire-cutting proceeding vigorously. Recce instructions and artillery programme in support of raid to be carried out by 13th/14th Battns Y&L. on the night of 6/7. Aeroplane registration of 'F' Barrage.	
	Nov 6		Wire cutting on front and support lines between the 'POINT' and Point 60 — third line at K24 a 6.3. Hows on K24 b 7.3 and PIG TRENCH. Bombardment of German Trenches in preparation for raid.	

Army Form C. 2118

Page 38
Vol 9

WAR DIARY
or
INTELLIGENCE SUMMARY
(Erase heading not required.)

Place	Date	Hour	Summary of Events and Information	Remarks and references to Appendices
COLINCAMPS K19c6½.1½	Nov 7		18 Pdrs. vigilant look-out for movement & working parties. How's bombarding trench junction (K17d4.6) GATE TRENCH. At night, in co-operation with 33rd Div. we fired bursts of fire at enemy wire at 5.30 P.M. and 6.45 P.M. Bombardment in support of raid. The southern raid failed, the northern one bringing in 4 prisoners.	
	Nov 8		18 Pdrs (A & B/169) actively cutting wire. Hows C & D/169 on GATE TRENCH and K17d4.6¾. At night we co-operated with 33 D.A. firing bursts on enemy wire. Hows on western exits of PUISIEUX.	

Page 39 Vol 9

Army Form C. 2118

WAR DIARY or INTELLIGENCE SUMMARY

Place	Date	Hour	Summary of Events and Information	Remarks and references to Appendices
COLINCAMPS K19c6&2			18 Pdrs wire cutting. Hows bombarding GATE TRENCH and K17 d 4. 6 3/4.	
	Nov 9	5.30 p.m. and 6.15 p.m.	Concentrated bursts by 18 Pdrs and Hows on LA LOUVIERE FARM	
		4.30 A.m.	Burst of fire on enemy front and support line wire.	
	Nov 10		'W' Bay. Bombardment of enemy trenches 5.45 to 6 a.m.	
		7 am to 5.45 p.m.	18 Pdrs wire cutting front and support lines. Hows wire cutting 3rd & 4th lines, and bombarding trench junctions. At night 18 Pdrs fired bursts at front line wire & the Hows bombarding LA LOUVIERE FARM	

Army Form C. 2118

Page 40 Vol 4

WAR DIARY
or
INTELLIGENCE SUMMARY
(Erase heading not required.)

Place	Date	Hour	Summary of Events and Information	Remarks and references to Appendices
COLINCAMPS K19c 6½.½	Nov 11		'X' Day. 18 Pdrs wire-cutting – B/164 assisting 33"Div with wire behind CRATER	
	Nov 12	5.45-6 AM	Y Day. Bombardment of enemy trenches.	
		7 AM to 5.45 PM	18 Pdrs wire-cutting. 4.5 Hows bombarding western defences of PUISIEUX.	
	Nov 13		'Z' Day. Zero hour 6.5 A.M. Enemy barraged CABER and ROB ROY, and also shelled K19c heavily with 10.5 c.m. and gas shells.	

Army Form C. 2118

WAR DIARY
or
INTELLIGENCE SUMMARY
(Erase heading not required.)

Pages 11
Vol 4

Place	Date	Hour	Summary of Events and Information	Remarks and references to Appendices
COLINCAMPS K19c6.5	Nov 14		Relief of 92nd 493rd Inf Bde by 94th Bde. Right Group (Lt Col W.S Craven) covering front held by Right Battalion K17 d 0.2 to K23 d 7.2.	
	Nov 15		Hostile Artillery active. Roads and vicinity of Battery Positions shelled at intervals during the day.	
	Nov 16		Hostile Artillery normal. 4.5 How Anti-gas zones amended to :— C/169 K23 d 6.4 – K17 d 2.5½ D/169 K23 d 7.2 – K23 d 4.4	
	Nov 17		Hostile Artillery active – principally in vicinity of our battery positions and roads.	
	Nov 18		Enemy Artillery Active – shelling usual areas. We fired bursts in the early morning and during the night.	

Army Form C. 2118

Page 42
Vol 4

WAR DIARY
or
INTELLIGENCE SUMMARY
(Erase heading not required.)

Instructions regarding War Diaries and Intelligence Summaries are contained in F. S. Regs., Part II. and the Staff Manual respectively. Title Pages will be prepared in manuscript.

Place	Date	Hour	Summary of Events and Information	Remarks and references to Appendices
COLINCAMPS	Nov 19		Hostile Artillery — normal. Occasional shelling of communication trenches — roads and tracks.	
	Nov 20		Hostile Artillery below normal. The roads and tracks in vicinity of Battery positions being lightly shelled occasionally during the afternoon. 517 Howitzer Battery attached to 169 Bde. Battery wagon lines at 19.d.1.1. Section of 517 Battery relieved section of C/169 in action at K.20.c.5½.5½ Supposed relief of German Brown Torpedo on front — all roads and communication trenches were swept throughout the night.	
	Nov 21		C/169 remaining section relieved by 517 How Battery. C/169 in reserve at wagon line J.3.c.8.5. Hostile Artillery very quiet.	
	Nov 22		Hostile Artillery normal. Occasional movement observed and dealt with.	
	Nov 23		Hostile Artillery normal during the day — very quiet at night. Enemy aircraft active throughout the day.	

1875 Wt. W593/826 1,000,000 4/15 J.B.C. & A. A.D.S.S./Forms/C.2118.

WAR DIARY or INTELLIGENCE SUMMARY

Place	Date	Hour	Summary of Events and Information	Remarks and references to Appendices
COLINCAMP K19C 6?.??	Nov 24	5 P.M.	Hostile Artillery normal. RIGHT GROUP (commanded by Lt Col W.S.D. Craven) composed of A,B,D/169. 517 How. Battery. D/170, A/170 and C/165. Covering both Battalions - 94th 2nd Bde — from SUNKEN ROAD to JOHN COPSE.	
	Nov 25	2 P.M.	Lt. Col. W.S.D. Craven having proceeded on leave — Major W.D. Stillwell assumed command of Right Group	
		11.20 – 11.55 A.M.	Hebuterne shelled with 10.5 C.M. and intermittently during the day. Operations — Enemy movement dispersed. Bursts of fire on gaps etc.	
	Nov 26		Enemy has shown quite unusual unprovoked activity today, principally on our front and support line trenches.	
	Nov 27		HEBUTERNE and neighbouring valley shelled intermittently during the day. Night firing — 18 Pdrs bursts of fire on gaps. Hour communication trenches.	

Army Form C. 2118

WAR DIARY
or
INTELLIGENCE SUMMARY
(Erase heading not required.)

Instructions regarding War Diaries and Intelligence Summaries are contained in F. S. Regs, Part II. and the Staff Manual respectively. Title Pages will be prepared in manuscript.

Page 444 Vol 2

Place	Date	Hour	Summary of Events and Information	Remarks and references to Appendices
COLINCAMPS K19c6½.2	Nov 26	2 AM	Enemy Artillery active. In retaliation for the enemy shelling HEBUTERNE we bombarded PUISIEUX — 18 Pdrs firing Shrapnel & H.E., 4.5 Hows incendiary shell. A good deal of movement observed behind enemy lines, and engaged with good effect. During the night we fired bursts of fire at gaps in enemy wire, also shelling roads and tracks used by the enemy at night.	
	Nov 29 9-9 pm		Vicinity of B Battery Positions in K20c9d shelled with 10·5 c.m. No damage done. Normal night firing.	
	Nov 30		Hostile Artillery less active than usual. Ordinary night firing programme.	

Con. 24/69 4 B 32 TMB

CONFIDENTIAL.

WAR DIARY

OF

169th BRIGADE R.F.A.

From 1st DECEMBER 1916 to 31st DECEMBER 1916.

VOLUME XII.

169 IofBde R.F.A.

WAR DIARY
or
INTELLIGENCE SUMMARY. 1st Dec.1916 Page 1
to 31st Dec.1916.
VOL II

Army Form C. 2118.

Hour, Date, Place	Summary of Events and Information	Remarks and references to Appendices
COLINCAMPS K19c 6½.2. Dec 1.	Cold. Heavy mist — observation practically impossible all day.	
10.a.m.	Right Group — (169 Bde H.Q. A, B & D Batteries 169 Bde. 517 How. Battery A/170 Bde and C/165 Bde) Group H.Q. moved to SAILLY Quarries at J18c6.2. Communications were satisfactorily established. Enemy Artillery much more active.	
11.35 a.m.	Heavy hostile shelling of our line SOUTH of MARK COPSE, spreading at 12 noon as far north as K23 a & c. Continued until 12.50 p.m when it gradually slowed down. The counter-bombarded enemy lines opposite RIGHT Battalion front.	

Army Form C. 2118.

Page 2
VOL 19

WAR DIARY
or
INTELLIGENCE SUMMARY.
(Erase heading not required.)

Instructions regarding War Diaries and Intelligence Summaries are contained in F.S. Regs., Part II. and the Staff Manual respectively. Title pages will be prepared in manuscript.

Hour, Date, Place	Summary of Events and Information	Remarks and references to Appendices
SAILLY J18c6.2		
Dec 2nd	Cold - frosty. rain invariably.	
9.45 – 10 A.M.	2 Hostile 10.5 c.m batteries vigorously shelled our lines between the SUNKEN ROAD and 100 yds North of "THE POINT"	
10.5 – 10.15 a.m	Our trenches in K22 and K23a received attention.	
10-30 to 3.30 PM	Considerable movement observed behind enemy lines and effectually dealt with by Bomp Batteries. At night we fired bursts at enemy wire to prevent repair.	
Dec 3rd	Hostile Artillery normal.	
11.50 A.M	Enemy shelled our trenches in K23 central with about 50 10.5 c.m.	

(73989) W4141—463. 400,000. 9/14. H.&J.Ltd. Forms/C. 2118/10.

WAR DIARY
or
INTELLIGENCE SUMMARY.
(Erase heading not required.)

Army Form C. 2118.

Page 3
Vol 12

Hour, Date, Place	Summary of Events and Information	Remarks and references to Appendices
SALLY J18c 6½.2		
Dec 3rd (cont)		
2.45 – 3.30 p.m.	Hostile 10.5 c.m. battery searched the valley K20c9D through K26a towards COLINCAMPS.	
8.10 P.M. – 8.55 P.M.	Enemy shelled HEBUTERNE	
Dec. 4th		
	Cold – but fine. Thin light for observation. Enemy appears to have done a little work on his front line wire, despite continual Artillery and machine gun fire directed against it.	
7.30 am – 2.30 p.m.	Considerable movement observed behind enemy lines, no doubt due to the bad condition of his trenches. Many instances were observed of men climbing	

Page 4
Vol 10

WAR DIARY
or
INTELLIGENCE SUMMARY.
(Erase heading not required.)

Army Form C. 2118.

Hour, Date, Place	Summary of Events and Information	Remarks and references to Appendices

SAILY JISC 57.2
Dec 4th (Cont)

out of their trenches and running across the open.

Hostile Aircraft were very active today. Many endeavours were made to cross our lines, but all enemy planes were effectively engaged by our A.A. guns. At 11.25 AM an engagement took place between one of our own planes and an enemy plane immediately over SERRE. After a little manouvering and firing of machine guns, both planes made off for their own lines, to be immediately engaged by A.A. guns.

Dec 6th 6 - 6.45 AM

Infantry reported considerable movement in vicinity of STAR ALLEY. We fired bursts of fire during the early morning mists.

WAR DIARY
or
INTELLIGENCE SUMMARY.
(Erase heading not required.)

Army Form C. 2118.

Page 5
Vol 10

Hour, Date, Place	Summary of Events and Information	Remarks and references to Appendices
SAILLY J18C6,2 Dec 6th (cont)	Noble trench mortars active on our right flank (3rd Division front). Considerable movement observed behind enemy lines. Between 10 – 11 a.m. 2 parties of Germans (between 60 and 70 in all) were observed at L25 a 4.3. These troops were immediately engaged by our 18 Pdrs – and casualties inflicted. An Infantry patrol left our lines during the night to examine gap in enemy's wire a K17 c.0.2. The patrol reported that the gap is about 12 ft. wide, and the ground in front much cut up by our fire. Our ordinary night programme was carried out.	

Army Form C. 2118.

Page 6

Vol 12

WAR DIARY
or
INTELLIGENCE SUMMARY.
(Erase heading not required.)

Hour, Date, Place	Summary of Events and Information	Remarks and references to Appendices
SAILLY J18c 6½.2. Dec 6th	Very misty all day — making observation difficult. Enemy artillery active at intervals during the day — principally on our communication trenches. The concentrations. A little movement was observed during the afternoon, and effectively engaged. Commencing on the night of the 6th — in conjunction with the Corps Heavy Artillery we fired bursts of fire at night on enemy roads and tracks. Programme attached - Tables A & B (appendix 1)	

WAR DIARY or INTELLIGENCE SUMMARY

Army Form C. 2118.

Page 7
Vol 12

Hour, Date, Place	Summary of Events and Information	Remarks and references to Appendices
SAILLY J18c 6.2 Dec 7	Hostile artillery a little more active today, shelling our trench junctions and communications.	
11.15 A.M.	Enemy searched K15a and K14d with 77 m.m. shrapnel and gas shell – doing no damage.	
	Very foggy all day.	
	During the morning enemy working parties were actively repairing their front line trench North and South of NOHM COPSE. Their portion of the trench was kept under fire from time to time.	
2.30 P.M.	In an interval of light – a working party was observed at K24 b 9.1 digging in the trench. They were engaged, and work ceased.	

WAR DIARY
or
INTELLIGENCE SUMMARY.

(Erase heading not required.)

Army Form C. 2118.

Page 8
Vol 19

Hour, Date, Place	Summary of Events and Information	Remarks and references to Appendices
SALLY J18C6½.2 Dec 8th	Area - with heavy enemy shelling all day. During the day the enemy three engaged enemy trench junctions, strong points and ammunition trenches. 18 Pdrs on Zepps & enemy wire. Trench Mortars on his parapets. (See Appendix 1) Our heavy artillery shelling of our front & support lines during the day, and occasional bursts in R26d.	
9.55 P.M. – 10.20 P.M.	Bombardment of our trenches in K16d and K17c with 15 c.m, 10.5 c.m and 77 m.m. The counter bombarded enemy support lines and reserves.	

Page 9
Vol 10

WAR DIARY or INTELLIGENCE SUMMARY

Army Form C. 2118.

Hour, Date, Place	Summary of Events and Information	Remarks and references to Appendices
SAILLY J18c6½.2 Dec 9th	Cold - with heavy mist lasting all day - making observation practically impossible. Enemy shelled our support & third line trenches at intervals during the day - no heavy concentrations.	
10 P.M.	Re-allotment of Right Group Zones, the 3rd Division extending their front to JOHN COPSE. Right Group now covering 94th Inf. Bde (with 1 Battalion plus two Companies in the line). Front held - WARRIOR ST K17a.1.7 to K23a 85.55. Re allotment of battery zones attached (appendix 2).	

WAR DIARY
or
INTELLIGENCE SUMMARY.

page 10
Vol 14

Hour, Date, Place	Summary of Events and Information	Remarks and references to Appendices
SAILLY J18c 6½.2 Dec 10—	Fine and cold, good visibility. Hostile Artillery slightly more active – probably due to good visibility. Most of their efforts were directed against our communication trenches. The gap in enemy's wire at K.17.b.0.2 has been partly closed up – the enemy having thrown out "concertina". Considerable movement observed behind enemy lines today – and effectively engaged. We registered important points in new zone. Night 10/11 a Battery 170 Bde withdrew from action to their wagon lines at J.2.c (central)	W

WAR DIARY
or
INTELLIGENCE SUMMARY.

(Erase heading not required.)

Army Form C. 2118.

Page 11
Vol 10

Hour, Date, Place	Summary of Events and Information	Remarks and references to Appendices
SALLY J18 & 7.2 Dec 11th	Light rain in morning - becoming heavy towards 2 P.M.	
	Enemy showed a little more activity today - principally on our communication trenches.	
10.20 am	Enemy shelled HEBUTERNE with a few 10.5 c.m and 77 m.m.	
	The gap in enemy wire at K.17.b.0.2 has been partly reopened by us today.	
	Night passed without any incident worth recording.	
Dec 12th	A little snow during the night - thawing today. Fair visibility.	
	A party of about 50 Germans were observed walking	

WAR DIARY
or
INTELLIGENCE SUMMARY.

Page 12
Vol 16
Army Form C. 2118.

Hour, Date, Place	Summary of Events and Information	Remarks and references to Appendices
SAILLY SEC 62.2 Dec.12th (cont)	in file - carrying packs at K25.E. They were engaged by our m.g. after - at least 3 were seen to be driven into an adjacent trench.	
10.30 am	Other movement and working parties were observed and dispersed during the day. Enemy fired a few 10.5 C.m into HEBUTERNE	
10.45 – 11 a.m.	Enemy fired 4 rounds 10.5 c.m H.E. (3 were delivers) into A/169 (K20 d 1.2) gun position - killing 2 O.R., and 3 horses. No further work appears to have been done during night of 11/12th on enemy mine at K17 c 0.2. Orders received for concentration on enemy communication on night of 13/12/16, but later postponed for 24 hours. (appendix 5)	

WAR DIARY or INTELLIGENCE SUMMARY.

Army Form C. 2118.

Page 13   Vol 10

Hour, Date, Place	Summary of Events and Information	Remarks and references to Appendices
SAILLY J1rc G.2.2. Dec 12th (Cont)	Night 12/13th communications were tested by means of an SOS test. Batteries opened fire for 5 minutes. (Appendix 3) Conference met at Group Headquarters to discuss a 'Construction Scheme' – its objects being to construct dug-out accommodation for officers & men – ammunition dumps – gun platforms – covers. It was decided that Major W.L.Y. ROGERS R.F.A. (Cmdg. B/169) should take another, assisted by LIEUT MOORE (223 Coy R.E.) and a LIEUT REAY R.F.A. (170 Bde R.F.A. H.Q.) (Appendix 4)	
Dec 13th	Hostile Artillery active at intervals – principally on our communication trenches and roads. Very little enemy movement observed today – There are signs of repairs to enemy wire from 150 to 200	

Army Form C. 2118.

Page 14
Vol xd

WAR DIARY
or
INTELLIGENCE SUMMARY.
(Erase heading not required.)

Hour, Date, Place	Summary of Events and Information	Remarks and references to Appendices
SAILLY LABOURSE 2. Dec 13th (cont)	Ypres North of "THE POINT" No news except there have been done during the night on gap at K.17.b.0.2.	
Dec 14th	In conjunction with XIII Corps Heavy Artillery we fired bursts of fire at various times. Programme for Dec 14th, 15th, 16th & 17th attached (Appendix 6)	
12.15 C. 12.30 P.M.	Heavy T.M. shelled our advanced posts about K.17 c 5.0 with about 20 rounds. The T.M. was not located - but immediate retaliation with H.E. caused his fire to cease. A little fresh work was noticeable today on the gap at K.17.b.02. No other signs of repair were observed.	

WAR DIARY
or
INTELLIGENCE SUMMARY.

(Erase heading not required.)

Army Form C. 2118.

Page 15
Vol 10

Hour, Date, Place		Summary of Events and Information	Remarks and references to Appendices
SAILLY AU BOIS 2 Dec. 15th		Cold - fine - fair visibility. Hostile artillery showing less activity - nothing but small bursts of fire on our sector - mostly on communication trenches.	
	1 P.M.	Hostile T.M. opened fire on our trenches opposite the "POINT". Immediate retaliation causing it to cease fire. No further reply appears to have been done to the enemy - none during the night. About 150 rounds were fired at gap in K17 & 12, 13 with satisfactory results. Considerable movement observed during the day on the ACHIET-LE-PETIT — PUISIEUX road.	RR

Army Form C. 2118.

WAR DIARY
or
INTELLIGENCE SUMMARY.
(Erase heading not required.)

Page 16

Vol 16

Instructions regarding War Diaries and Intelligence Summaries are contained in F. S. Regs., Part II. and the Staff Manual respectively. Title pages will be prepared in manuscript.

Hour, Date, Place	Summary of Events and Information	Remarks and references to Appendices
SAILLY J18c 6.2		
Dec 15th (Cont)		
2.45 PM	A working party building a dug-out or emplacement at K17 d 3.4 were dispersed, and the work destroyed by our fire.	
Dec 16th.	Low visibility.	
	Enemy artillery normal.	
12.15 PM and 2.30 PM	HEBUTERNE was lightly shelled.	
	Enemy's reply to our bursts of fire during the night were very feeble.	
	Preparation for raids to take place at a near date — we fired short bursts at enemy front and supports — to accustom him to our fire at night.	RSF

Army Form C. 2118.

Page 17
Vol 10

WAR DIARY
or
INTELLIGENCE SUMMARY.
(Erase heading not required.)

Instructions regarding War Diaries and Intelligence Summaries are contained in F.S. Regs., Part II. and the Staff Manual respectively. Title pages will be prepared in manuscript.

Hour, Date, Place	Summary of Events and Information	Remarks and references to Appendices
SAILLY J18c63.2 Dec 17.	Low visibility. A few rounds were fired at enemy working the day. Hostile artillery showed much less activity. A very uneventful day. Heavy night firing.	
Dec 18th	Enemy artillery normal. Our communication trenches were lightly shelled during the day - mostly 77 m.m.. Operations. wire cutting during the day, and movement effectively engaged. Night firing as per programme. 3 Patrols left our lines night of 17/18th to examine enemy's wire, but no information was gained - the night being too dark.	

Army Form C. 2118.

Page 15
Vol N/1

WAR DIARY
or
INTELLIGENCE SUMMARY.
(Erase heading not required.)

Hour, Date, Place	Summary of Events and Information	Remarks and references to Appendices
SAILLY J18c.6½.2		
Dec 19th	A slight rearrangement of Battery Zones were made to allow for overlapping. New zones as follows:-	
	B/169 K23 & 3½.6½ to K17 d 2.3 } 16 Pdrs	
	A/169 K17 d 2.3 to K17 b ½.1	
	C/165 K17 b ½.1 to SUNKEN ROAD (inclusive)	
	D/169 SNUFF ALLEY to LOB STREET } 4.5 How.	
	517 Bty. LOB STREET to SUNKEN ROAD	
	For purposes of accurate description and speedy fire on any portion of the Group front - the Group Zone is split into 6 portions - each known as HELL. These are numbered from the right 1 to 6.	C.A.F.

Page 19
Vol 10

Army Form C. 2118.

WAR DIARY
or
INTELLIGENCE SUMMARY.
(Erase heading not required.)

Hour, Date, Place	Summary of Events and Information	Remarks and references to Appendices
SAILLY J18c 6.2.2. Dec 19th (cont)	Therefore, if Infantry require us to shoot on any portion of their front — the code word HELL followed by the number is sent to the Battery ensuring that particular zone, and will immediately open fire. (Appendix 7) Operations. Wire-cutting during the day at K17 b.0.2 and K17 d.0.8, in preparation for raids to take place at a later date. At night wire bombarded enemy trenches in support of raid made further north by 18th D.L.I. (Appendix 8)	

Army Form C. 2118.

WAR DIARY
or
INTELLIGENCE SUMMARY.
(Erase heading not required.)

Page 20.
Vol IV

Hour, Date, Place	Summary of Events and Information	Remarks and references to Appendices
SAILLY J.15.c.6½.2.		
Dec 19th (cont)	Hostile reply to our bombardment was fairly heavy - mostly around the neighbourhood of KNOX STREET.	
Dec 20th.	A quiet day - hostile Artillery shewing but little activity. Hostile minnewerfer dispersed. Hostile A-craft active until 11 P.M. Many fruitless efforts were made to envision same.	
Dec 21st	In preparation for raid to be made on the 23rd inst. we fired bursts of fire on enemy R.S.P.	

Page 21
Vol D

Army Form C. 2118.

WAR DIARY
or
INTELLIGENCE SUMMARY.
(Erase heading not required.)

Hour, Date, Place	Summary of Events and Information	Remarks and references to Appendices
SAILLY J18C 6.2. Dec 21 (cont) Dec 22nd	front and support lines to accustom him to smaller bursts of fire at night, in the hopes of making him take to his dug-outs whenever the guns open. During night of 21/22 two prisoners belonging to the 169 I.R. were captured by our advanced posts. Information gained from them was to the effect that a relief was in progress, and would continue on the night 22/23rd. They also stated that the whole relief was in a "muddle", and that they had lost their way.	(Appendix 9)

WAR DIARY
or
INTELLIGENCE SUMMARY.

(Erase heading not required.)

Army Form C. 2118.

Page 22
Vol 10

Hour, Date, Place	Summary of Events and Information	Remarks and references to Appendices
SAILLY J 18 c 67.2 Dec 22nd (cont)	Acting on this information we shelled vigorously all approaches and tracks behind enemy line until 2 a.m. 23rd Dec.	
Dec 23rd.	Hostile Artillery tonight. Enemy movement successfully engaged. At night an attempt of raid made by the 18th Y & Lancs on hundred yds of enemy trenches (Appendix 10) The raiding party entered the German trenches & bombed dug-outs - causing casualties. Enemy reply to our bombardment was very feeble. Very few shots were fired on our zone, but HEBUTERNE was lightly shelled.	

WAR DIARY
or
INTELLIGENCE SUMMARY.
(Erase heading not required).

Army Form C. 2118.

Page 23 Vol ?

Place	Date	Hour	Summary of Events and Information	Remarks and references to Appendices
SALLY J18c6½2	Dec 24th		Hostile Artillery normal. Active principally against our communication trenches and areas in rear. Enemy movement successfully dealt with during the day. At night we fired bursts on enemy communications.	(Appendix 11)
	Dec 25	10:30 a.m.	Hostile Artillery very quiet. Only one 77mm battery active on our front. We fired frequent bursts on enemy communications. A German was seen to enter NO MANS LAND from the 'POINT', and appeared to enter our trenches at J523 &o.3.	(Appendix ?)
	Dec 26	10:30 a.m.	Hostile Artillery much more active during the day. We counter-bombarded enemy trenches. Light. van from A new liaison scheme between Artillery and Infantry, drawn up by Group Commander.	(Appendix 12) Col

WAR DIARY
INTELLIGENCE SUMMARY.

Page 24
Vol No V

Place	Date	Hour	Summary of Events and Information	Remarks and references to Appendices
SAILLY J18c63.2	Dec 27th		Our trenches in K16 & and K17.c were shelled with 15c.m and 10.S.C.m. We counter-bombarded enemy trenches in our front. (Hostile aircraft active. Several attempts were made to cross our lines but were driven off by A.A. guns. At night bursts of rifle or enemy communications and front line repeated. (Appendix 12)	
	Dec 28th	10.35a 11.a.m	{HEBUTERNE was lightly shelled with 77 m.m & 10.5 c.m. Situation. Enemy movement distinct. At night – bursts of fire on enemy communications trenches & trenches. The S[ome] one aeroplane flying over PUISIEUX was brought down by German A.A. guns.	AR

Army Form C. 2118.

WAR DIARY
or
INTELLIGENCE SUMMARY.
(Erase heading not required.)

Page 25
Vol 10

Place	Date	Hour	Summary of Events and Information	Remarks and references to Appendices
SAILLY J18c62.2	Dec 29th		Hostile Artillery normal. A few enemy parties were dispersed by us. At night - burst of fire on enemy tracks & roads.	
	Dec 30th		Hostile Artillery quiet. Some working parties observed behind enemy lines were dispersed. At night - burst on roads and tracks (Appendix 12) The 517 Bty attacked to Pt. Group, having 3 guns temporarily out of action (due to pits being flooded) the right lines of P/16g were watched to cover their guns. (Appendix 13)	
	Dec 31st		A prepared raid to be made by the Division on our left was postponed owing to weather conditions. At night - fire on enemy communications and roads. (Appendix Doc 14) P/16g were ordered to withdraw their two forward guns at K2kc2.2, this position being required by 3rd Division. AAF	

CONFIDENTIAL.

WAR DIARY.

OF THE

169TH BRIGADE R.F.A.

FROM JANUARY 1ST TO JANUARY 31ST 1917.

VOLUME XIII

169 Battery

WAR DIARY or INTELLIGENCE SUMMARY.

Army Form C. 2118.
1st January 1917 / 31st January 1917
Page 1
Vol XIII

Place	Date	Hour	Summary of Events and Information	Remarks and references to Appendices
Sailly 18c 6½.2	Jan 1st 1917		Visibility very low. A little movement observed behind enemy lines and effectively dealt with.	
		4:30 p.m.	Infantry (9th Inf. Bde) reported a relief taking place in enemy lines in neighbourhood of the 'POINT'. We fired vigorously on this area and also on communications in rear. In addition, we fired several bursts of fire on roads, tracks, and exits from PUISIEUX. (Appendix I.)	
	Jan 2nd		Visibility low. Raining slightly. Enemy heavily shelled HEBUTERNE. We counter-bombarded PUISIEUX.	
		11 a.m.	At night – we fired bursts on enemy communications and PUISIEUX (Appendix II) B Battery, 86th Bde R.Fa. 19th Division, attached to Right Group as reinforcing battery. At present, they remain at their wagon lines, until a position is made for their occupation.	
	Jan 3rd		Raining – light very poor. Enemy movement dealt with. At night, we fired bursts of fire	C.W.

Army Form C. 2118.

Page 2

WAR DIARY
or
INTELLIGENCE SUMMARY.
(Erase heading not required.)

Vol 1.

Place	Date	Hour	Summary of Events and Information	Remarks and references to Appendices
SAILLY J18cb2.2	Jan 3rd (cont)	5:30 p.m.	on enemy communications - roads - tracks etc. Lieut Craven D.S.O. R.G.A. (Commanding R Group) lectured at 31st Div. School VACHELLES on "Liaison between Artillery and Infantry".	
	Jan 4th	4:30 a.m. to 5:30 p.m.	Hostile Artillery active - searching through K21 with 15 c.m. One O.R. 8/169 killed. Enemy aircraft very active throughout the day, but attempts to cross our lines failed. One 18 pdr Battery Right Group (C/165) co-operated with 42nd Heavy Artillery Group in "Road Strafe" (Appendix III)	One O.R. 8/169.
		11 p.m. to 11:30 p.m.	During the night we fired bursts on enemy front line, and communications (Appendix 4) A/169 withdrew two 18 pdrs from forward position at K21 c1.9 to K20 d1.2. B/86 Bde, 19th Div. went into action at K21 c1.9	

Army Form C. 2118.

WAR DIARY Page 3
or
INTELLIGENCE SUMMARY. Vol 1

Place	Date	Hour	Summary of Events and Information	Remarks and references to Appendices
SAILLY J18c6½2	Jan 5th	11 a.m.	Hostile Artillery unusually active on our trenches in K17c, K23 & E. We counter-bombarded enemy trenches, and a hostile battery at L19 & 78.91 (reported by aeroplane) was also engaged.	
		4 p.m.	An enemy 'plane crossed our lines, and fired on a party of our Infantry in K20 E. This was twice repeated a little later, our A.A. guns being unable to secure a hit. The usual small parties were observed throughout the day in K7c, and effectively dispersed.	
	Jan 6th	1 p.m.	Hostile Artillery again showed increased activity. He bombarded our front and support lines from K23 a 4.7 to K11 c1.3 with 10.5 c.m. and 77 m.m. Rate of fire, about 30 rounds a minute, slowing down at 1.3 p.m. to half that rate. There were two 1 minute pauses at 1.5 p.m and 1.9 p.m. At 1.12 p.m. the 77 m.m. batteries ceased fire, and the 10.5 c.m. concentrated heavily from K17c55 to K17 a 5.6. During this bombardment, enemy Trench mortars were also active.	

WAR DIARY
or
INTELLIGENCE SUMMARY.

Army Form C. 2118.

Page 4   Vol 1

Place	Date	Hour	Summary of Events and Information	Remarks and references to Appendices
SAILLY J18c6½2	Jan 6th (cont)	4 P.M.	The 10.h. bombardment was repeated. It is thought from enemy images, that he is contemplating a raid on this front. Precautions are being taken accordingly.	
	Jan 7th	11.30 AM 4 P.M.	Hostile Artillery - below normal. Visibility very low, and very little movement observed. 8 hostile planes endeavoured to cross our lines, but were driven off by our A.A. guns. At night, we fired bursts of fire on enemy communications.	(Appendix 5)
	Jan 8th		Hostile Artillery normal. A Battery 170 Bde, came into action at K15c7.4 as reinforcing battery. C/169 at K14a9.1 ditto. At night we bombarded enemy trenches and communications	(Appendix 6)

WAR DIARY

INTELLIGENCE SUMMARY.

Page 5. Vol I

Place	Date	Hour	Summary of Events and Information	Remarks and references to Appendices
SQUEY J18c6½.2	Jan 9		'X' day of Artillery Programme of preparation of attack to be made by 7th Division on MUNICH TRENCH (Appendix 7) Enemy retaliation to our bombardment was very feeble.	
	Jan 10		'Y' Day. Bombardment programme carried out as per Appendix 7. The enemy offered no prompt retaliation. That of this fire was directed against HÉBUTERNE and near S.W. of it. Hostile Aircraft very active. Several enemy planes, flying very low, attempted to cross our lines, but were driven off by A.A. guns. A large gap has been cut by us today at K.17 & O.2 at night, the enemy seemed to be very nervous in this neighbourhood. He was continually throwing up Very lights, and occasionally golden rain rockets – but with no apparent results.	

WAR DIARY or INTELLIGENCE SUMMARY.

Army Form C. 2118.

Page 6 Vol 1

Place	Date	Hour	Summary of Events and Information	Remarks and references to Appendices
SAILY J18c6.2	Jan 11th		"Z" Day. Attack on MUNICH TRENCH by 7th Division. Zero hour - 6.40 P.M. At Zero minus 3 minutes we opened fire - barraging areas South and South West of SERRE, one battery being detailed to engage any enemy movement. At Zero plus 14 minutes, the rate of fire slowed down, but a continued barrage at a slow rate was kept on these areas all day and through the night — at request of the 7th Division, who found that the very useful, and prevented hostile flank machine gun fire. A/170 and C/169 withdrew from action to their wagon lines.	
		5. P.M.	We carried out a steady bombardment of enemy trenches, also wire - cutting South of "THE POINT". The gap at K17.B.0.2 was further enlarged.	
	Jan 12th		Night firing commenced at 5.30 P.M., and continued until 7 a.m. 14th. (appendix 5) The enemy fired very little attention to our trenches, confining himself principally to back areas.	CaB

Army Form C. 2118.

WAR DIARY
or
INTELLIGENCE SUMMARY.

(Erase heading not required.)

Page 7 Vol I

Place	Date	Hour	Summary of Events and Information	Remarks and references to Appendices
SAILLY J18c6½2	Jan 13th		A very quiet day. Enemy inactive during the morning, and unusually quiet in the afternoon. Considerable enemy movement observed throughout the day. Three large parties each of about 20-25 men, were fired on, and casualties inflicted - (1) L8c1.1 (2) L7d1.1 (3) L7c5.1. There has been considerable less movement by the enemy in his forward areas recently - no doubt due to the vigilance of our 18 pdrs.	
	Jan 14th		Hostile Artillery normal. Commencement of relief by 19th Divisional Artillery. One section of B/169 relieved by A/87. One section A/169 relieved by section B/87. One section D/169 relieved by D/87.	
	Jan 15th		Relief of A, B & D/169 completed, and withdrawn to wagon lines. 517 How Bty withdrawn to wagon-line.	

Army Form C. 2118.

WAR DIARY
or
INTELLIGENCE SUMMARY.

Page 8
Vol. I.

(Erase heading not required.)

Place	Date	Hour	Summary of Events and Information	Remarks and references to Appendices
SAILLY J18c6½.2	Jan 16th		H.Q. 169 Bde A, B, C & D Batteries marched to rest billets:— A & B Batteries to MEZEROLLES H.Q., C & D Batteries to FROHEN-LE-PETIT. 517 How. Battery marched under orders of 170 Bde to LA QUESNEL FARM.	
FROHEN-LE-PETIT	Jan 17th		C/169 marched to BEALCOURT. 517 How. Bty, attached to 169 Bde, and marched from LA QUESNEL FARM to BEALCOURT.	
	Jan 18th		This time was spent in cleaning horses and vehicles etc.	
	Jan 19th			
	Jan 20th		Reorganization of Divisional Artillery. A/169 and 1 section C/169 ordered to proceed to join 3rd Div. Arty. on morning of 21st. This order was subsequently postponed until the 24th.	RaS

WAR DIARY
or
INTELLIGENCE SUMMARY.
(Erase heading not required.)

Army Form C. 2118.
Page 9
Vol. I.

Place	Date	Hour	Summary of Events and Information	Remarks and references to Appendices
FROHEN-LE-PETIT	Jan 21st		Training and recreation. Gun & driving drill. Signalling. Lectures.	
	Jan 22nd		— do —	
	Jan 23rd		— do —	
	Jan 24th		A/169 and ½ C/169 marched to join 3rd Divisional Artillery at ST LEGER-LES-DOMART. One section D/169 absorbed by D/170 — the other by D/165. The following changes of billets took place. 517 How. Bty. BEALCOURT to MEZEROLLES ½ C/169 Bde BEALCOURT to FROHEN-LE-PETIT ½ D/169 Bde FROHEN-LE-PETIT to OUTRES BOIS	
	Jan 25th		One section 517 How Bty marched to join 62nd Div, and one section to 32nd Div	CAP

Army Form C. 2118.

WAR DIARY
or
INTELLIGENCE SUMMARY.

Page 10

Vol 1

(Erase heading not required.)

Place	Date	Hour	Summary of Events and Information	Remarks and references to Appendices
FROHEN-LE-PETIT	Jan 26th		D/165 moved into FROHEN-LE-PETIT and absorbed ½ B B/169.	
	Jan 27th		At 12 noon B/169 and ½ C/169 were taken on the strength of the 7th Division, but remain at MEZEROLLES, and attached to 31st D.A. for rations.	
	Jan 28th		At 12 noon B/169 re-designated C/14.	
	Jan 29th		—	
	Jan 30th		Orders received for move of 31st Divisional Artillery to ST OUEN area.	
	Jan 31st		Advanced parties sent to ST OUEN, to arrange and prepare billets.	[sgd]

A. Renee Midd[?]
An[?] Lt Col
169 Bde [?]
Comdg.

Appendix I

a/c Battery

SB 57

O/c Battery.

You will fire bursts of 3 rounds gun fire tonight at times and objectives as follows:—

8.20 P.M.   } Area between STAR
9.40 P.M.   } ALLEY and LOUVIERE
            ALLEY in K18d.

8.40 P.M.   } Western exits of
9.50 P.M.   } PUISIEUX. L14c & L20a

1-1-17

Appendix II

SB 59

O/c Battery.

1. There will be patrols and wiring parties out in Rt Group front tonight 2/3rd between the hours of 11 P.M and 1 a.m.

2. You will fire bursts of 2 rounds Gun fire on roads and tracks in K18 c & d at the following times
   8.15 P.m
   8.45 P.m
   9.30 P.m —
The last burst to be followed by 2 rds G.F. in Western exits of PUISIEUX.

2-1-17

Appendix III
SD 0?

O/c C/165.

1. The following is an extract from "Programme of Road Strafes". XIII Corp Heavy Artillery.

Thurs. Jan 4th 11.0 P.m to 11.30 P.m } 42nd Group
Fri. Jan 5th 1 a.m to 1.30 a.m   } 50 rounds
                                         Road
                                         L.14 c.0.0.6
                                         K.18 d.8.4

2. Right Group will co-operate with one 18 pdr. Battery (C/165) during each of above periods, sweeping either side of the road named for 100 yards.

C.A Pearce 2Lt R.F.A.
for Adjt R F Group

1-1-'17.

Appendix VI

S861

O/C 4.5 How. Battery's

1. There will be patrols and wiring parties out tonight 4/5 between the hours of
(i)   6 P.m – 9 P.m
(ii) 11 P.m – 12 a.m

2. You will fire a burst of 2 rds G.F. on roads and tracks in rear followed by a salvo on Night lines at the following times

5 P.m
6.30 a.m (Jan 5th)

Cabeau M L th
for Lt Col Comg

4-1-17

Appendix 4.
SB 60

O/c 18 Pdrs Battery.

1. There will from be shooting on the front lines tonight of 5th Jan. between the hours of

(1) 6 P.m to 9 P.m (Patrols)
(2) 11 P.m to 2 a.m (Wiring)

2. You will fire a burst of 2 rounds G.F. on support line followed by a salvo on front line at the following times.

5 P.m
6.30 a.m (5th Jan)

C. Beane M.R.A.
for Adjt R.A. Group

4-1-17

Appendix 5.

All Batteries

SB 63

O/c Battery.

There will be patrols out on all roads tonight between the hours of 8.30 P.M and 12.30 a.m.

In addition there will be patrols out by Boxes 3 and 4 between 2 a.m and 5 a.m.

You will fire a flight of 3 rounds gun fire on roads and tracks in K18d followed by a salvo on night lines at 8.15 P.M. 6. A.M. 8th inst.

C. A Pena 2Lt RFA
for O/C R Group.

7-1-17.

SECRET.

Appendix 6.
SB64

O/c all Batteries.

1. Night firing on enemy communication will take place on the night 8/9th in accordance with attached Tables.
2. Watches will be synchronised by telephone at 3.0 P.M. on 8th Inst.
3. Batteries barraging roads and tracks will sweep to cover 100 yards on either side of the track.
4. H.E. will be used.
5. Acknowledge.

Catcaner M.R.H.
for Adjt R.A. Group

8-1-17

Communication Shoot.
Night 8/9th

Time	Battery	Objectives	Rates of Fire
5.30 to 6.0 P.M.	4.5" Hows	A. Junction BOX ALLEY and STAR ALLEY. Railway and trench junction K18d9.4. Trench junction K18d9.6	60 rds per battery.
6.5 P.M.	18 Pdrs & 4.5 Hows	B. Road and Railway K18d9.4 to L13d9.2 to L14a 0.2 Road K12d9.3 to L7d4.7	18 pdrs. 3 rds Gun fire 4.5 Hows 2 rds Gun fire sweeping either side of tracks. To be repeated 3 times as rapidly as possible with searching effect till the whole length of objective has been cov
6.15 P.M.	18 Pdrs & 4.5 Hows	C. BOX ALLEY from K18d8.2 to L13d5.2 STAR ALLEY K18d9.6 to L13d6.8	18 Pdrs 3 rds G.F. 4.5 Hows 2 rds G.F. To be rapidly repeated with searching effect etc.

2.

Time	Battery	Objective	Rate of fire and Amm. Allotment.
7.0 P.M	All Batteries	As in B	
7.15 P.M	— do —	As in C.	
8.10 P.M	— do —	As in B	
8.12 P.M	— do —	As in C	
10.20 P.M	— do —	D. Dugout Lane, LA LOUVIERE FM. TOUVENT FM ROAD	
10.25 P.M	— do —	As in B	
10.30 P.M	— do —	As in C	
12.30 A.M	— do —	As in D	
12.35 A.M	— do —	As in B	
12.37 A.M	— do —	As in C	

Cakane Wrath
for Lt/R Group

SECRET   War Diary
                            Copy No 3   [Appendix]

31st Divisional Artillery Order No 54.

7th Jany 1917.

1. A bombardment will take place on a date to be notified later, in accordance with XIII Corps Artillery Instructions No 20 notified.

     The XIII Artillery Bombardment will consist of:—
     (a) Wirecutting. Right Group on right, Left Group on left.
         Belt 35 yards wide in the front line wire.
     (b) Bombardment by 4.5" Hows, 15" T.M's and Heavy T.M's.
     (c) Intense bombardment by all guns at hours stated in para. 4.
     (d) Practice of S.O.S. barrages.

3. Firing will be continued day and night except during the hours specified in para. 15 of XIII Corps Artillery Instructions No 20 when there will be a complete cessation of fire.

4.   Hours for intense bombardments will be:—
       "X" DAY   1:20 to 1:30 P.M.
                     4:50 to 5:0 P.M.
       "Y" DAY   1:0 P.M to 8:10 P.M.
                     5:30 P.M to 5:40 P.M.
     Zones and objectives are shown in Table 'B' attached.

5. S.O.S. barrages will be practised on "Y" day at 11:50, 3rd Division, including mutual support from Right Group, 31st Division.
     "Y" day, 11:50, 31st Division including mutual support from Divisions on right and left.
     S.O.S. barrages will be opened by watch time.
     18 pr. H.E. will be used.

6. Ammunition allotment is shown in Table "B" attached.

7. Throughout the operations each Group will select one officer to report in detail on (a) the hostile retaliation, (b) the accuracy of the barrage put up, specially noting if there are any gaps.
     Each of these officers will have a telephone line to O.C. 165th Bde., who will take up his position at an O.P. to be selected by him.
     O.C. 165th Bde. will collate these reports and forward accurate information on the following points:—

       (i) Time German barrage is put on.
       (ii) Its intensity, number and nature of shell.
       (iii) Direction from which it comes.
       (iv) The effect of our own H.E. on enemy barrages (a) as to guns killed, (b) as a curing it an

CONTINUED   2

    (v) The accuracy of our S.O.S. barrage.

    Reports to Head D.F.H.Q. at 9.0 P.M. daily.
In addition to the above each Group will send a report as follows:—
    (i) At 6 P.M. by telephone, progress in wire cutting.
    (ii) General Intelligence, 6 A.M. to 6 P.M. (written report)
    (iii) General Intelligence 6 P.M. to 6 A.M. (written report)

The D.R.D. will call at 165th Bde. H.Q. for the above reports at the following times:—
    9:30 P.M. nightly
    9:15 A.M. daily

8. The firing is to be continuous whatever the light; advantage will, however, be taken of intervals of good light to increase the rate of fire.

9. Watches will be synchronised by telephone from this office at 9:30 P.M. on "X" and "Y" days.

10. Programme for "Z" day will be issued later.

11.   ACKNOWLEDGE.

PROGRAMME
"X" DAY

8.0 a.m.	Wire cutting commences
9.0 a.m.	4.5" How. bombardment commences
10.0 a.m.	2" and H.T.M's fire as opportunity occurs any time from 10.0 a.m. onwards, except during pauses.
11.20 a.m. to 11.50 a.m.	No firing.
1.20 p.m. to 1.30 p.m.	Intense bombardment front and second line trenches, each Battery on S.O.S zone.
4.30 p.m. to 4.45 p.m.	No firing
4.50 p.m. to 5.0 p.m.	Intense bombardment front and second line trenches, each Battery on S.O.S zone.
5.0 p.m.	Night firing commences
5.40 p.m. to 9.40 p.m.	No firing
9.40 p.m. to 7.0 a.m.	Night firing continues.

"Y" DAY

8.0 a.m. to 8.10 a.m.	Intense bombardment as on 'X' day.
8.15 a.m.	Wirecutting commences
9.0 a.m.	4.5" How. bombardment re-commences
10.0 a.m.	2" T.M's and H.T.M's fire as opportunity occurs from 10.0 a.m. onwards except during pauses.
11.30 a.m. to 11.40 a.m.	S.O.S Division on our right, Right Group only (as for HELP SAUCE).
11.50 a.m. to 12 noon	S.O.S.

(CONTINUED)

"Y" DAY (CONTINUED).

1.0 pm to 1.20 pm } no firing

4.30 pm night firing commences.

5.0 pm to 5.20 pm } no firing

5.30 pm to 5.40 pm } Intense bombardment as on "X" day

5.40 pm to 9.40 pm } no firing

9.40 pm to 7.0 am } night firing

"Z" DAY

Programme will be issued later.

TABLE OF OBJECTIVES.   TABLE "B"

GROUP	WIRE-CUTTING	4·5" HOW BOMBARDMENT	NIGHT FIRING	INTENSE BOMBARDMENT
RIGHT	K17 b 05-15 5/9 5/9 5/9 5/9 5/9 5/9 5/9 5/9 10/9	(i) Selected points front system K17 & K17 d (ii) LA LOUVIERE ALLEY (iii) K17 d 35·10 (iv) K17 d 75·25 (v) PUB STREET (vi) LOB STREET (vii) NIEMEYER WEG (viii) LA LOUVIERE FARM (ix) From line LA LOUVIERE FARM to BOX WOOD	(i) Gaps in Wire (ii) Communications in Enemy zone	Each 18-pdr Battery on its S.O.S. zone. 4·5" Hows on selected points Reinforcing Batteries of Left Group on whose this is possible, other Batteries to have place on the line can be taken by a reinforcing Battery, concentrated on GONNECOURT first 2 mins on front trench next 2 " " Second " next 4 " " Third " next 2 " " Second " 18-pdrs 3rds per gun per minute 4·5" Hows 2 " " " "

Appendix 8.
SB 79.

O/c   Battery

1. Night firing commences at 5.30 P.m. and will be continued until 7.0 a.m 13th Inst. except between the hours of 6.0 P.m to 9.15 P.m.

2. Expenditure from 5.30 P.m to 7.0 a.m 13th Inst.

60 A
60 Ax } 18 Rds per Battery.

80 Bx } 4.5 Hours per Battery.

3. Acknowledge.

12-1-17

C. A. Pearce 2/Lt R.F.A.
Fr. Adjt. R Grp

Programme of night Shooting. 12/13 January 1917.

Time	Battery	Objectives	Rate of fire
9.30 P.M.	18 Pdrs & 4.5 Hows	(A) NIGHT LINES	18 pdrs 3 rds G.F. 4.5 Hows 2 rds G.F.
10.0 P.M	18 Pdrs & 4.5 Hows	(B) Road and Railway K18d9.4 to L13d9.2 to L14a0.2	— do —
10.15 P.M.	18 Pdrs & 4.5 Hows	(C) Junction BOX ALLEY and STAR ALLEY	— do —
11.0 P.M.	18 Pdrs & 4.5 Hows	(D) BOX ALLEY from K18d8.2 to L13d5.2	— do —
11.20 P.M. to 7 a.m.	18 Pdrs & 4.5 Hows	Occasional bursts on objectives A.B.C.& D	Remainder of allotment.

WO95/23495

WO95/23495

31ST DIVISION
DIVL ARTILLERY

171ST (HOW) BDE R.F.A.

~~MAR — JUL 1916~~
1916 MAR — 1916 AUG

FROM EGYPT

BROKEN UP

Vol II

171st (Howitzer) Bty: RFA.
38th Division
VIII Corps
Fourth Army

Page 1
Army Form C. 2118.

WAR DIARY
or
INTELLIGENCE SUMMARY.
(Erase heading not required.)

Hour, Date, Place	Summary of Events and Information	Remarks and references to Appendices
1st March ALEXANDRIA	Embarkation at ALEXANDRIA. 1st train arrived at Docks about 7 AM. Commenced entraining Horses & Baggage to BOHEMIAN (England Line), other trains followed in succession & Embarkation proceeded. The arrangements for loading the Gun Carriages were very bad indeed. Goods lift door-edge was curved & wheels & trays in one case a ship broke to about six feet; several roofs in traces were ventilated, but boards broken & ground near tent. The hatches were far too small & the payout load that they took was quite insufficient, as also parts of harbour & Reins of T. Subriages. Insufficient deck space to be fitted for the 20 Lbs of Vehicles carried, namely:— 12 Guns 40 Wagons 1 Telephone Wagon. Ship sailed about 9 p.m. 704 officers & men all ranks written took to sea struck up a ALEXANDRIA had been embarked the day before with 169 Bogans.	Mar '16 July '16

Vol II

WAR DIARY
or
INTELLIGENCE SUMMARY.

14th (War/Sup) 1918 Army Form C. 2118.
31st Div. Page 2

(Erase heading not required.)

Hour, Date, Place	Summary of Events and Information	Remarks and references to Appendices
At Sea	Usual cases of land sick occurred during voyage, sick 3 officers. No casualties amongst men.	
7th March /16	Life on board Karachi Maru known at 10 P.M., 20 casualties. Ink store.	
8th MARSEILLES	BOHEMIAN came alongside at 8.30 A.M., commenced disembarking horses 10 A.M., very speedily carried out. Have 9 carriages here 2nd Jewelry closed at 4.5 P.M. Headquarters & A Battery turned in a Train at 8.30 P.M. Train very crowded H.O. for officers at Baggage. Horses alright. B-C & AC followed at about 3 hours interval.	
8th/9th March Train	Halts for hot tea & some tea. Badly arranged. Rec. Dix. for a long time before getting tea at horses had a	
10th March Train	Forward PONT RE MY (Val-Fran 11-30 p.m.) Extremely difficult without assistance, hot water provided for. No bustle tea.	

Vol II 111th (How) Bty RFA

WAR DIARY
or
INTELLIGENCE SUMMARY.   31st Division.
(Erase heading not required.)

Army Form C. 2118.
Page 3 /hr

111th (How) Bty RFA

Hour, Date, Place	Summary of Events and Information	Remarks and references to Appendices
March 11th ALLERY (ABBEVILLE District)	H.Q. - C & A arrived during the course of the day, having entrained at 12.2 ltrs from Station at PONT REMY. D. Battery had arrived on the evening of the 9th March. The whole Brigade in Billets & Billetage Yards known under cover. Present in afternoon 5 Master Cards, 5 Officers' Servants, 1 Ambulance Cart, took horses & harness complete, also 4 Heavy horses with Artillery Class GS Transport Horses.	
ALLERY 15.3.16		HMMoncrieff Col Comm. 171 Bay RFA

HMMoncrieff Col
Comm 171 Bay RFA

Vol II

179 Bry RFA
31st Division

Page 4
Army Form C. 2118.

WAR DIARY
or
INTELLIGENCE SUMMARY.
(Erase heading not required.)

Instructions regarding War Diaries and Intelligence Summaries are contained in F.S. Regs., Part II. and the Staff Manual respectively. Title pages will be prepared in manuscript.

VIII Corps - Fourth Army

Hour, Date, Place	Summary of Events and Information	Remarks and references to Appendices
ALLERY (SOMME) FRANCE 12th March /16	The Division now incorporated in VIII Corps. Fourth Army. Considerable difficulty in obtaining Rations & Forage as Great shortage of both, & at present 20 cwt only of forage.	
13th March	SSO bivouacked in respect of supply, and rations furnished & authority given to make good shortage by local purchase, with exception of Oats & Hay, which are requisitioned by French Government. Indents for Ordnance Stores, to complete, & Clothing (Waterdress) submitted also for Renown-to-complete establishments. Being so difficult of throwing supplies from Railhead Point of Baggage Wagons Rams, allowed the Brigade on loan.	
17th March	Brass of sick, & destitute horses for Inspection by GOC.RFA. Total deficiency to look after 136 horses.	
18th March	Party of 8 Officers & 24 men conveyed by motor buses to firing line at MAILLY-MAILLET for instruction - all BCs with one 2nd Br Bates	
20th March	37 Cast horses sent in to ABBEVILLE with 2 2nd Br Bates, who returned with 30 Remounts	

Vol II

171 (How) Bty. R.F.A.
31st Division

WAR DIARY
or
INTELLIGENCE SUMMARY.
(Erase heading not required.)

Army Form C. 2118.
Page 5

Hour, Date, Place	Summary of Events and Information	Remarks and references to Appendices
20th March/16 ALLERY	G.O.C.-R.A. held conference at ALLEN COURT	
22nd March	Party returned from firing line about 5-30 p.m.	
23rd & 24th March	Weather became very cold, with snow.	
25th March	"A" & "B" Batteries with 1/2 A.C. left ALLERY G.J.R. en route for Front, marching via ARRAINES – SOUES – HANGEST – BOURDON to YZEUX when they Billeted for the night. Inspected by G.O.C.-R.A. on the road, who expressed his satisfaction with the turn out & march discipline. 106 Remounts arrived from ABBEVILLE 9.10 p.m. – 170 Brigade.	
26th March	Head Qrs., "C" & "D" Batteries & 1/2 A.C. left ALLERY, following same route as preceding batteries yesterday and billeted. Left ALLERY in pouring rain. Were inspected by G.O.C.-R.A. on the road, also noted the same sight of approval. Supplies received at YSEUX, very short & Head Quarters see 2 20 pent: bread or biscuit, just tea & cheese. Billets comfortable – Head Quarters at Chateau.	Appendix A. Letter from G.O.C. R.A.

Vol II   191 (Howz/Boul) R.F.A.
                    31st Division.

Page 6
Army Form C. 2118.

WAR DIARY
or
INTELLIGENCE SUMMARY.
(Erase heading not required.)

Hour, Date, Place	Summary of Events and Information	Remarks and references to Appendices
YSEUX 27th 2nd week 9 AM	Left YSEUX marched via BELLOY – LA CHAUSEE – VIGNACOURT – HAVERNAS & WARGENIES where billeted – A & B Batteries had billeted roof for night before. Accommodation for men rather indifferent – Horses in open on good lines. Head Qrs in Chateau	
9 AM 28th March WARGENIES	Left WARGENIES for SARTON, Via NAOURS – VERT GALANT Farm – BEAUQUESNE – ORVILLE. "C" "D" & "½" Column billeted at ORVILLE. Head Quarters went on to SARTON, where "A" & "B" Btys/½ A.C. had already established. Road being filly & in places bad. Both villages ORVILLE SARTON rather congested with Hy Arty. "A" Battery from 2 Staffs – "B" & divn – "D" Howr Divies – HQ ½ in Te-for Archies. Supplementary to Brecon – Biscuit. Ride issued to Lum, which it was impossible to cook. Weather very very cold, took snow during afternoon.	
SARTON & ORVILLE 29th & over		
SARTON 30th	One Section of "A" & one of "D", marched out to MAILLY (2 id.) to take over Guns & Emplacements from Le Batterie's Ley return in the string time. They took ration for 3rd day's and took over communications of 108 Hou By of Northumbl Div Artillery	
31st	Relief completed by the other Section of A & D Head Quarters remain at SARTON	

(signature)

Appendix A

Officer Commanding
171 How Bry RFA

I am directed to inform you that the GOC. RA was much gratified by the appearance, turn out, & march discipline of C & D Batteries of your Brigade whom he saw near LE QUESNEY.

It was all the more creditable in face of the adverse circumstances under which their march was being conducted, & he trusts you will convey his appreciation to all ranks.

(Sd) Chilton Major RA
Brig Major 31st Div Art'y

DAHQ
26.3.16

True Copy

H.K. Aldworth Col
Comm'd 171 Brig RFA

Confidential

DAG 3rd Echelon

War Diary 171st How. Brigade R.F.A. for
month of April, forwarded herewith.

H.H.Dermington Col
Comm'd 171 Brig RFA.

HQ 171
13.5.16

Vol IV

171st Bde RFA
31st Division
VIII Corps
Fourth Army

Army Form C. 2118.

WAR DIARY
or
INTELLIGENCE SUMMARY.
(Erase heading not required.)

Instructions regarding War Diaries and Intelligence Summaries are contained in F.S. Regs., Part II and the Staff Manual respectively. Title pages will be prepared in manuscript.

Hour, Date, Place	Summary of Events and Information	Remarks and references to Appendices
Head Quarters SARTON (France) 1st April /16	A & D Batteries in Action. Rear MAILLY-MAILLET. Lorry taken over position & ammunition 15th Brigade R.F.A. B Battery in SARTON. C Battery & A at ORVILLE. A & D Brdes taken over own position by sections at a time. Battery Commanders assumed control Friday.	
2nd – 3rd – 4th – 5th	Batteries in Action. Engaged in checking Registration of Targets. C Battery moved to MAILLY – MAILLET Dug 4 5th April & took over position from A Battery. A Battery returned to Billets at SARTON, D & C unchanged in Action.	
6th April	On receipt of 5th April German Quarterly bombarded our front line about 6pm – 7 to 30pm. Second probably directed on to a Relief in progress of the 2nd Brigade. 2 wounded to date. The Batteries are distributed as follows :— A Battery .... SARTON Corps Reserve B " .... do attached Left Group 31st Divn R.A. C " .... MAILLY do Rept. D " .... MAILLY "	

Page 2

VOL IV

WAR DIARY
or
INTELLIGENCE SUMMARY.
(Erase heading not required.)

171 (How.) Brigade RFA
37th Division
VIII Corps. Fourth Army

Army Form C. 2118.

Hour, Date, Place	Summary of Events and Information	Remarks and references to Appendices
	Disposition (continued)	
	Brigade Ammunition Column — ORVILLE	
	Brigade Head Quarters — SARTON	
13th April	Brigade A.C. moved to AUTHIE	
14th April	O.C. Brigade with Capt. ROLLESTON 13/17 Lack a reconnaissance of ground between MAILLY-MAILLET and HEBUTERNE, as French off Biel., two positions were finally selected for A & B Batteries. A. to the Gridiron Trench behind the SUCRERIE about 3/4 mile SE of COLINCAMPS. B on SUCRERIE-HEBUTERNE road about 1200 yards due E of COLINCAMPS.	
16th April	Capt. ROLLESTON, 2nd Lt BARTLETT and a party of 27 men, proceeded to MAILLY to commence digging Gun Emplacements. Work	
17th April	started following day. The 1st Gun H.W. cart to BUS Road Line 5-2 Kilos distant & conveyed the position to G.S. Majors. A very short proceeding & another considerable difficulty to find difficult cross cult roads & one step to find great difficulty in the respect received from Pioneer Battalion KOYLI	

Pp 3

Vol IV

171st (How) Brigade R.F.A.
39th Division
VIII Corps
Fourth Army

Army Form C. 2118.

WAR DIARY
or
INTELLIGENCE SUMMARY.
(Erase heading not required.)

Hour, Date, Place	Summary of Events and Information	Remarks and references to Appendices
17th April	"B" Battery - Capt Williams with 1 Officer and a party of men went to Billets in COLINCAMPS to commence their replacements also. C/D remain in Motor and One Horses employed in altering & reconstructing Gun Emplacement Work on Emplacement much retarded by mild weather.	
17th to 22nd		
22nd	Made reconnaissance with Capts ROLLESTON & 2nd Lt JACKSON of proposed position for a Howitzer in BASIN WOOD. In position R.O.D. primarily a fortune in other respects, was rejected on account of the great difficulty of getting the Howitzers there & of being hopelessly flooded. The position is only some 1200 yards from front line, would be exposed to a cross fire from 2nd front & N. Great improvement in weather condition.	
23rd		
BEAUSSART 24th Day	Head Quarters of Brigade moved to BEAUSSART, Very bad accommodation & Billets & absurcity of Water.	

Army Form C. 2118

WAR DIARY
or
INTELLIGENCE SUMMARY

(Erase heading not required.)

Vol IV

171 (Heavy) Bry. R.G.A
31st Div.
XIII Corps
Fourth Army.

Instructions regarding War Diaries and Intelligence Summaries are contained in F.S. Regs., Part II. and the Staff Manual respectively. Title Pages will be prepared in manuscript.

Place	Date	Hour	Summary of Events and Information	Remarks and references to Appendices
MAILLY	29/30		Very heavy Bombardment commencing at 11.30 P.R. Hostility till about 2 a.m., then continuous of raid made by 29th Division, but however failed to accomplish any useful work, & caused to us considerable casualties.	
	13.5.16			

H.H. Wainwright Lt-Col
Comm. 171 Bry: R.G.A

171 Inf. Brigade A.F.A.
31st Div.
VIII Corps
Fonquevillers

Vol IV
1st week of April/16

Page 1

WAR DIARY
or
INTELLIGENCE SUMMARY

Vol I   171st (Hants) Brig. D.F.W.
          31st Septr.
          VIII Corps
          Army

Army Form C. 2118

Place	Date	Hour	Summary of Events and Information	Remarks and references to Appendices
MAILLY	May 1st/16		Head Quarters of Brig. moved from BEAUSSART to MAILLY-MAILLET. A Battery reported 2 Gun Emplacements ready for occupation, good work taken but construction had weaken & difficulty experienced in cutting & procuring & transporting timber & RE Material.	
	6th		Inspecting of A Battery Working Party with Capt ROLLESTON returned to SARTON, Remy. a small party with 2 oil Jacks to complete	
	8th		"A" Emplacements completed, with exception of Platforms which are not yet quite firm. "B" Emplacements proceed slowly. "D" Have made Emplacements for a battery of 4th Divn "C" Have reconstructed & altered the Gun End of Reserve emplacements Head Quarters "Battle Station" under construction near APPLE TREES	
	7/8th		Heavy firing during night, between 12 midnight & 2 A.M.	
	11th & 12th		Arrangements being made for Telephone Communications, Loneyhouse Brigade in connection with Divisional Signalling Officer.	

Page 2

171st Brigade RFA
31st Division
VIII Corps
Fourth Army

Vol I

Army Form C. 2118

WAR DIARY
or
INTELLIGENCE SUMMARY
(Erase heading not required.)

Instructions regarding War Diaries and Intelligence Summaries are contained in F.S. Regs., Part II. and the Staff Manual respectively. Title Pages will be prepared in manuscript.

Place	Date	Hour	Summary of Events and Information	Remarks and references to Appendices
HdQrs MAILLY-MAILLET	May 15th		In consequence of scheme for re-organization of Ammunition Columns, the Brigade Ammunition Column is abolished & becomes one of the Echelons of Divisional Ammunition Column, this change takes effect from 12 noon May 15th. Officers handed over — Capt. Stockward. 2nd Lt. Atherington & 2nd Lt. Bloor.	
"	22nd		Re-organization of Brigade takes effect from 12 noon this date. A/171 - Capt. McIlwain Heaton — becomes B/165 B/171 - " A Williams — becomes B/169 C/171 - " Kenoth Hough — becomes B/170 In other to ease the following are transferred to 171st Brigade. — B/165 - Capt. Walker — becomes A/171 B/169 - Major Sir C. Owen — becomes B/171 B/170 - Capt. Fitzgerald — becomes C/171 The re-organised Brigade is now composed of 3-18Pr & 1-4.5 Hour Batteries. Head Quarters being un affected by the change.	

171 RFA
Army Form C. 2118
No. 31

Vol V
Page 3

WAR DIARY
or
INTELLIGENCE SUMMARY
(Erase heading not required.)

171st Brigade R.F.A.
31st Div
VIII Corps
Fourth Army

Vol 3

Place	Date	Hour	Summary of Events and Information	Remarks and references to Appendices
MAILLY-MAILLET	1st to 31st	3.5 p.m.	Brigade disposed as follows:— "A" Battery in Action rear COLINCAMPS attached to 48th Division " " Wagon Line at ST LEGER "B" " in Corps Reserve at ORVILLE "C" " in Action rear COLINCAMPS (Formerly) Wagon Lines BUS WOOD "D" " in Action rear MAILLY-MAILLET Wagon Lines BERTRANCOURT " " in Action rear Trench Mortar in Le Quadrilateral, Aisne "Y" Battery knocked out a Heavy Trench Mortar 1000 yards N of BEAUMONT-HAMEL Nothing of Interest.	

W H MacArthur Col
Comm 171 Brig RFA

WAR DIARY or INTELLIGENCE SUMMARY

Army Form C. 2118

Vol VI June 1916

171 Brigade R.G.A.
31st May
VIII Corps
Fourth Army

Place	Date	Hour	Summary of Events and Information	Remarks and references to Appendices
Hdqrs MAILLY-MAILLET	1st June		A/171 2nd Capt H. WALKER in Section – COLINCAMPS Sector LEFT Group. B/171 2 gun sec. C. NIXON in Reserve at ORVILLE 10k. behind Battery dripping. Em placement near La SUCRERIE C/171 Capt HC FITZGERALD in Action. Attached to RESERVE Group. COLINCAMPS Sector, troop completing Gun Position. D/171 Major W. STILLWELL in Action near MAILLY-MAILLET, attached to RIGHT GROUP	
	2nd "		2 reserve & heavy Howitzer firing 3/171 started to command firing at 12.20 & light 3³/₄⁵ I continued till 10.p.m. B/Sec Bt 15 rounds. Ammunition Brought to & sto-ro- Tends completed.	
	5th "		Head Quarters B/171 moved to COLINCAMPS & teams attached to RESERVE GROUP. but emplacements not having been got completed 2-Gun a.m. not Brought up.	
	7th "		B/171 Commenced dipping forward emplacements in SACKVILLE STREET, working under great disadvantages owing to Inclement weather.	
	11th "		B/171 Brought up their guns & placed them in position & re-	

Page 2

WAR DIARY
or
INTELLIGENCE SUMMARY
(Erase heading not required.)

Army Form C. 2118

171 Brigade R.F.A.
31st Division
VII Corps
Fourth Army

Place	Date	Hour	Summary of Events and Information	Remarks and references to Appendices
HQRs MAILLY MAILLET	13th		Lieut. O'Brien Moore with 5-9 Shell This Battery's Telephone Central Contact with good forward Telephone equipment, also cameralites.	
	14th			
	15th		A/171 completed ammunition pits at SACKVILLE STREET & carried 1000 up ammunition last night.	
	17th/18th		The batteries fired 1600 rounds. A/171 had been brought up by night, were safely placed away. The position was ready for occupation.	
	19th		B/171 2nd also constructed a forward position near LA SIGNY FARM which was completed this day.	
	21st		BOMBARDMENT which had been originally fixed for this, postponed the 24th	
	22nd		HQrs Brigade moved into day out BATTLE STATION 2cm L- Upper Trees MAILLY- SUCRERIE. The OC Brigade took charge of Howitzer Groups which batteries formerly constituted 171 Heavy (How) Brigade.	
	24th		"U" Day 9 Bombardment commenced at 6 a.m. - All Batteries of Brigade employed Wire cutting for Special Bombardments.	

WAR DIARY or INTELLIGENCE SUMMARY

Army Form C. 2118

Vol VI

171 Bnt. B.348
31st Div.
VIII Corps
Fourth Army

Place	Date	Hour	Summary of Events and Information	Remarks and references to Appendices
BATTLE of Q near MAILLY	25th June "V" day		BOMBARDMENT continued throughout day according to PROGRAMME. D/171 burst a gun. Enough Premature explosion of Bore, fortunately no casualties. Board held & Secondary Report et'd..	
	26th June "W" day		BOMBARDMENT continued.	
	27th "X" day		Do. Lieut Gen. arrived for B/171 & Rotary Lord st. Forward Poster. SACKVILLE STREET 9.30 P.2. No Casualties among 2 me. B/171 also Lord & their forward Poster near LA SIGNY FARM — 20 casualties.	
	28th "Y" day		Do. to according to Programme. Do. rest of to: Forward Posters relied 2nd open fire. New emits Batteries continued Programme. 20.3 Ammunition pit of "G" Battery transferred to falling taken round to accompany facing rain taken the Yard rest. No protection was in any way important practically acted as a "SUMP"	
	29th Y1 & 30th Y2		Hard & Bombardment and last Day has sufficiently effective few Two extra days here added to Programme	

War Diary
171 Brigade R.F.A.

VOL VI
June /16

31st Division.

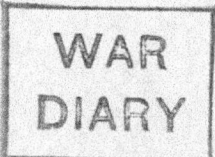

171st BRIGADE R. F. A. (HOW)

1st to 31st JULY 1 9 1 6.

Vol 5.

Confidential

War Diary

of

171st Bde R.F.A.

31ST DIVISION

July 1st to 31st 1916.

WAR DIARY or INTELLIGENCE SUMMARY

Army Form C. 2118

171 Brigade R.F.A.
34th Division
VIII Corps
Fourth Army

Vol VII

Place	Date	Hour	Summary of Events and Information	Remarks and references to Appendices
BATTLE H.Qrs	1st July "Z" Day		BATTLE of the SOMME on 31st Division front commenced with a Heavy BOMBARDMENT by Artillery of all Calibre & for the last 10 minutes before Zero (7.30 a.m.) became INTENSE.	
		7.30	Infantry got out of their TRENCHES & commenced Assault on SERRE under cover of Artillery Barrage. Divisional Artillery was very carefully prepared & thoroughly PROGRAMME for Divisional Artillery was very carefully prepared & thoroughly explained to all Batteries before hand. The times of LIFTS were minutely detailed and tasks allotted to GROUPS and by Group Commanders to Batteries.	
		9.55 a.m	Major ND STILLWELL, who was in O.P. was wounded in the Arm by a machine gun bullet. Lt Scott relieved him at the OP who commanded the Battery. No Brigade during the Bombardment.	Whilst taking Forward Position Rear LA SIGNY FARM Shell Fire
			The following casualties occurred :- Subsequent Operations, MS:	
	28th June		2016671 Br HAGAN J 13/1/71 Seriously wounded	" " "
			16274 Br BUCKLEYNE 13/1/74 "	" " "
			16102 " FIRTH-A "	" " "
			102068 " WILLIS-EG " Slightly	" " "
			4949 " WADE "	" " "
			16418 " TATTERSALL "	" " "
			73414 " TIDSWELL J "	" " "

Page 2 VOL VII   191 Brigade R.F.A.
                                                   31st Division
                                                   VIII Corps
WAR DIARY   Fourth Army
or
INTELLIGENCE SUMMARY
(Erase heading not required.)   Army Form C. 2118

Place	Date	Hour	Summary of Events and Information	Remarks and references to Appendices
BATTLE HDQRS near MAILLY	1st July		Casualties	
			Major W.D. STILLWELL 8/171 Wounded Left Femur	
			2nd Lt P.FENWICK 8/171 Wounded & Missing – Was 700 Yards from about	Wounded between
			13659 Bdr RICHARDSON 8/171 " " 30 yards in Fintzofen Trenches	SERRE
			13538 a/B" RILEY H " " Wounded	
			80741 S.S.YARROW 13/171 Wounded by Shell Fire in WAGON LINES	
			16692 Gr COLEBROOK " " at BUS WOOD	
			5044 " CLARKE " " which was subjected to a good deal of shelling	
			16117 " LOMAS S " " from a Heavy Battery.	
			16090 " UNDERWOOD " "	
		3pm	Brought up a fresh supply of ammunition, under considerable	
		1pm	difficulties owing to the Trenches each side it had to be brought through	
			Helped by wounded men.	
	2nd July		Bombardment resumed at intervals	
	2nd/3rd		Night 8/171 removed guns to old position at MAILLY nicknamed 10 layer	
			Trades of Manchester. No casualties.	

Page 3   VOL VII   171 Brig: R.F.A
31st Div.
Army Form C. 2118

WAR DIARY or INTELLIGENCE SUMMARY
(Erase heading not required.)

Place	Date	Hour	Summary of Events and Information	Remarks and references to Appendices
BATTLE HQ Bus MAILLY	3rd July		Batteries mostly employed in destroying German working parties. Enemy trenches especially in MUNICH TRENCH & PENDANT ALLEY WEST left right tire at irregular intervals. SALVOES were fired	
	4th July		Much the same procedure during the day.	
	5th	night-up	371 removed all un damaged ammunition from dumps in SACKVILLE STREET. This battery employed in taking 4 pm-4 pm interval in order to stoke 2. One other of 375 when?, all btys safely moved by DAC	
	5/6th		A/171 right. Very good bit of work to see N shared splendidly.	
	6th/7th		Batteries evacuated positions during event. & drivers carrying to retired to HQ Reserve. The Brigade reached during last night Starting Point near BUS KNICK 2	
	7th July		Brigade invited for first time at AMPLIER Got orders to return to Entrans next	

Page 4 VOL VII

171 Brigade R.F.A.
31st Div.

WAR DIARY or INTELLIGENCE SUMMARY
Army Form C. 2118

Place	Date	Hour	Summary of Events and Information	Remarks and references to Appendices
AMPLIER	8th July		"B" & "C" marched to HAZECOURT with many horses in 2 following day to Fair	
			"B" Battery at AUXI LE CHATEAUX	
			"C" " at CONTEVILLE	
	9th	2PM	Head Quarters marched to FRÉVANT followed by "A" & "D" Batteries.	
	9/10"		Entrained during night, arrangements to Great	
	10th	6.30AM	Detrained H.Q. "A" & "D" Batteries at STEENBECKE marched to ST VENANT about 6 miles, where also "B" & "C" arrived during the course of the morning. All Batteries fairly close together, each in its separate farm.	
	12th		"D" Section off at GUARBECQUE. Inspection of all guns & harness brigade by JunR II Corps, R.A.& Corps Brigade 2nd Helops.	
	13th		36 Numerant arrived at BERGUETTE for Le Brijean	
	15th		31st Div. Art. Hvy. H.Q moved to FOSSE from ST VENANT. "A" "B" & "C" Batteries attached 9 Art. to 3rd Australian Div. Art. Arty.	

WAR DIARY or INTELLIGENCE SUMMARY

Army Form C. 2118

171 Brigade R.F.A.
31st Division
XI Corps
First Army

VOL VII

Page 5

905

Place	Date	Hour	Summary of Events and Information	Remarks and references to Appendices
H.Q. at ST VENANT	15th July		Arc marched last night to FLEURBAIX. Rear H.Q. place positions had been selected. Major Davies at SAILLY SUR LA LYS.	
	15th/16th	12.30pm	"B" Battery marched to FLEURBAIX & picked up 1 pm at LESTREM en route. Mr 3 Batteries in different GROUPS.	
	16th/17th		Capt HUSSEY joined Y.Tob. over command of 8/171 vice STILLWELL	
	16th		A & C Batteries Registering & wire cutting	
	19th		A - B & C assisted in attack by 5th ANZAC Division on 1st & 2nd line German Trenches. The attack was successful on the left, but, owing to heavy Machine gun fire failed on right.	
	20th		Casualties in Batteries NiC. Ch.St. St. Aubut sent letter following wire from Corps Commander – "The Corps Commander congratulates your 9th and 10th Brigades by Battery" – This was the 96th "A" Battery.	

Army Form C. 2118

Page 6   71 Brig. RFA
VOL VII   3/Lct Div.
           XI Corps Artillery

WAR DIARY
or
INTELLIGENCE SUMMARY
(Erase heading not required.)

906√

Place	Date	Hour	Summary of Events and Information	Remarks and references to Appendices
MERVILLE	22nd July		4th Brigade Again collected at a place about 1 Kilometre Sof MERVILLE. Brigade Hers good messy quarters.	
	23rd		Orders came for Brigade to take up positions in FERME DU BOIS sector - Brig Comm' & BCs went out & reconnoitred positions, held at present BCs at LACOUTURE	
	24th		Batteries marched out to take over positions occurred in by Jackson's Taking over gen'l fire pln. HQ Qu moved to LESTROM	
LESTROM HQ	25th		Batteries completed Taking over.	
	26th		HQ Qu marched to LACOUTURE - Batteries told off to Sres - OC Brigade took over GROUP at 10th.	
	27th		Shifted HQ Qu from rear LA TOURET (Communications established but not very satisfactorily. But	
	27th/28th		SOS Call for German attack on LEFT SECTOR - Lt Buveyes & Vahergue Rg affected assistance to LEFT GROUP.	

Page 1

VOL VII

171 Brig RFA
3rd Bgd
II Corps
First Army

WAR DIARY or INTELLIGENCE SUMMARY

Army Form C. 2118

Place	Date	Hour	Summary of Events and Information	Remarks and references to Appendices
LA TOURET	Jan 1916 29th 30th 31st		Batteries employed Registering new zones. Selection of O.Ps. present some difficulties owing to shortage of wire. Communication is not as good as it ought to be.	

A.H. Hotchkiss Lt Col
Comm'g 171 Brig: RFA

WAR DIARY
and
INTELLIGENCE SUMMARY

171 Brigade H'drs

VOL VII

July/16

Vol 6

CONFIDENTIAL.

WAR DIARY.

of

171st BRIGADE R.F.A.

From AUGUST 1st, 1916 to AUGUST 31st, 1916.

VOLUME VIII

8118

171 Brigade R.F.A.
31st Division
XI Corps
First Army

Army Form C. 2118.
Page 1

WAR DIARY
or
INTELLIGENCE SUMMARY.
(Erase heading not required.)

Instructions regarding War Diaries and Intelligence Summaries are contained in F. S. Regs., Part II. and the Staff Manual respectively. Title pages will be prepared in manuscript.

Hour, Date, Place	Summary of Events and Information	Remarks and references to Appendices
August 1st 1916 Head Quarters Rear LE TOURET (FERME DU BOIS SECTOR)	All Batteries of 171 Brigade in action in his sector – Centre Group. 31st Distribution, reinforced by A/155 & C/165. Positions. Ref. Maps 36C/NW & SW BETHUNE (enclosed sheet) A/171 J7d.6.6 C/171 S13d.1.5 B/171 M32c.9.8 A/155 X17a.x.17&5.6	
Aug 2nd	Turned a considerable retaliation on German front line. Concentrated fire on a battery found attacking our crops front.	
Aug 5th	Major H Walker transferred to T. B. Walker from command of A/171. Head Quarters moved to LACOUTURE	
Aug 15th	Concentrated retaliation on BOAR'S HEAD	
Aug 19th	German took a strong attack on the FESTUBERT Right, which called for our support from Centre Group.	

2118 171 Brigade 0718 Page 2

Army Form C. 2118.

WAR DIARY
or
INTELLIGENCE SUMMARY.
(Erase heading not required.)

Instructions regarding War Diaries and Intelligence Summaries are contained in F.S. Regs., Part II and the Staff Manual respectively. Title pages will be prepared in manuscript.

Hour, Date, Place	Summary of Events and Information	Remarks and references to Appendices
23rd August.	92nd Infantry Brigade made a raid, preceded by a bombardment by 6 into Groups & Third all batteries 171/ Brig. The raid was most successful & 20 prisoners were taken. 2nd Lt ILES 13/171 was wounded by a shell burst (in our support trenches), he had ten feet or thereon with 6 mm Support party, for Dutch Party.	
25th & 26th	LACOUTURE Shelled 9 Brigade HQ cause to some extent. One shell (4.2") struck the officer's latrine & buried a Cpl's Orderly - he took & from clad very - PARR, orderly room clerk, slightly in the head & lightly wounds Colonel. Major General MERCER - 2nd RA Inspected trench in position & ordered them from C/171. The front of the position to vicinity of the line was. Thirty men, stationed of had been the cause of men throwing away waters of from the gallery taken in our line.	C/170 C/171

Vol 8

171 Brigade 0708 Page 3

Army Form C. 2118.

WAR DIARY
or
INTELLIGENCE SUMMARY.
(Erase heading not required.)

Hour, Date, Place	Summary of Events and Information	Remarks and references to Appendices
27 May/16 LE TOURET	Shifted HQrs to Le Touret. Orders issued for breaking up of the Brigade, in consequence of the reorganization of Divisional Artillery on a 6 gun basis. The following dispositions were made of HQrs & of Batteries. Head Quarters Brigade Commander with Staff taken over 165 Brig. A/171 transferred 1 section to 16.1/165 " " 1 " to B/165 " " 1 " to C/165 B/171 " 1 " to C/170 " " 1 " to 1/170 C/171 " 1 " to 1/170 " " 1 " to Major St C Bisson from commanding B/171 & command of B/165.	

Part 8

171 Brigade RFA

Page 6

Army Form C. 2118.

WAR DIARY
or
INTELLIGENCE SUMMARY.
(Erase heading not required.)

Hour, Date, Place	Summary of Events and Information	Remarks and references to Appendices
27th Sep	Capt Fitzgerald from onward of C/171 to command C/169. B/171 receives C/169 & in Lealy tattery of the proposed 171 How Brigade. Left intact.	
29th Sep	Being a wet & cloudy day, was particularly favourable for the shifting into position of new batteries, full advantage was therefore taken of the circumstance to get by night time all moves of units completed.	
29th/30th Sep	At 12 noon this day 171 Brigade RFA ceased to exist.	MW Newcombe Lt Col Comd'g 171 Brigade RFA

War Diary
171 Brigade R.F.A.

Original

Vol 8 August/16

171 R 7A
Vol 1

www.ingramcontent.com/pod-product-compliance
Lightning Source LLC
Chambersburg PA
CBHW081430300426
44108CB00016BA/2344